TRYST DESTINY

Free India's First Half-Century

PAUL R. DETTMAN

TIMES BOOKS INTERNATIONAL
Singapore • Kuala Lumpur

© 1997 Times Editions Pte Ltd

Published by Times Books International
an imprint of Times Editions Pte Ltd
Times Centre, 1 New Industrial Road
Singapore 536196
Tel: (65) 2848844 Fax: (65) 2854871
e-mail: te@corp.tpl.com.sg

Times Subang
Lot 46, Subang Hi-Tech Industrial Park
Batu Tiga, 40000 Shah Alam
Selangor Darul Ehsan, Malaysia
Fax and Tel: (603) 7363517

Printed in Singapore

ISBN 981 204 826 X

To Jean and our children, who were with me during the years in India and shared the writing journey that followed

Contents

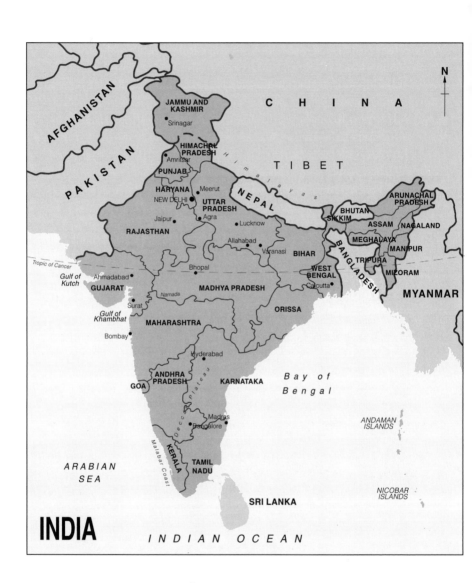

N

AFGHANISTAN

PAKISTAN

CHINA

JAMMU AND
KASHMIR
• Srinagar

HIMACHAL
PRADESH
Amritsar •

TIBET

Himalayas

PUNJAB

HARYANA
NEW DELHI •
• Meerut

NEPAL

UTTAR
PRADESH
• Agra

ARUNACHAL
PRADESH

Jaipur •

• Lucknow

BHUTAN
SIKKIM

RAJASTHAN

Allahabad •

ASSAM

NAGALAND

Varanasi •

MEGHALAYA

MANIPUR

BIHAR

BANGLADESH

TRIPURA

Tropic of Cancer

• Bhopal

WEST
BENGAL

MIZORAM

Gulf of
Kutch

Ahmadabad •

Calcutta •

GUJARAT

MYANMAR

Narmada

MADHYA PRADESH

Gulf of
Khambhat

Surat •

ORISSA

MAHARASHTRA

Bombay •

Bay of
Bengal

• Hyderabad

ANDHRA
PRADESH

Deccan Plateau

GOA

KARNATAKA

ANDAMAN
ISLANDS

ARABIAN
SEA

Malabar Coast

KERALA

• Madras
• Bangalore

TAMIL
NADU

NICOBAR
ISLANDS

SRI LANKA

INDIA

INDIAN OCEAN

❖

Preface

Two months prior to the 50th anniversary of India's Independence on August 15, 1997, the Central Government announced its plans for celebrating this important milestone in the country's history. The chairman of the Implementation Committee revealed that the Central Government had intended all along that the celebration would not be limited to the anniversary day itself but would go on during the entire year that followed. Thus, the celebrations scheduled for August would be only the beginning of a year-long series of events that would take place throughout the nation as a whole.

According to the Central Government's plan, all of Delhi's public buildings and national monuments will be illuminated on August 14 and 15, and dance and music concerts will continue until August 31 in the city's auditoriums. Similar cultural programs will mark the 50th anniversary in all of India's villages, cities, and districts. Parliament will be in special session at the August 15 midnight hour to hear again the words of, among others, free India's founding fathers—Mahatma Gandhi and Jawaharlal Nehru. These events will be preceded on August 9 in Delhi by a "March of the Nation" in which India's various social and regional groups will be represented. And all of these festivities will be only the highlights of a long litany of activities, projects, and products that will be organized to celebrate 50 years of freedom from colonial rule.

The critic of the Central Government might explain the Implementation Committee's statement that the 50th anniversary celebration will continue throughout the year as political cover for the lateness of the date on which the plans for the celebration were announced. After all, he could argue, a planning committee had been set up under the chairmanship of the Central Government's Human Resources Development Minister in June 1996. Five months later it had to be reconstituted, and then it took another six months to complete its work. The net result was that the plans which it worked out had to be announced from Delhi only two months before the anniversary date, a very short time in which to carry them out on a national scale if the day itself was intended to be their focal point. But, if that date was to be only the beginning of a year-long celebration, then the June 1997 announcement allowed plenty of time for the nation as a whole to join in the festivities launched in August from Delhi.

This critic's argument could gain strength from the loftiness of the goals laid out by the Central Government for the 50th anniversary celebration—to rekindle the spirit of patriotism and promote cultural harmony, national integration, social justice, and political freedom. How could the plans announced by the Implementation Committee, even if carried out in a spectacular fashion over a full year, achieve positive results on such a broad front in dealing with such deep-seated problems? Isn't this, the critic could ask, another example of a Central Government's good intentions which would never end up becoming a reality in the country's life?

This critic can be answered in a way which puts the Central Government's celebration plans in a positive light. The goals which it has set may indeed be ambitious, but they have the virtue of focusing attention on serious problems in the nation's life which need to be addressed during the years ahead. In formulating these goals, the Central Government is not saying to the Indian people: "Let us celebrate 50 years of Independence in order to remind ourselves of what a wonderful state we are in as a nation and how rosy our future looks," but "Let us celebrate 50 years of Independence in order to remind ourselves of the areas in our national life in which we need to make progress if our future is to be what we would like it to be." So, whether it was intended from the beginning of the planning process or was introduced at the end as a political cover, placing the celebration's center of gravity on the year following the anniversary rather than on the anniversary day itself turns out to be a wise and useful move. For, if any significant progress is to be made toward achieving the 50th anniversary celebration goals, it will take time, and a full year of holding those goals before the eyes of the Indian people will accomplish more than a celebration that lasts only a few days.

Even that one year will accomplish little unless it is the beginning of a national effort of consciousness-raising that continues for decades. As *Tryst with Destiny* attempts to make clear, rekindling a spirit of the high-minded patriotism that guided India's founding fathers—self-sacrificing service to their country—and promoting communal harmony, national integration, social justice, and political freedom during India's second half-century will not be easy. But to quote a Chinese saying that has become somewhat hackneyed through frequent use but is, nevertheless, very appropriate in this context: "A journey of a thousand miles begins with a single step." Pursuing the goals set forth by the Central Government for the celebration of the 50th anniversary of Indian Independence during the year that follows August 15, 1997, could become India's first step along the long road it has to travel to become the nation envisaged by its founding fathers and desired by its people.

❖

Remembrance of India Past

Why should I be writing about free India's first half-century at this particular time in my life and at this particular point in its history? I am not a professional writer; nor am I a scholar who has devoted his life to the study of the Indian scene. But I did live and work in India for 15 years in the 1950's and 60's, when India was still in its infancy as an independent nation. Those were the years when Mahatma Gandhi was more than a memory. Even though he had died four years before my arrival in 1952, his spirit was still alive in Indian politics and society.

Those were the years when Jawaharlal Nehru was India's Prime Minister, and the eloquent words which he had spoken from the Red Fort in Delhi at midnight on August 15, 1947, were still fresh in the minds of the Indian people:

"Long years ago we made a tryst with destiny and now the time has come when we shall redeem our pledge. At the stroke of the midnight hour, while the world sleeps, India will awaken to life and freedom. A moment comes, which comes but rarely in history, when we step out from the old to the new, when an age ends, and the soul of a nation, long suppressed, finds utterance."

Those were the years when a substantial part of my life was an infinitesimally small part of the life of India. So the India of the 1950's became my India, not in a proprietorial sense or in the sense that I had Indian roots, for I was a foreigner. It was my India in the sense that it was the India that unfolded to me when I arrived in 1952 and which I continued to carry in my mind for more than 25 years after I returned to the United States in 1969.

Why did I visit India again in 1996 and find that my India had been lost? Farfetched as it may seem, the answer lies in the conjunction

11

between my personal life and the life of free India. In 1994 my wife and I celebrated our 50th anniversary. It also marked the 25th year following our departure from India. The coming together of these two personal milestones made us decide to see India again before more years had gone by.

Moving from the level of personal life to the level of national life, we realized that India would be celebrating 50 years of Independence in 1997. Symbolically speaking, India's "Golden Anniversary" year would have been the appropriate time to visit once again the places that had been our home when both we and free India were young. But, realistically speaking, we knew that India would be caught up during 1997 with public celebrations that would obscure the realities of Indian life and that, if we wanted to see what India was really like 50 years after Independence, we would have to journey there before the pomp and circumstance had begun. So we decided to travel in India during the first two months of 1996.

Is it presumptuous to link a milestone in an individual's personal life with a milestone in the life of a nation, especially when the individual is a foreigner and that nation has a population approaching one billion people? Perhaps it is, but I was encouraged to do so when I encountered just such a link in Salman Rushdie's *Midnight's Children*. In this curiously and wonderfully contrived story, Rushdie merges the life of the narrator, Saleem Sinai, with the life of independent India. Saleem and independent India are born at the same moment, midnight on August 15, 1947, and, from the moment of their births, their lives are fused. What happens to Saleem happens to India:

"The monster in the streets has begun to run, while in Delhi a wiry man is saying—'At the stroke of the midnight hour, while the world sleeps, India awakens to life and freedom.' And beneath the roar of the monster there were two more yells, cries, bellows, the howls of children arriving in the world, their unavailing protests mingling with the din of independence which hangs saffron and green in the night sky—'A moment comes, which comes rarely in history, when we step out from the old to the new; when an age ends and when the soul of a nation long suppressed finds utterance'...while in a room with saffron and green carpet, Amed Sinai is still clutching a chair when Dr. Narlikar enters to inform him, 'On the stroke of midnight, Sinai brother, your Begum Sahalia gave birth to a large healthy child: a son!'" I was also encouraged by recalling a story from the *Mahabharata* in which Krishna is portrayed as a mischievous child who steals some of the butter that has been churned by the milkmaids with whom he has been playing. When his mother, Divali, makes him open his mouth to see if he is eating the stolen butter, she does not see butter inside but the whole world spread out before her. The point of this story for the millions of Indians who have heard it through the centuries is that Krishna is not a mischievous child, but a god. For me, its point was that the wide expanse and teeming life of the Indian scene could be encapsulated in an individual's observations and written down so that another individual could share them.

Although neither of these stories of India was directly related to my situation, both of them told me that it was not absurd to link a milestone in an individual's life with a milestone in the life of an entire people, to act on the basis of that linkage by undertaking a personal journey to observe a whole people's journey through a part of their history, and then to write about both journeys. Accordingly, I undertook a personal journey to India and, during its course, glimpsed something of the journey that India had taken during the 50 years that had followed its independence from British rule.

Inevitably, my reaction to what I heard and saw during this personal journey was framed in terms of the changes that had taken place since the 1950's. I found these changes to be substantial and, for the most part, negative in nature. I would be exaggerating to say that I was shocked, but to say that I was merely disappointed would be putting it too mildly. My feeling was somewhere between shock and disappointment—a sense of loss, a sense that my India had been lost during the course of India's journey to the 1990's.

This sense of loss drove me to ask questions. How did this happen? What were the forces behind it? What does all this augur for India's future? Given India's state at the end of the first half-century of its independence, what will it be like in another 50 years' time? These

13

were the questions that plagued me while I traveled through India and after my return to the United States. During my visit to India, I saw, if I may use a metaphor which is poles apart from India's climate, what appeared to be the tip of an iceberg. During the year that followed, I attempted to explore the terrain of the iceberg itself.

The result of this exploration is the description, diagnosis, and projection of free India' first half-century that follows. It takes as its starting point observations made during my journey of 1996. These observations were subsequently deepened and augmented by consulting the writings of others who had followed the Indian scene more extensively and over a longer period of time. These raw materials became grist for a mill which consisted of all that I had experienced and learned about the Indian way of thinking and acting during the years that I had lived and worked in India—corrected, refined, and enriched by the reading and reflection upon the broad panorama of Indian life that had been a part of my life during the more than a quarter-century that had gone by since my return to the United States.

My life in India began in 1952 when my family and I landed in Bombay on a TWA flight from Rome. Three days later we boarded the Deccan Express for three days and two nights of hot and dusty journeying to Madras. Our stay in Madras was just long enough to change from Central Station to Egmore Station and catch the overnight Trivandrum Express to Madurai, the city which was to be our home for the next 12 years. In 1964, we moved 75 miles and 6,000 feet up from Madurai to a hill town in the Western Ghats called Kodaikanal. Three years later, it was back to the South Indian plains, this time to Madras, the metropolis of southeastern India. Here we lived for the two years that preceded our return to the United States in 1969, enduring a high degree of heat and humidity broken by an occasional sea breeze from the Bay of Bengal.

Almost 27 years later, in January 1996, my wife and I visited the three places where we had lived in Madras State, today's Tamil Nadu (Land of the Tamils), as the first stops on our "pilgrimage". to revisit India. From Madras we flew to Bombay and then to Goa. After a week studying the 1990's Indian scene from the beautiful vantage point of Callangute Beach, followed by a short hop back to Bombay, we were once again on an Air India flight, this time to Delhi. From Delhi, we traveled overland to Agra, Jaipur, and Mandawa, before closing the "Golden Triangle" loop by returning to our starting point in the nation's capital. Our return visit to India, which had begun as a sentimental journey and subsequently became the springboard for a serious probe into the contemporary Indian scene, ended two days later when we caught Air India's February 14 flight from Delhi's Indira Gandhi International Airport to Heathrow Airport in London.

Covering thousands of miles in such a short time meant that my impressions of contemporary India were the product of what I saw and heard during fleeting moments of time rather than the result of an in-depth study of what I had encountered. They were also filtered through the lens of the memory of my India which I had brought back with me, the remembrance of an India that had existed almost 50 years earlier. These impressions left me with the distinct feeling that my India had been lost, that the India of the 1990's which I saw and heard was not only a different place, which I could have expected, but a far less attractive place, which I had not expected. This feeling came to me wherever I traveled, but it was strongest in the cities. I should have been prepared for this urban onslaught because I had been advised months earlier by both Indian and American friends who had visited India recently: "Stay out of the cities." Obviously, this was not advice that I could have followed to the letter because most of the places that I wanted to visit or had to pass through were the cities against which I had been warned. Still, their warnings should have made it easier for me to encounter the drastic degree to which the city life that I had known during the 1950's had deteriorated during the decades that had followed. But they did not make it easier, and I was shocked! Not shocked in an absolute sense, because the urban India of the 1990's was not different in kind from my urban India. Most of the problems that bedevil urban life today were there when I lived in Madurai and did social work in Madras's slums—overcrowding, poverty, congested streets, chaotic traffic, rundown and inadequate housing, slums, pavement dwellers, poor sanitation, degraded water and air quality, and uncollected rubbish. But shocked in a relative sense because these problems had become so much worse. They were present in my India but to a degree where urban life was not only tolerable, but enjoyable. By the 1990's, their seriousness had escalated to the point where urban life was on the verge of becoming intolerable.

Urban life verging on the intolerable was most apparent in the major cities: Madras, Bombay, Delhi. But medium-sized cities like Madurai, Agra, and Jaipur were not far behind, and even towns like Mahabalipuram and Kodaikanal had not escaped a precipitous decline in quality of life. All these urban settlements seemed to be bursting at their seams. It appeared that twice as many people were packed into living spaces that were already overcrowded 50 years ago and that three times as many motorized vehicles were being driven on streets that had been jammed for decades. A steady and increasing stream of pollutants were spewing into atmosphere and watercourses that had long been fouled. More and more rubbish was piled upon the mounds that had always littered the roadsides and open grounds. To be sure, many new middle-class houses and shiny high-rise buildings had been built, but even these improvements were plagued by chronic shortages of electricity and water, a result of a vast increase in demand outrunning a limited increase in supply.

To some extent, the geographic base of the cities had been expanded to absorb the tremendous increase in people, vehicles, and buildings, but not on an extensive scale. The widespread suburban expansion that had accommodated the growth of America's cities could not be repeated in India. Most of the poor immigrants who had swollen India's city populations had come from the countryside looking for any kind of work which they could do with their limited education and skills. Since the jobs that they found were poorly paid, and usually near the city's center, they could not afford to spend money on transportation or find decent housing. They had to live close to their work, and in degraded surroundings that better-off urban residents had spurned. So the millions of ruralites who had become urbanites during the 50 years since Independence had to pack themselves into the already overcrowded inner city rather than settle on the city's fringes. Slums had proliferated, and most of the limited amount of open space which used to be free of habitation was now covered with huts. At an even lower level of shelter, in the pits of urban society, were tens of thousands of urban immigrants who could not even find a place in the slums but were forced to live on the pavements, with nothing but pieces of cardboard and tattered plastic sheets to protect them from the elements.

Contrasting with these signs of urban decay was obvious evidence of improvements in city life which glossed over to some extent the dismal living conditions that lay underneath. Glitzy hotels, elegant office buildings and bungalows, and more and bigger automobiles attested to the fact that the rich had become richer during the past 50 years. This was no surprise. What was surprising were the obvious signs of a substantial urban middle class and the beginnings of a consumer society. More well-dressed men, women, and children walked the streets and rode on motor scooters or in taxis. Shops displayed television sets, VCR's, watches, cameras, household appliances, and other commodities that had been few and far between in the city shops of my India. Equally impressive evidence that India's middle class now had the "disposable income" characteristic of its Western counterpart was provided by the proliferation of Indian sightseers at places like Mahabalipuram, Kodaikanal, Goa, and Agra, which, 50 years ago, were largely the preserves of Western tourists.

City technology was also greatly improved, not only in degree but in kind. There were numerous public telephones, where 50 years before there had been none, and thousands more telephones in private homes. The telephone system was still full of bugs, but its service area had been extended. Telephones there were in 1950's India, but they were scarce commodities. The American College, where I served as bursar during that decade, had one telephone to take care of 1,000 students and 60 faculty members. Totally new in today's India was the array of computers and printers that were busily at work in shops and offices. Transportation technology had also been modernized, with buses, trucks, vans, taxis, scooters, and motorized rickshaws, much more than bullock and camel carts, horse drawn *jutkas*, cycle rickshaws, and hand-drawn carts, crowding the city streets.

Technological advances and a growing middle class bear witness to the fact that a substantial degree of economic development had taken place and that its impact had been felt especially in the cities. But it was also plain that the benefits of that economic development had not "trickled down" to the great majority of the population who still lived in varying degrees of poverty. Evidence of the continuation of poverty even in the face of substantial economic development was everywhere, concentrated in the cities and diffused in the countryside. Droves of unemployed men inhabited the metropolises, the cities, the towns, and the villages, waiting for work. Even greater numbers of underemployed men and women used every device at their disposal to eke out a livelihood—in V.S. Naipaul's words, "many small hands doing many small things." It might well be that the urban and rural poor of the late 1990's were no poorer than they were 50 years before, but they were obviously no better off, and it was also obvious that there were many more of them.

A Country Study of India published in 1985 by the American University painted a vivid picture of India's underemployment:

"There were thousands of washers, pressers, rickshaw drivers and pullers... Businesses divide and subdivide jobs; retail stores employ a clerk to total the bill, to collect payment and still another to wrap and deliver the order to the customers... There are ear cleaners and cotton fluffers and those who sell the Ganges' sacred mud and myriad statues of sundry deities. There are delivery services that cart lunches from suburban homes to downtown businesses. People sort the garbage for potentially recyclable or resaleable items... Literates station themselves outside post offices to write letters for those unable to do so; a portable typewriter and table enable one to type documents for those in need. And the telephone system works so erratically that companies hire women whose sole job it is to dial and redial numbers until a connection is made."

Just as the signs of poverty were widespread, so also were the signs of the malnutrition that it spawned. While the January 1996 newspapers reported almost verbatim the speeches of Central Government ministers taking credit for the fact that India had become a food exporting nation, India's streets and byways were full of men, women, and children who obviously did not have enough to eat. The absence of famine conditions and the availability of some grain for export showed that the increase in food production that had been achieved since Independence had managed to keep pace with the increase in population. What had not kept pace were the incomes of those on the bottom rungs of India's socio-economic ladder who could not buy enough food to maintain bodily health.

It has often been said that India is a land of contradictions, and here was an obvious case in point: a growing middle class with "disposable income" and the beginnings of a consumer society on the one hand, and widespread poverty and malnutrition on the other. Contradictory as these developments were, they merged in the question that inevitably came to the mind of one who, like myself, observed them through the lens of 1950's India: What had happened to the ideal of *sarvodaya* (service) which Mahatma Gandhi had preached? Gandhi envisaged free India as a society in which people followed a simple rural way of life, spurning modern gadgets and appliances and dedicating themselves, not to the pursuit of worldly goods, but to moral development, social harmony, and care for one another. What I saw of the India of the late 1990's made it plain that his vision had evaporated during the almost five decades of urbanization, industrialization, and economic development that had followed his death.

Traveling through the India of 1996 also made it plain that another of Mahatma Gandhi's ideals had been forgotten, *ahimsa* (non-violence). The Indian Army was battling Muslim separatists in Kashmir and using military force to keep the peace in the Punjab and Assam. Newspaper headlines proclaimed the successful testing of a missile with a range of 250 kilometers and powerful enough to carry a nuclear weapon. The country's leaders were exulting over India's development of this missile because its range encompassed many of Pakistan's major cities and thus put much of the population of India's major opponent under the potential threat of nuclear attack. That India was determined to keep its potential nuclear threat alive was evidenced by its refusal to sign the Nuclear Test Ban Treaty even in the face of intense pressure from the United States and other members of the world community. The sad irony here is that it was Nehru who originated the idea of the treaty in 1954. Some 40 years later, it was India that had blocked the adoption of this agreement.

Although a state of peace existed with Pakistan, 1996 India was replete with signs of a national conviction that it must be prepared for the worst from Muslims living both within and outside its borders. The roads of Rajasthan which we traveled were congested with convoys of infantry and artillery units heading northwest, either for the Pakistan border or for Kashmir. Passports were checked over and over again in an apparent effort to detect foreign terrorists who might plant bombs or otherwise cause damage and unrest—by the clerk in the hotel, by airline staff and police personnel at the airport—when baggage was checked, when seats were assigned, during the security check, at the entrance to the gate waiting room, and even at the door of the aircraft. Going through these numerous passport checks and watching the army convoys roll by gave one the impression that the land of Mahatma Gandhi, the apostle of non-violence, had moved so far in the direction of militarization that it appeared to be living on a semi-war footing.

Reinforcing this impression was the fact that the Indian Air Force had been given control of the airspace over Delhi. Civilian aircraft flying in and out of the Indira Gandhi International Airport were restricted to a single corridor, despite the fact that incoming and outgoing flights had increased from 170 to 290 per day since 1993. This meant that aircraft taking off and landing at the same time had to fly at the same heading and could be separated only by an altitude difference of 1,000 feet. The space limitation was one of the factors that caused a Kazakh freight plane and a Saudi Arabian passenger plane to collide on November 12, 1996, resulting in 349 deaths, the fourth worst aircraft accident on record. Shortly after this accident, an organization of Indian air traffic controllers recommended that corridors for civilian aircraft landing and taking off be separated. According to the Indian Air Traffic Controllers Guild statement, the collision "could have been averted if there had been separate arrival and departure routes at Delhi airport." In fact, Indian air traffic controllers had been making this request for a long time, but the Indian Air Force, which uses part of the airport as a military airfield, has steadfastly refused to give its approval.

Less than two months after the disaster, Indian newspapers reported a near collision between an Indian Airlines plane and an Air India plane, which had both landed at the same time in the Delhi airport's one corridor open to civilian aircraft. The Civil Aviation Department hastened to deny that any such incident had occurred, asserting that the two aircraft had been separated by 2,000 feet. Given this official denial, no investigation was conducted to ascertain what had actually happened, but the Central Government's speedy and emphatic defense of the "one corridor" policy showed that it had no intention of diminishing the degree to which India's military controlled the air space surrounding the capital's major airport.

Sharing the front pages of India's newspapers in January and February 1996 with the report of the successful testing of the 250-kilometer missile was a barrage of stories about the Jain brothers corruption scandal. The Jain brothers, prominent Delhi businessmen, were being investigated by the Central Bureau of Investigation (CBI) for possible violation of India's foreign exchange laws. During a raid on one of their homes, the CBI unearthed a notebook in which the Jain brothers had kept a record of payments which they had made to leading politicians in exchange for favored treatment in the awarding of government contracts. Although bribing government officials and politicians was an old story, two features of the Jain brothers' influence buying operation had brought it to the front pages: firstly, the total amount of the bribes involved—63 crores ($18 million)—a large figure by Indian standards and one which shocked even the most cynical of India's political observers and activists; and, secondly, the high status of the politicians who had received Jain brothers' money. Seven were Cabinet Ministers and one was the president of the Bharatiya Janata Party (BJP), the Congress Indira Party's major political rival. All eight of them had to resign their Parliamentary posts when the scandal broke.

The Jain brothers scandal became the talk of the country only because Prime Minister Narasimha Rao, under whose authority the

CBI operated, had allowed the investigation findings to be made public. Rumors circulated that one detail that was not revealed to the public was that Narasimha Rao's name was among those found in the Jain brothers' notebook. Rao's political enemies, and even one of the seven Cabinet Ministers who had resigned, charged him with authorizing the CBI to go public in order to discredit the leading Congress Indira Party politicians who might rival him for the Prime Minister's post if the party won the general election scheduled for the following April. As an added political bonus, the Jain brothers scandal had implicated the president of the BJP, the Congress Indira Party's major opponent in the coming general election. The BJP had been trumpeting itself as the more honest of the two parties, and showing the public that its president was corrupt would give the lie to that claim.

There were those in the press who praised Narasimha Rao for letting the chips of the CBI investigation fall where they might, even when the result was the resignation of seven of his Cabinet Ministers. But most commentators explained Rao's motives in terms of his political interests rather than in terms of his opposition to political corruption. And all of them agreed that, whatever Narasimha Rao might have had in mind, the Jain brothers scandal highlighted the astonishing degree to which political corruption had escalated during the years when "Permit Raj" had given way to a more or less free market economy.

Although the newspaper stories did not raise the question, apparently because Indian reporters and editors of the late 1990's had forgotten what he stood for, the query that came to my mind as I read about the Jain brothers' notebook was: "What has happened to Mahatma Gandhi's *satyagraha* (moral force) which was the foundation of his strategy for winning freedom from British rule and which, after that freedom had been won, was a political principle that was still honored, if not always observed, in my India's political life?" Gandhi believed and put into practice the conviction that it is moral strength that provides the power for successful political action and, therefore, that moral principles should be the guide followed by free India's political leaders. The Jain brothers scandal, coming as the high point of a history of ever increasing political corruption, made it clear that, more often than not, it was the bribes that were offered and received rather than moral principles that determined the actions taken by India's 1990's political leaders.

These evidences of the demise of the three pillars of Gandhian political philosophy—*sarvodaya, ahimsa,* and *satyagraha*—shocked me in much the way that I had been shocked when I saw what had happened to the physical dimensions of Indian life. But here, at the level of the things that determine the spirit of a nation, my sense of shock was even more profound. On the physical side, India of the 1990's was different from the India I had known in degree, not in kind. The problems were not new, only more serious. In the realm of India's national spirit, however, the difference was one in kind. The problem was new. My India had a clear political and social vision, conceived by Mahatma Gandhi and, except for its economic dimensions, carried into practice by Jawaharlal Nehru. So far as I could see, India of the 1990's had no political and social vision. The masses of the poor were understandably preoccupied with the struggle to survive. The goal of the middle class and elite appeared to be to acquire more material possessions in order to lead a more comfortable life. The aim of the Narasimha Rao government was to promote a free market economy that would accelerate economic development and thus build support for the Congress Indira Party so that it could win the next general election and stay in power.

Not only did I experience a more profound sense of shock as I saw the evidence that the vision which had inspired my India was no longer there in 1996, but I was also overcome by a feeling that was not far from despair. All I could think of was the oft-repeated statement that a people who have lost their vision will perish. That feeling verging on despair came from the realization that there is an intrinsic connection between the challenges that a people face and the vision needed to inspire them and lead them to find the strength and the means to meet those challenges. If they have that vision, they will overcome their challenges. If they do not have that vision, their challenges will overcome them. And, if this truth holds for nations in general, does it not hold for India?

The feeling of shock at the deterioration of India's physical world struck me most forcefully on two occasions during our tour. The first was in Madras when we were catching the bus to Mahabalipuram, the site of the shore temple and the rock carving of "Arjuna's Penance," produced by South India's eighth-century Pallava dynasty. The bus started from the Mofussil (Suburban) Bus Stand, which turned out to be a combination of foul shambles and vehicle gridlock, rather than a functioning bus terminal. Garbage and rubbish were heaped everywhere. The surrounding shops had not been washed and the drains had not been flushed since the northeast monsoon had ended two months earlier. Dozens of buses entered through a single narrow lane and left through a single exit. The result was one incessant traffic jam. Buses moved inch by inch, their horns blaring. Drivers cursed each other for refusing to give way, and passengers took their lives in their hands trying to find and board the buses that would take them to their destinations.

The streets of the Madras that I had lived in during the 1960's were certainly crowded, but they were not overtaxed. They could manage the traffic without it grinding to a halt and without straining human nerves and endangering life and limb. But the streets of the Madras of the late 1990's, as exemplified in the Mofussil Bus Stand, were overtaxed, almost to breaking point. That scene, almost like a glimpse of hell, made it plain that Madras's old urban life—easy going and relatively stress-free — had been lost and had been replaced by one where people and vehicles and the environment within which they moved were subjected to pressures that threatened to overwhelm them.

The second occasion was in Agra, during a visit to the Taj Mahal. I had seen the Taj Mahal once before, in 1968, and thought that it was so beautiful that it belonged in a fairyland, not in our drab and dreary world. It was a joy to see in 1996 that, at least to the naked eye, the building looked much the same as it had 28 years earlier. During the intervening time, Agra had grown roughly threefold to become a city of one and a half million people. The smoke stacks of the numerous factories that had been built in its vicinity were spewing out what the Uttar Pradesh Government admitted was five times as much sulfuric and nitric acid as the marble of the Taj Mahal can tolerate over the long term without suffering serious harm. The "acid rain" damage that had occurred thus far was not yet visible from a distance. Nor had the city's growth infiltrated the buildings' immediate surroundings. Fortunately, the Mogul emperors built their mausoleums within extensive parks surrounded by high walls. With this protection, even though shops and taxi stands had moved right up to its gates, neither they nor any of Agra's other urban accouterments had spoiled the beauty of the 25-acre park which surrounds the Taj Mahal.

Nevertheless, there was one point at which Agra's growth had damaged the Taj Mahal's setting, not in a way that one could see but in a way that one could smell. That was at the rear of the mausoleum, where the Yamuna River flows by. Agra dumps its untreated sewage and waste water into the river. As the city had tripled in size, it had become so polluted that, during the low flow conditions that prevail during all but the monsoon months, it stinks. When I smelled that stench, I was brought back from fairyland to the real world. To my nose, the magical beauty of the Taj Mahal in its impressive setting on the high bank of the Yamuna River, the beauty that I had relished on my first visit 28 years earlier, had begun to lose some of its luster. At the same time, I was thankful that, although its setting was already beginning to suffer degradation, the building itself had not yet lost its glory. But, even as I took comfort from this thought, I could not forget that Agra's factories were raining down showers of "acid rain" day in and day out and that, if these "acid" showers continue unchecked, the Taj Mahal's untarnished glory will be a memory before another 28 years have gone by. If that happens, what a tragic loss it will be for India and for the whole world!

Especially poignant on those occasions in Madras and Agra, but developing steadily throughout my travels, was this growing feeling that my India had been lost during the decades leading up to 1997, when India would be celebrating its first half-century of freedom. This growing sense of loss brought to mind some words which, while the meteorological metaphor which is at their heart is totally out of place in India's climate, encapsulated my feeling. They were written centuries ago in medieval France by François Villon as the refrain of a poem entitled *Ballade des Dames du Temps Jadis* (Ballad of Ladies Past). In this poem, he laments the loss of the renowned and beautiful women who had been celebrated in myth and history before his time by asking: *"Mais où sont les neiges d'antan?"* ("But where are the snows of yesteryear?") These famous ladies had disappeared like last winter's snow had disappeared when the spring sun had begun to shine.

Villon's question referred to the loss of the celebrated women of times long gone. He wanted to know why they had become only a memory. My mind transposed his question to the loss of my India. Villon used the metaphor of the snow which piles up in the winter and then disappears completely when spring comes. Despite the fact that the Indian language that I know, Tamil, does not even have a word for snow, my mind applied that metaphor to the hot and humid Indian world. My India of the 1950's had seemed a substantial and enduring reality but, when I encountered the India of the late 1990's, I found that it had disappeared. And, following Villon's mind, I wanted to know what had happened to it. That question led me to a second, which Villon did not ask. He did not ask why these celebrated women had disappeared because, in their case, that question had a simple and straightforward answer. As time had passed, they had either died, had been killed, or had lost their notoriety. But the process by which the life of a nation is lost is not simple and straightforward. As I contemplated the loss of my India, I had to ask, and try to answer, a second question: "Why had it disappeared?"

~ PART ONE ~

FREE INDIA'S FIRST
HALF-CENTURY DESCRIBED

❖

Population, Economy, and Society

Although I was convinced when I returned to the United States that the India of the 1950's had been lost in the India of the 1990's, I had to recognize that this conviction was based upon observations made during a short stay and upon travels through only a few regions and cities. Obviously, I had to probe further and deeper before I could be sure that what I had seen were glimpses of an accurate picture that held throughout the country as a whole. The first written evidence that I found confirming that my impressions were not an aberration but a window into what had happened to India during the first 50 years of its independence was a dispatch written in 1993 by Barbara Crossette, the *New York Times'* Delhi correspondent:

"Despite the free market economic policies thrust on India in 1991, this ancient nation remains divided on how to tackle the challenges ahead. Parts of India are slipping into the levels of sub-Saharan Africa as far as quality of life is concerned... It had been a grave disappointment to many Indians that in a half century of independence so much optimism about the strength of Indian society has turned to uncertainty and heartbreak... In 1947 India was a pioneer and model of the post-colonial age. No other nation emerging from imperialism had a towering figure like Mohandas Kamarchand Gandhi. ...Jawaharlal Nehru ranked among the great international personalities of the age... Half a century later India seems to be bent on self-destruction."

Since they were supported by observations made over several years and covering the whole country, Barbara Crossette's words reinforced my impression that the promise of a better life for all its people with which India had embarked upon its Independence era had been lost by the 1990's. They also made it clear that it was worthwhile probing further to see why we agreed that, on the whole, India had gone downhill during the decades that had followed 1947. First and foremost, we saw that free India's population had exploded during its first half-century. When I first came to India in 1952, it was approaching half a billion. By 1997, it was approaching one billion. In the year of their 50th anniversary, the people of free India consisted of approximately 950 million men, women, and children—almost two and a half times the number counted 49 years earlier on the first Independence Day. India's population problem was exacerbated by two considerations over and above the astronomical numbers involved. Firstly, its vast population was concentrated in a relatively limited area: one-seventh of the world's population living on one-fortieth of the world's land mass. Secondly, a higher proportion was now packed into cities with boundaries not much larger than those of 50 years ago. During the 1950's, approximately 20% of India's population were urban dwellers. The 1990's urban proportion was 50% higher. Twenty cities had populations exceeding 1 million, four of them reaching or exceeding the 5-million mark (Bombay with 13 million, Calcutta with 11 million, Delhi with 8 million, and Madras with 5 million).

Rapid population growth in India's major cities had not only continued unabated for 50 years, but the rate of increase had accelerated. Between 1975 and 1985, for example, countrywide urban population increased by 46%. The rate of increase in some cities was much higher. Bangalore led the way at 75%, followed by Jaipur at 57%, and Delhi at 56%. Even though the rate of increase in the "big four" cities other than Delhi fell below the 46% national figure, their already large populations rose at a substantial rate during this one decade: Bombay up 37%, Madras up 34%, and Calcutta up 30%. As a result, "big city" population density had reached unbelievably high figures by 1997. Bombay's population density was 150,000 per square mile, and Calcutta's was 55,000 per square mile, compared with 22,000 per square mile in Tokyo and 10,000 in New York.

On the positive side, the socio-economic stratification of this burgeoning population had undergone a marked change. Since

Independence, particularly during the 1980's and 1990's, India had developed a substantial middle class. It is difficult to define a middle class because a person's sense of his or her socio-economic status is a matter of self-perception as well as standard of living, but most observers agree that India's middle class now constitutes roughly 20% of the population. One cannot even guess what its size was during the 1950's because it was not very noticeable in a country where the major socio-economic division was between rich and poor, and there were relatively few people in between. Nevertheless, the development of this substantial middle class, positive as it was, did not change the continuing hard fact of Indian life, that about half of its population lived below the poverty line, as India defines that poverty line. Relative to other socio-economic groups, the proportion of poor people was not any higher than it was during the 1950's. But, in absolute terms, the number of poor people had increased approximately 100% because they still accounted for 50% of a population that had roughly doubled.

At the dawn of Independence, India outwardly displayed most of the characteristics of a "Third World" developing country. By 1997, it outwardly displayed many of the characteristics of a modern industrial and commercial nation. There were numerous colleges, steel mills, manufacturing and chemical plants, mines, offices, and scientific establishments. India had also developed computer-based service industries, nuclear power plants, and a space program, none of which had even been imagined during the 1950's. Expanded educational opportunities had produced a large cadre of scientists, engineers, and computer programmers.

The average annual rate of increase in Gross National Product produced by economic development had exceeded 5% during the 1980's and, after a fall in 1991, had gone up again to a high point of 7% in 1996, a rate of growth that put even the United States to shame. Between 1980 and 1995 the structure of the economy had undergone a significant shift in the direction of a developed country. Agriculture's share of the Gross Domestic Product had fallen from 38% to 28%. Industry's contribution had increased from 26% to 31%, and the service sector had expanded from 36% to 41%.

But underneath the modern, developed surface lay a solid residue of a "Third World" society. Poverty was still massive and endemic. Unemployment and underemployment were rife. Almost 70% of the population still depended upon agriculture for its livelihood. Millions of children still did not go to school, with the result that literacy among the general population had not risen above 50% and was much lower than that among women.

While the rapid industrialization that had taken place during the first 50 years of Indian independence had put India among the top 10 industrialized nations in the world, its factories operated at a low level of efficiency, and most of them turned out products that could not compete on world markets. Supporting these industries was an inadequate and shaky infrastructure that placed limits on factory productivity. Electricity and water were in short supply. Transportation and communication facilities were overtaxed and poorly maintained, with the result that they could not be relied upon to function wherever and whenever needed.

Along with substantial economic and industrial development, the bright spot among India's achievements in the last half-century was in the area of food production, which was 250% higher in 1997 than it had been during the 1950's. India had experienced a "green revolution." High yield seeds, increased use of fertilizers and mechanization, better irrigation techniques, and more land under cultivation had combined to increase wheat production many fold, and rice and corn yields to a substantial degree. Not only was more food available for consumption, but food reserves to guard against famine were at record levels. Some grain was even being exported.

Unfortunately, malnutrition still persisted among the half of the population who lived at or below the poverty line. The "green revolution" had kept the increased number of "have nots" from starving, but it had not enabled them to eat better. Former Prime Minister Indira Gandhi, speaking before her assassination in 1984, candidly admitted that this was the dark shadow in the bright food production picture: "The (food) battle is far from won. Hunger is far from vanished. Many old problems persist... Although India achieved comparative self-sufficiency in food, malnutrition is still prevalent. Not because of lack in the market but because many people do not have enough money in their pockets to buy it."

Not only were the structure, functioning, and productivity of India's 1990's economy very different from what they had been during the 1950's, but the economic policies pursued by the Central Government bore little resemblance to those followed during the 1950's. Under the leadership of Prime Minister Jawaharlal Nehru and with the support of the Congress Party, the Central Governments of the first decades after Independence were committed to Fabian socialism—parliamentary democracy on the political front and a mixed, command/free market system on the economic front. Following Five-Year Plans prepared by a Central Planning Commission, resources were allocated to meet the goal of rapid industrial development. Since these resources were limited and rapid industrialization increased demand, a permit system was instituted to ration everything from steel products and cement to wheat flour and sugar. Congress Party critics called this system "Permit Raj" and complained that its burden was almost as onerous as that of the British Raj which had only recently given up its control of Indian economic life.

In line with the principle espoused by Mahatma Gandhi and endorsed by Jawaharlal Nehru that India should be, as far as possible, economically self-sufficient, foreign investment was discouraged by limiting the degree to which Indian enterprises could be owned by foreigners and by instituting currency regulations that made it all but impossible to convert the Indian rupee to other currencies. In order to make sure that the limited amount of foreign exchange in Indian hands was used to purchase investment rather than consumer goods, no item costing more than $10 could be imported without a permit from the Central Bank in Delhi. In this way, "Permit Raj" jurisdiction was extended to foreign as well as domestic economic transactions.

India's transportation and communication facilities had been government-owned since British days. What the Congress Party's pursuit of Fabian socialist principles did was to add to the public sector the irrigation and power generating projects, the steel mills, the cement factories and the coal mines that were constructed under the early Five-Year Plans. At the same time, important segments of the economy remained in private hands, most notably the agricultural sector. Agricultural lands were not taken over by the government and collectivized, nor were state farms established. The Nehru governments did not even take effective steps to break up large land holdings into small plots that could be acquired by the millions of landless farm laborers. Some states did pass laws limiting the acreage that an individual could own, but these laws were easily circumvented by giving individual members of a family title to the maximum acreage allowed but keeping control of the total acreage in the hands of the family elders. By following this practice, large landowners succeeded in turning such land redistribution laws as were passed into expressions of good intentions rather than effective tools for land redistribution. Commercial activity and production of consumer goods also remained in the private sector. Not only small shops but also major companies continued to be privately owned and operated. Industrial magnates like Birla turned out Ambassador automobiles in Calcutta, and an exception to the rule that heavy industry should be in Central Government hands was made for Tata's steel mill in Jamshedpur.

On balance, then, India's economic system in the 1950's was a mix of public and private sectors with the emphasis on the public side. In the 1990's, on the other hand, it was the private sector that was the center of gravity. No doubt, a significant residue of the command economy and the "Permit Raj" still remained. A Five-Year Plan was still in effect, although it was more a statement of goals and objectives than a guide to be followed in allocating Central Government resources. The fact that the Planning Commission's 1996 meeting was the first held in three years was evidence that the Five-Year Plans were not what they used to be. Some commodities were still distributed by permit, but they were comparatively few in number. Central and State governments still played important economic roles through the decisions they made in spending the considerable public funds at their disposal. Finally, and perhaps most strikingly, given the substantial shift in favor of the private sector, well over half of India's industrial assets remained in government hands, despite the fact that, due to their gross inefficiency, they produced only about one-fifth of the country's industrial goods.

While the public sector still played an important economic role, India's economy of the 1990's was more market driven than government directed. The changeover from a predominantly command economy to a predominantly market driven economy, begun slowly during the 1980's under Prime Minister Rajiv Gandhi, accelerated rapidly during the 1990's under Prime Minister Narasimha Rao. During the regimes of these two Prime Ministers, the Fabian socialism of Jawaharlal Nehru, which had provided India's economic guiding light during the early decades of the Independence era, was replaced by a new economic model: free market capitalism.

Nor was Narasimha Rao concerned, as was Jawaharlal Nehru, about fostering economic self-sufficiency. In fact, he took exactly the opposite tack by encouraging foreign investment and opening the Indian market to foreign consumer goods. In 1991, laws were passed allowing foreign investors to own a majority of shares in Indian companies and making the Indian rupee convertible into US dollars and other foreign currencies. These changes in economic policy produced quick and spectacular economic and social results. In the economic realm, the GNP's growth was stimulated by a major infusion of foreign capital, which rose from $30 million in 1990 to $5 billion in 1995. The annual rate of increase in GNP, which had averaged 3.5 % between 1950 and 1980 and had fallen as low as 1.2% in 1991, shot up to 6–7% within five years. Exports increased at an annual rate of 25%, and foreign exchange reserves, which stood at $1.2 billion in 1991, reached $22 billion in 1996. Despite this rapid acceleration in economic activity, the inflation rate fell from 17% to 5% during the same five-year period. In the social realm, the pace of development of India's consumer oriented society was stepped up because greatly sought after foreign goods could now be freely purchased by the growing middle class.

In many ways, then, the official functioning of the 1990's economy was a very different story from its official functioning during the 1950's. If, however, one looked at unofficial ways of doing business, one would find that the difference between these two eras was not so great. Although the power of politicians and public officials to make decisions that had a direct impact on economic activity was not as extensive as it was during the days of Fabian socialism and the "Permit Raj," it was still considerable. Some commodities were still distributed through permits, and government approval had to be received for joint ventures between Indian and foreign investors. Most importantly, State and Central governments still allocated substantial resources through the contracts which they granted. Since decisions regarding who would be granted permits, what joint ventures would be approved, and who would get government contracts were in the hands of politicians and public officials, political influence and bribes were frequently used to induce them to do favors for clients who paid in money or votes rather than to follow the economic path that led to the public good. Such practices were widespread and constituted a substantial residual of the command economy of the 1950's.

❖

Demise of Gandhianism and Nehruism

Substantial as was the difference between the economic system of the 1950's and that of 1997, the changes that had taken place in political life were even more striking. The most dramatic among them was the complete demise of the political vision that had inspired India during its first years of Independence. That vision was mainly the product of the trio of principles taught and exemplified by Mahatma Gandhi: *sarvodaya* (service), *ahimsa* (non-violence), and *satyagraha* (moral force). Added to Gandhi's basic triumvirate was his conviction, which was written into India's Constitution and supported by the words and deeds of the first Prime Minister, Jawaharlal Nehru, that India should be a pluralistic secular society. Although the Indian people were overwhelmingly Hindu, although much blood had been shed in the clashes that had taken place between Hindus, Muslims, and Sikhs at the time of Partition, Gandhi and Nehru steered India away from the natural inclination to set itself up as a Hindu state. They launched the new nation with a consensus that India should be a pluralistic secular society in which all Indians, whatever their religion or caste, were equal citizens, entitled to equal protection under the law.

Tragically, when Gandhi tried to carry this principle from the political realm into the deeper level of social relations, he was rebuffed in his efforts to give untouchables (whom he named *Harijans*—God's People) the status of decent human beings, and paid with his life for his empathy with Muslims. Nevertheless, the degree of acceptance of his belief that free India should be a pluralistic secular state with equal rights for all its citizens was sufficient to make it possible for successive Congress Party governments to implement an "affirmative action" program aimed at improving the political and economic position of untouchables and members of India's numerous tribes. Legislative seats and administrative posts were reserved for untouchables and tribals, and scholarships were granted to children belonging to what the Central Government called "backward and scheduled castes and tribes."

It was Nehru, Gandhi's devoted follower, who began the process by which the Congress Party began to eclipse the Gandhian vision for a free India. While he affirmed and supported much of Gandhi's political program and all of Gandhi's social program, Nehru differed sharply with his mentor on two fronts. In the first place, he rejected Gandhi's economic notion that India should remain a traditional, rural country deriving its livelihood from agriculture and village handicrafts. Nehru believed in and carried into practice the idea that India could become a prosperous and influential country only by modernizing and industrializing, which also meant that India would urbanize.

Secondly, although he espoused the ideal that political disputes should be settled by peaceful means, Nehru refused to follow Gandhi's principle of *ahimsa* in every situation. Where military force was, in his view, necessary to pursue India's national interests, he was prepared to, and did, use it. When Pakistan irregulars threatened in 1948 to take over Kashmir, he dispatched the Indian Army to secure the two-thirds of that state that India has continued to hold to the present day. When the Portuguese refused to follow the British and French examples by giving up their Indian holdings, he lost patience in 1961 and ordered Indian troops to take over Goa and the other Portuguese enclaves. A year later, after he had failed to settle border disputes with China in Ladakh and the North East Frontier Agency by diplomatic means, he decided to strengthen India's hand by ordering the Indian Army units assigned to the disputed areas to act more aggressively to pressure Chinese troops into withdrawing. The Chinese responded by sending in a large scale invading force that approached the border of Assam before unilaterally withdrawing, thus dealing a humiliating defeat to the Indian Army and a crushing blow to Nehru's policy of basing India's Greater Asian policy on friendly relations with China.

The erosion of Gandhianism, which Nehru began in the economic sphere as early as in 1947 and continued until the early 1960's in the military sphere, was complete by the end of free India's first half-century. Gandhi's vision was totally absent from the 1997 political scene. No doubt, Gandhi's name was still venerated, but, as a demigod, not as a flesh and blood political prophet whose "Experiments with Truth" guided the Indian nation. Some politicians still wore the *khadi* (homespun cloth, woven from the thread which Gandhi urged all Indians to spin), not because they still followed his principles, but because they believed that associating themselves with Gandhi's memory would give them a moral image in the eyes of the voters superior to that of their opponents.

One occasion on which the demise of Gandhian influence was clearly displayed was the Congress Indira Party's 1985 celebration of the 100th anniversary of the founding of the Indian National Congress. One would have expected that Gandhi's dominant role in the party's history would have been highlighted, but it was not. Even more demeaning was Gandhi's absence from the anniversary brochure that was circulated. On its cover were pictures of the men and women who had led the party down through its history. Gandhi's was not among them. An even more obvious sign of Gandhi's absence from the 1990's political scene was an empty pedestal standing at the intersection of the two main boulevards that run through Delhi's Central Government enclave. During the days of the British Raj, a statue of King George V stood on that pedestal. Obviously, that statue had to be, and was, removed when India became free. After Gandhi's assassination in 1948, the suggestion was made that King George's statue be replaced by a statue of Mahatma Gandhi. Almost 50 years later, the pedestal was still empty. Gandhi's statue was conspicuous by its absence. There is now talk of erecting a statue of Gandhi in Antarctica to commemorate free India's 50th anniversary!

It was almost as if contemporary India did not know what to do with Gandhi as he became more and more a memory and less and less a moral and political force. For 48 years after his assassination, his ashes were kept in the vault of a branch of the State Bank of India in Orissa. How and why they had ended up in this depository was never made clear. In January 1997 officials announced that Gandhi's ashes would be delivered to his great-grandson. This announcement came after the Supreme Court had ruled, in response to a request that it order a chemical test of their authenticity, that the ashes were really Gandhi's and that they should be handed over to his family. According to the official announcement, his grandson would take them to several places around the country where important events had taken place during Gandhi's non-violent campaign to end British rule. Thereafter, a Hindu ceremony would be held at the confluence of the Ganges and the Yamuna rivers, India's most sacred spot, during which Gandhi's ashes would be immersed. To be sure, the procedure that was finally agreed upon was an appropriate way to honor Gandhi's contribution to Indian freedom and to dispose of his remains, but why it had taken 48 years for official India to devise and implement that scenario remained a puzzle.

One part of the answer, of course, was the dragging out of the legal proceedings, but another obvious part was the indifference of both the leaders of the Central Government and the Congress Party. They made it plain at the close of the 48-year process that they were not concerned about when or how Gandhi's ashes were disposed of, not only by taking no action to speed up the court proceedings, but also by absenting themselves from the immersion ceremony when it finally did take place. One would have expected the Prime Minister to be there when the remains of the man who had been regarded as the father of free India were laid to rest, but he had an excuse in that he was from a rival party. What was inexcusable was the absence of the leaders of the Congress Indira Party. Even though the latter owed their position of political power and influence to what Gandhi had done during the days of the liberation struggle, they did not want to be identified with him any longer when he was buried.

The Prime Minister's absence from the ceremony was all the more striking as a repudiation of what Gandhi stood for because of a ceremony which he had attended a week earlier. That ceremony had been held to commemorate the 100th anniversary of the birth of Subhas Chandra Bose, and it had been accompanied by the declaration of a national holiday and the issuing of a stamp bearing his image. The high point of the celebration had been the unveiling of a statue of Bose which stood in the courtyard of Parliament Building. Only six other leaders of India's Independence movement had statues in the courtyard, and Mahatma Gandhi was one of them. The placing of Bose's statue adjacent to Gandhi's had created a strange juxtaposition of these two Indian political leaders because, during their lifetimes, they had espoused dramatically opposed political philosophies and strategies. These sharp differences had inevitably led to open conflict. Bose had tried to convince the Congress Party that using violent means was the way to achieve independence from British rule. Gandhi had succeeded in convincing the party that it should use only non-violent means. The clash between Bose and Gandhi had come in 1939. Gandhi had emerged the victor, and Bose had been expelled from the Congress Party.

His reaction had been to leave India and travel to Berlin and Tokyo, where he was welcomed with open arms by Axis leaders who assured him that an Axis victory in its struggle with Britain would lead to an independent India. Won over by their assurances, Bose had thrown in his lot with the Axis and eventually had taken on the role of commander of an "Indian National Army" made up of three divisions recruited from among the thousands of Indian soldiers who had been captured by the Japanese and Indian civilians caught up in the Japanese Occupation of Malaysia and Singapore. Members of this "Army" had fought alongside the Japanese when they invaded Assam in 1943, and the result was that, at this point in World War II, Indian troops under Mountbatten had exchanged fire with Indian troops under Bose. The fighting in Assam had been the high point in Bose's military career, which had ended 12 days after Hiroshima when he was killed in a plane crash while seeking refuge in Taipei. His reputation as an Indian nationalist leader had ended when the Axis powers had been defeated, and Mahatma Gandhi had led India to freedom following his strategy of non-violence.

The celebration to install Bose's statue in the Parliament House courtyard had been designed to rehabilitate Bose's name and restore his reputation as an honored leader of the Independence movement. By placing his statue alongside Gandhi, his 1939 political defeat at

Gandhi's hands had been made good, and the tarnish had been removed from his memory, both as regards his having used violent means to pursue Independence and his having sided with the Fascist powers that had sought to destroy democracy. As he unveiled Bose's statue, Prime Minister Deve Gowda had praised him as an ardent Indian nationalist who had been prepared to use any means and ally himself with any powers that would help to free India from British rule. Deve Gowda had no qualms about praising a nationalist leader who had taken a line dramatically opposed to Gandhi's political principles even though he knew that one week later Gandhi's ashes would finally be disposed of in a ceremony which could not help but bring to some Indian minds the crucial role which Gandhi had played in freeing India from British rule. He had no qualms because he knew that most Indians had come by 1997 to view what Gandhi stood for as a venerable memory that had no relevance to free India's present political situation and to view Bose's political philosophy as a more realistic and useful guide in the world of the 1990's.

The rehabilitation of Subhas Chandra Bose was bad enough, but what was a more heartrending repudiation of Mahatma Gandhi had come from the segment of India's population that he had nurtured even more than the Muslims whom he had supported at the cost of his life. The most important element in his program of social reform was to give India's untouchables a respectable place in society. Since their traditional place had been that of "outcastes" who had no power within the political, economic, or social system to promote their cause, Gandhi named them *Harijans,* people who had no one to care about them except God. While the untouchables of the 1950's were glad to be called by the name that Gandhi had bestowed on them, the untouchables of the 1990's had rejected it. They insisted upon being called *dalits* (the oppressed). They maintained that the word *Harijan* was a euphemism for children of temple prostitutes and refused to be labeled with a term that they thought made them unclean. The tragedy here was that, in coining the word *Harijan,* Gandhi was trying to get away from the caste Hindu tradition of considering untouchables to be ritually unclean. To do so, he came up with a term that connoted

41

the opposite of unclean by linking untouchables with God. In rejecting the name that Gandhi had given them on the ground that it labeled them as unclean, untouchables of the 1990's were turning against the man who, along with Dr. B.M. Ambedkar, an untouchable who became the principal framer of India's Constitution, had done more than any of the other Indian political leaders to improve their lot.

Untouchable rejection of the name that Gandhi had chosen for them reflected a rejection that went much deeper—rejection of the man himself. They had come to feel that, during his lifetime, Gandhi had led them astray on two counts. Firstly, they had followed his teaching that there was no need for them to abandon the Hindu fold because they could find a place there. Secondly, he had forced Dr. Ambedkar to accept his argument that untouchables could be best represented in India's legislature by reservation of legislative seats on the basis of untouchable candidates rather than untouchable voters. Untouchables of the 1990's had become convinced that their experience of the first 50 years of free India's history had proved Gandhi wrong on both these counts. They had not found a place in the Hindu fold, and the untouchables who had represented them in its legislatures had sold out their interest in order to please the caste Hindus who had elected them. The most bitter expression of Gandhi's rejection by the untouchables had come from Mayawati, their leader in Uttar Pradesh, who, significantly enough, the Congress Indira Party was backing, despite her attack on Gandhi, to become Chief Minister of that state. She had called Gandhi "our greatest enemy." During his lifetime, untouchables had regarded Gandhi as their greatest friend.

It was Dr. Ambedkar who, more than a decade before Independence, had proposed that untouchables call themselves by the Sanskrit word for the oppressed, *dalits*. At that time, he was engaged in a contest with Mahatma Gandhi for leadership of the movement to improve the status of untouchables, especially concerning the political role that they would play in a post-British Raj India. This contest came to a head over the issue of whether the legislative seats that would be reserved for untouchables would be defined as seats for which only untouchable candidates could stand or as seats in which only

42

untouchables could vote. Gandhi had advocated that the former definition be adopted in India's Constitution. Ambedkar insisted on the latter. In order to win this important political debate, Gandhi undertook one of his "fasts unto death." Faced with the threat of being held responsible for Gandhi's death, Ambedkar had been forced, against his better judgment, to give in and accept Gandhi's position, which was subsequently written into the Constitution that India adopted in 1950. So Gandhi had won the battle over the form in which untouchables would be assured of representation in India's legislature. But 60 years later, the tables were turned when Ambedkar won the battle over the name by which untouchables would identify themselves.

Not only had Ambedkar, by the 1990's, won out over Gandhi on the issue of the term that untouchables would use to identify themselves, but the working of the Constitution's provisions had vindicated the position that he had taken on the question of how untouchables' representation should be guaranteed in India's legislatures. Reserving seats for untouchables had resulted in untouchable representation in name only. Political parties had been obliged to select candidates who were untouchable, but these candidates were men whom Afro-American activists would call "Uncle Toms," untouchables who were acceptable to the caste Hindus who dominated the political parties and who constituted the majority of the voters. The result was untouchable legislators who backed programs and policies that were supported by the Hindu party bosses who had selected them and the caste Hindu voters who had elected them rather than programs and policies that would benefit the ranks of untouchables from which they came.

V.S. Naipaul has described this death of Gandhianism in a memorable passage:

"A multitude of nationalists...had brought the country Independence. A multitude of nationalists new to responsibility but with no idea of the state—businessmen, money hoarding but pious; politicians, Gandhi capped and Gandhi garbed, had worked to undo that Independence. Now the Nationalists had begun to be rejected and India was discovering that it had ceased to be Gandhian... Now of Gandhianism there remained only the emblems and the energy; and the energy had turned malignant. India needed a new code but it had none... Gandhi swept through India but he left it without an ideology."

Paradoxically for India, the land of Mahatma Gandhi, the champion of non-violence, the one institution which had maintained and even augmented its stature during the first 50 years of Independence was the military establishment. India's armed forces had continued to follow the British military tradition out of which they grew, practicing British "spit and polish" in their manners and military way of life, remaining subject to civilian control and direction, and keeping out of politics. In these respects, the military of the 1990's was the same as the military of the 1950's. During his recent travels throughout India, Jonah Blank encountered an Indian Army colonel who stated the continuing British connection in plain terms: " Let us be frank. In training, rules, discipline, this is still the British army... The English system is a fine one, none better in the world." In one important respect, however, free India's military was different: it was much larger. By the end of the 1980's, the armed forces numbered 1.3 million, making them the fourth largest in the world.

So also had India's armaments industry become much larger, having grown even more than the armed forces because, when Independence came, it had hardly existed. Following India's defeat in the 1962 border war with China, the Central Government embarked upon a program to make India more self-sufficient in equipping its armed forces. While the Soviet Union continued to supply sophisticated, high-tech weapons until its dissolution, more and more conventional weapons and other equipment were supplied by Indian factories. Expansion of the "military/industrial" complex continued for more than 30 years, to the point where, by 1997, it was the second largest component of India's manufacturing sector, employing more than 300,000 workers.

Just as evident in the India of the 1990's as the absence of Gandhianism as a guiding principle, but much more surprising, was the demise of the economic and political philosophy of Jawaharlal Nehru which had dominated 1950's India. Nehru's principles were much less utopian than Gandhi's, and he was India's unchallenged leader for the first 16 years of its existence, whereas Gandhi never held public office and died the year after Independence. For both these reasons, one would have expected Nehru's economic and political philosophy to have enough staying power to make it a major influence right down to 1997. But Nehruism was almost as dead as Gandhianism as India prepared to celebrate the first half-century of its Independence.

Both the concept and practice of Fabian socialism were downplayed in the speeches and policies of Nehru's grandson, Rajiv, and were conspicuously absent from those of Rajiv's successor, Narasimha Rao. The other pillar of Nehruism, pluralistic secularism, was still honored in words and still used as a political weapon by so-called "secular" parties to attack the forces of Hindu fundamentalism but had lost much of its potency as a determinative political principle. More and more politicians had come to rely on Hindu votes to win office and more and more Indians had come to see India as a Hindu nation and its 82% Hindus as the "true blue" Indians. The dangerous flip side of that coin was that Muslims and other minorities were more and more regarded as second-class citizens who must be treated accordingly. A political party, the Bharatiya Janata Party (BJP), had emerged to give a political shape to these growing anti-secular and anti-pluralistic sentiments. The BJP had hardly been heard of in the general election and Parliamentary debates of the early 1980's, but had rapidly gained strength during the decade that followed and had emerged from the 1996 General Election with more seats than any of its rivals.

BJP's basic ideology was the very antithesis of Nehru's pluralistic secularism. Its supporters believed that India should be Hindu India, that Hindu law should be the law of the land, and that religious minorities should follow that law. Accordingly, one of the specific planks in the BJP platform was that the special law code which was adopted for Muslims during the early days of Independence should be abolished. These Hindu fundamentalist positions did not yet dominate the political scene, but their power was on the rise. To the considerable extent that free India had by the late 1990's moved toward Hindu fundamentalism, it had repudiated Jawaharlal Nehru's political vision of pluralistic secularism, just as free India's conversion to free market capitalism had repudiated his economic vision of Fabian socialism.

The "affirmative action" program, conceived by Mahatma Gandhi, implemented by Jawaharlal Nehru, and supported by the country for over 25 years, had also come under attack during the 1980's and 1990's. Caste Hindus were arguing that they were suffering from "reverse discrimination" because they were excluded from filling the legislative seats and official posts reserved for untouchables and their children did not receive the scholarships available to children from "backward and scheduled castes and tribes." When V.P. Singh, who succeeded Rajiv Gandhi in 1988 as Prime Minister of a coalition government, had tried to more than double the number of seats and official posts reserved for untouchables, his government had been forced to resign in the face of the storm of caste Hindu protest which had ensued.

That the principles of Gandhi and Nehru were no longer taken seriously in the thinking of 1990's India came across loud and clear in the words of a young, well-educated, Westernized Brahmin which Michael Ward recorded during a visit to Madras in the early 1990's:

"Look, let's be honest about it. Gandhi sold this image of eternal India; *ahimsa*, non-violence and all that. But India is one of the most violent societies in the whole world. I'm not sure that Gandhi didn't resurrect something that was an aberration in our history and make it appear the norm. It was an ideal, not the reality. Gandhi was wily, canny; this was his great quality. He understood the people. He focused the message which was right for the time. But it's one thing to fight a liberation struggle, to fight against the oppressor. You have to define yourself clearly, say what you are fighting for. Gandhi did this, defined us in terms of an image which we liked—and of course you Westerners liked it, too. But 50 years on the message is more complicated. All the debates in the Anand Bhavan (Parliament) are irrelevant now. Nehru is irrelevant now. No one talks about him any more. The Socialist-type experiment took us in the wrong direction. It delayed the growth of the country for much of the last 50 years. But it's over now. Material improvement is the only answer for India. People want to get on. None of us are Gandhian now."

For this young Madrasi Brahmin, Gandhi had become irrelevant for the life of 1990's India. For Mayawati, the leader of Uttar Pradesh's

46

untouchables, he had become an enemy. While one can easily understand why a member of India's highest caste who believed that "material improvement is the only answer for India" would turn a deaf ear to Gandhi's teachings, it is more difficult to grasp why a member of a traditional pariah group which, during his lifetime had regarded Gandhi as its greatest friend, would now see him as its "greatest enemy." Part of the answer to this puzzle is to be found in the results of the 1996 General Election. Of the 79 Parliamentary seats reserved for untouchables, 30 had been won by BJP candidates. Of the 18 Parliamentary seats reserved for untouchables in Mayawati's state of Uttar Pradesh, 14 had been won by BJP candidates.

How did it happen that so many Parliamentary seats reserved for untouchables had been filled by candidates of the party which was most opposed to the "affirmative action" program? It happened because Gandhi had forced Dr. Ambedkar by threatening a "fast unto death", to write into the Indian Constitution the Gandhian stand that legislative representation reserved for untouchables should be based upon untouchable candidates, and not, as Dr. Ambedkar had argued, upon untouchable voters. Taking advantage of this provision, the BJP had selected token untouchables to run under its banner in reserved constituencies, and these token untouchables had been elected in those constituencies where there were many BJP supporters among the caste population that comprised the majority of voters. Since the State of Uttar Pradesh was a BJP stronghold, almost all of the reserved Parliamentary seats had gone to the BJP. It is no wonder that Mayawati, who is not only an untouchable but a bitter political opponent of the BJP, would regard the man who had created this "Uncle Tom" form of untouchable representation as her community's "greatest enemy."

❖

Public Administration and the Rule of Law

Not as damaging as the loss of Gandhi's and Nehru's political, economic, and social vision, but damaging enough, was the decline that had taken place in standards of public administration. The British had left behind a civil service with traditions of honesty and impartiality which were world renowned and were still followed to a substantial degree during the early years after Independence. Indian civil servants of the 1950's administered a rule of law that was also a carry-over from British days. Not only had free India adopted that rule of law, but it had kept in place the institution that the British had set up to administer it, merely changing its name from the Indian Civil Service (ICS) to the Indian Administrative Service (IAS). As Indian ICS veterans had retired, the IAS recruits who replaced them had been trained to do their work in the honest and impartial way that had been the standard of the Indian members of the ICS who had been recruited by the British. Fifty years after Independence, that tradition of honest and impartial public administration had gone by the boards. Ved Mehta describes in uncompromising terms the change that had ensued. "By the beginning of the 90's, the Indian Civil Service, its judiciary and other once stable autonomous institutions had been compromised to the point where they were mere appurtenances of politicians. Corruption and intimidation at every level of society had brought into being a moneyed class which exercised ruthless power. Examples of corruption abound."

A number of cases of political corruption had been revealed to the Indian public at the time when one political party had lost power and another had taken over. The winning party now had control of the investigative agencies that could uncover incriminating evidence and the losing party could no longer protect former officials. As was to be expected, this scenario was played out when the Congress Indira Party lost power after the General Election of 1996 and the United Front took charge. Shortly after the Deve Gowda government was sworn in, the Central Bureau of Investigation raided the house of Sukh Ram, the former Minister of Telecommunications. Its officers found 3.61 crores (over $1 million) in cash hidden there, which turned out to be a small part of the former minister's total take, estimated at 30 crores ($8.5 million). Thereupon, they raided the house of his deputy who had been in charge of negotiating large contracts for the purchase of telecommunications equipment. There they found 3 crores (about $850,000) in cash, plus considerable amounts of gold and jewelry.

The investigation that followed the finding of these caches of "ill-gotten gains" uncovered the fact that, during the three years that the minister and deputy minister had held their posts, they had regularly received kickbacks from companies to which they awarded contracts for supplying telecommunications equipment. Since these were years in which the Central Government had been implementing a major program to extend communication facilities, the total value of these contracts was approximately 20,000 crores (almost $6 billion). With this volume of expenditures, the minister and deputy minister were able to amass large fortunes by Indian standards within a relatively short period of time. The companies to which they had given contracts and from whom they had received kickbacks had also done well. One firm that they particularly favored increased its sales from 7.17 crores (just over $2 million) to 155 crores ($50 million) during the years the minister and his deputy minister were in office.

Another, and much more spectacular, instance of political corruption being revealed when there was a change in the political power equation occurred at the state level in Tamil Nadu. Following the death of its founder, C.N. Annadurai, a star of Tamil movies named M.G. Ramachandran had wrested control of the Dravida Munnetra Kazagham from M. Karunanidhi, Annadurai's chief lieutenant and heir apparent. As a result, Ramachandran had replaced Karunanidhi as Chief Minister of the Tamil Nadu government. When he died in

1991, his widow, a movie star named Jayalalitha Jayaram, had succeeded him as Chief Minister. In 1996, thinking that the Congress Indira Party would win the upcoming general election, Jayalalitha had entered into a political alliance with Narasimha Rao. This move proved to be a disastrous miscalculation because the Congress Indira Party was soundly defeated in Tamil Nadu at both national and state levels.

As soon as Jayalalitha lost the Chief Minister's post and Karunanidhi had taken over, retribution set in for her with a vengeance. She was charged with having enriched herself through corrupt practices while in office and, in December 1996, was jailed on a charge of having received kickbacks from the Tamil Nadu government's purchases of hundreds of color television sets for village centers at the inflated price of $400 each. At the same time, the CBI raided two of her houses. They found valuables worth approximately $14 million which had not been accounted for in her income tax returns for the previous five years. These valuables included 62 pounds of gold and diamond bangles, 1,700 pounds of silver ornaments and dinner plates, 10,500 saris, 91 wristwatches, and 750 pairs of shoes.

One of the houses that was raided contained 27 rooms equipped with 44 air-conditioners. In addition to the valuables, the CBI unearthed deeds and other proprietary documents showing that Jayalalitha owned several other houses valued at $7 million. To Tamils in the political know, these revelations came as no surprise. During her five-year tenure as Chief Minister, the Tamil Nadu Government had been popularly known as the "10% government" because it was generally understood that substantial kickbacks had to be paid by those wishing to do business with it. A good share of those kickbacks seem to have gone to Jayalalitha because she had amassed millions of dollars starting from scratch and with little or no legitimate income along the way. She had even declared bankruptcy before assuming office and, in order to show that she did not intend to enrich herself from public service, had agreed to draw a token salary of only one rupee (3 cents) per year.

By the beginning of free India's 50th anniversary year, such instances of political corruption had become so commonplace that political parties no longer regarded charges of corruption as a reason for disqualifying a candidate from party endorsement and, if elected, from public office. The Congress Party was the last to hold to the tradition that it had followed from the days of Mahatma Gandhi that it would not endorse as a party candidate any member who was under investigation or charged with misuse of political power or illegally gorging from the public trough. In fact, this tradition was cited by Sitaram Kesri and his followers during their late 1996 campaign to deprive Narasimha Rao of any leadership position in the Congress Indira Party. They made much of his having been charged with three criminal offenses following his ouster from the Prime Minister's position and his having to engage since that time in a struggle to stay out of jail.

Following Narasimha Rao's resignation as chairman of the Party's Parliamentary Committee, the party line on the question of political corruption had changed. The change took place in connection with an intra-party debate that arose over whether or not it should endorse a former Congress Indira Party MP, Kamal Nath, who had been denied a party ticket for the 1996 General Election on the ground that he had been charged with political corruption. In order to make sure that the party continued to hold his Chindwara seat, its backing was given to his wife, who was duly elected. Less than a year later, she dutifully resigned her MP's office in order that the seat might be vacated for another election. By this time Narasimha Rao had been deprived of all his party offices, and the party's tradition of dissociating itself from political corruption was no longer needed as a political stick with which to beat him. Accordingly, the ticket for the Chindwara Parliamentary seat was given to Kamal Nath.

This official change in the party's policy on political corruption came as no surprise to those observers of Indian politics who had earlier seen several former party leaders quietly return to the party after they had been forced to resign their positions and party memberships because of their involvement in the Jain brothers or some other corruption scandal. At the time of their resignations, they had accused Narasimha Rao of cutting their political throats by allowing the CBI to make public the evidence against them. When Narasimha Rao came under political attack by the Sitaram Kesri forces, they expressed their desire to rejoin the party. Without any serious debate, their applications to rejoin the party had been accepted, despite the fact that criminal charges were still pending against them.

As one of the post-Narasimha Rao Congress Indira Party leaders had put it, "There is a change in leadership, and this must be followed with other changes." Apparently, one of those "other changes" was to discontinue the party's practice of refusing to endorse candidates who had been charged with political corruption. In taking this step, party leaders pointed to the fact that other parties had never bothered to follow that tradition. While L.K. Advani, the BJP president, had reacted to his involvement in the Jain brothers scandal by resigning from his Parliamentary seat, he had continued to occupy his party post. The president of the Janata Dal Party, Laloo Prasad Yadav, who was also Chief Minister of Bihar State, was under investigation by the CBI, in what was reputed to be the largest misuse of public funds of the post-Independence era. When the report was submitted in June 1997, the "charge sheet" alleged that, during a period of more than 10 years, Laloo Prasad Yadav and 55 other Bihari politicians and State officials had pocketed 950 million crores ($270 million) that had been supposedly spent to buy fodder for cattle and to fund rural development projects that did not exist. To be sure, Laloo Prasad Yadav might, in the end, be exonerated by the Bihar court, but, as the new leaders of the Congress Indira Party pointed out, neither his Janata Dal Party nor the State of Bihar had in any way clipped his political wings during the CBI investigation because of its allegation that he was involved in the "fodder scandal." A spokesman for the post-Narasimha Rao Congress Indira Party expressed the political parties' prevailing indifference to corruption by saying that "if the people elect a leader, the (corruption) charges have no meaning." In his view, it was not up to the political parties but up to the voters to decide whether or not to put into office a politician who is under investigation or has been charged with corruption.

Since political corruption had become rife among India's politicians and civil servants, it was not surprising that respect for the whole system of law and order had waned among the rank and file of the population.

It was the common view of police officials, informed observers, and citizens in general that crime had increased substantially during the 50 years since Independence, and especially during the past decade. This common view was substantiated by the crime statistics that had been compiled during the early 1990's. According to a 1994 report from the Central Government's Home Ministry, not only had violent crimes been on the rise, but white-collar crime had gone up 31% between 1984 and 1994. The National Commission on Women reported that the incidence of crimes against women had increased sharply between 1987 and 1991—molestation and rape up 26%, kidnapping and abduction up 36%, and dowry-related deaths up a shocking 170%. The 1995–96 Report of the Ministry of Welfare showed that crimes against untouchables and tribal members had risen 34% and 37% respectively between 1993 and 1994. In order to grasp the true extent to which the crime situation had deteriorated by the 1990's, one has to take into account the fact that crime statistics are based upon police records which do not reflect the numerous cases where crimes are not reported or, if reported, are not entered into police records.

Exacerbating the seriousness of the 1990's crime situation was the fact that the police establishment which now had to cope with more frequent and more serious crimes was less capable of doing its job than it had been 50 years earlier. Policemen were held in very low esteem, and perceived as being brutal, corrupt, undisciplined, and incompetent. The result was that policemen were paid low wages, had to put up with poor working conditions, and received little or no cooperation when they attempted to track down and arrest criminals. Their effectiveness in dealing with crime was further undermined by the policy of using them to provide security for politicians and political activities and to quell India's frequent civil disturbances. Not only did these diversions from regular police work consume time and energy, but crowd control made the police more unpopular with the public because force often had to be used to bring unruly crowds under control. Personal and institutional stress had combined to produce, since the 1970's, police demonstrations and strikes for better pay and working conditions, demonstrations and strikes that were unheard of during

53

the 1950's. The worst of these backlashes on the part of the police took place in 1982, when the Indian Army had to be called in to restore order after a paramilitary force had failed to quell striking policemen who had themselves become rioters.

The marked increase in crimes similar to those committed in Western countries had been accompanied by an increase in a style of crime that is peculiarly Indian: *dacoity*. *Dacoity* had been stamped out by the British Raj as part of its program to bring law and order to India. After Independence, it had made a comeback, and its practitioners had even begun to be glamorized in some parts of the country because of the way they taunted the much maligned police force. *Dacoits* were armed gangs of five to 20 members, who operated in remote rural areas. They descended on a village and camped there, sometimes for several days, lording it over the inhabitants, looting, raping, and eliminating anyone whom they thought would report them to the police. When they departed, they sometimes took with them a member of the wealthiest family, who was later returned after payment of a ransom.

Not only did *dacoity* become more common, but more adulation was given to the *dacoits* by India's common folk. In those regions where they were most active, especially in Uttar Pradesh and Madhya Pradesh, as the police became more unpopular, the *dacoits* who defied and taunted them became more popular and even took on a kind of "Robin Hood" image. Trevor Fishlock attended and described for readers of *The London Times* the festive gathering which took place in June 1982 when Malkhan and his gang, one of Madhya Pradesh's most notorious bands of *dacoits*, surrendered to State authorities:

"It says much about the status of a bandit like Malkhan that the surrender was received at an astonishing public ceremony... At a police barracks a dais of bricks, six feet high, was hurriedly erected, covered with a white cloth and shaded by an awning of red, green, and yellow. It was hung with photographs of Mahatma Gandhi, Mr. Nehru, and Mrs. Gandhi, the Prime Minister... Film music was playing loudly over a public address system. Reporters and All-India Radio were in attendance, along with numerous police officers and State officials. A crowd of 25,000 people, who had traveled on foot, by bus, pony cart, and bullock cart, were in roped off spectator enclosures... Malkhan fell at the feet of the Chief Minister (who had arrived by helicopter) and touched his shoes in homage... He then turned to the crowd, holding his rifle above his head. He placed it reverently on a chair, on which was a picture of the goddess Durga, and added his revolver, dagger and belt. The rest of his gang followed suit and Malkhan's long reign of terror was over. As the Chief Minister left the dais, one of the spectators remarked sardonically, 'A big bandit gets a big minister.'"

Malkhan's surrender was followed by the capture of Phoolan Devi, a female *dacoit* known as the "Bandit Queen." She was held without trial for 11 years during which a Bombay studio made a film based on her life. In 1994, after she had been released from prison, she announced that she was going to enter politics. Her opportunity came two years later during the 1996 General Election. Campaigning on the basis of her low caste origin and the lady "Robin Hood" image that she had acquired as a *dacoit*, she won a seat in Parliament.

❖

Political Process

India's politics had undergone drastic changes between the 1950's and the 1990's, not only at the ideological level, but also lower down in the nitty-gritty of party organization. During the early years after Independence, the Congress Party was dominant in all regions of the country, both in the cities and in the countryside. Led by Mahatma Gandhi, Jawaharlal Nehru, and Sardar Patel, it had subsumed the nationalist movement that had freed India from British rule and had inherited the reins of government both at the Central and State government levels. The only opposition party of any consequence were the Communists, and their strength was confined to two widely separated States: West Bengal and Kerala.

Relegated to the fringes of 1950's political life were militant Hindu fundamentalist groups like the Rashtriya Swayam Sivak (National Self-Service Organization), popularly known as the RSS, and the Hindu Mahasabha. Because these two groups had conspired together to organize the plot to assassinate Mahatma Gandhi, they were looked upon with disgust by most Indians. The best they could do politically was to keep their fanatical members together and out of jail and to carry on secret meetings and quasi-military exercises. Forming a Hindu fundamentalist party that could take part in the political process in opposition to the Congress Party was out of the question during the early decades following Gandhi's death because the militant Hindu organizations that would have had to put it together were the very ones that had sentenced him to die.

Within the Congress Party that dominated the political life of 1950's and 1960's India, the paramount figure was Jawaharlal Nehru. When Independence had come in 1947, the party was led by a triumvirate, but when both Mahatma Gandhi and Sardar Patel died within the next three years, Nehru became the uncontested head of both the Congress Party and the Central Government. He ruled for the next 16 years as a democratic autocrat. He was an autocrat in the sense that he made all the final decisions, and those decisions were carried out by lesser party leaders and government officials with no questions asked. But he was democratic in the sense that he consulted with both lesser party leaders and government officials and took their views into account when he made his decisions. Thus, under his regime, both lesser party leaders and government officials had a voice in the formulation of party and Central Government policy.

Regional party leaders also played an important role in the structure and functioning of the Congress Party of Nehru's day, a role that gave them prominent positions in State governments. Although he was its unchallenged leader, the Congress Party of the 1950's was not Nehru's personal following. It was a well-organized institution with strong regional branches which controlled almost all of the State governments. Underneath Nehru's overshadowing political umbrella, lesser Congress Party leaders like Kamaraj Nadar in Madras, Sanjiva Reddy in Andhra Pradesh, S. Nijalingappa in Karnataka, Y.D. Chavan in Maharashtra and Morarji Desai in Gujarat acted not only as regional party bosses but also as Chief Ministers of their respective states.

By the 1990's, the Congress Party that had dominated the politics of the 1950's existed in name only. By then, even its name had been changed. It was now the Congress Indira Party, named after Indira Gandhi when she reconstituted the party in order to regain her Prime Minister's post after her defeat in the 1978 General Election. This was her second restructuring and renaming of the party, the first having been carried out in 1969, when she had gutted the political power of the regional party bosses and split the party. At that time, the remnant that remained under the control of the regional bosses was designated the Official Congress. The breakaway majority who supported Mrs. Gandhi became the New Congress.

These two changes in the character of the Congress Party put Mrs. Gandhi in the position of a political autocrat, pure and simple.

Her father may have been an autocrat, but he consulted with and listened to lesser party leaders. In the New Congress Party of 1969 and the Congress Indira Party of 1980, there were no lesser party leaders. All members were Mrs. Gandhi's followers, and their role was to abide by her decisions or get out. Given the dominant role which the New Congress and the Congress Indira parties came to play in the functioning of free India's governmental processes during the 1970's and 1980's, the change in the nature of the party led inevitably to a change in the way the Central Government's legislative branch functioned. When the Congress Party became Mrs. Gandhi's personal following, Parliament, controlled as it was by a majority made up of MP's elected under her party banner, became a body that rubber-stamped whatever edicts she sent for approval.

Paralleling this change in the Central Government's legislative branch was a change in the nature of its executive branch that was equally striking. Independent India had taken over from the British a parliamentary form of government in which the Prime Minister, not the President, was the executive head and the Prime Minister was chosen by the majority party or coalition of parties in Parliament. From 1947 to 1996, when the Congress Party in one form or another dominated Parliament for all but four years, almost all of the Prime Ministers were bound to come from that party. This was, in itself, a deviation from the model of parliamentary government, which requires that there be two strong parties if the pitfall of one party rule is to be avoided. What made India's deviation much more radical was the fact that during all of the 45 years of Congress Party domination, the Prime Ministers were members or confidantes of one family, the Nehrus.

The emergence of a Nehru dynasty was by no means inevitable even though a step in that direction had been taken when Jawaharlal Nehru held the Prime Minister's post for an unbroken period of 16 years and relinquished that post only when he died in 1964. When Sardar Patel died in 1950, Nehru's only rival as leader of the Congress Party was removed from the political scene. Still, there were several regional party bosses, members of what came to be known as the "Syndicate," who might have been elevated to take Nehru's place after the collapse of his policy of friendship with China and India's disastrous defeat in the ensuing border war, especially when these political blows led to a rapid decline in his health. It was one of the "Syndicate" members, Morarji Desai, who gave his own explanation of why this did not happen. He accused Nehru of planning from the start of his tenure as Prime Minister to establish a family dynasty and of preparing the way by seeing to it that none of the regional party leaders who might have been nominated for the Prime Minister's post came into prominence as his likely successor. While there is no convincing evidence that Desai's accusation is well-founded, it is true that Nehru must bear responsibility for creating the conditions in which the emergence of a Nehru family dynasty became possible. It is fair to say that, while he did not designate a member of his family to take his place, his silence on the question of who would succeed him opened the way for just such a development to take place.

His daughter, Indira Gandhi, held the Prime Minister's post for 17 years. During her time in office, her actions made it plain that, whatever dynastic ambitions her father might or might not have had, she was determined that one of her sons should succeed her as Prime Minister. Her first choice was her younger son, Sanjay, but, before he could take over, he died in a flying accident. She then turned to the elder, Rajiv, and converted him from piloting Indian Airlines planes to preparing to run the Central Government. He did succeed in serving as Prime Minister, from 1984 to 1989, but he too met a tragic end when he was killed by a Tamil extremist bomb. By this time, the Nehru dynasty had such a stronghold on the Congress Indira Party that its leaders asked Rajiv's widow, Sonia, to succeed her husband as party president despite the fact that she was Italian by birth and Roman Catholic in religion. If she had accepted the offer, she would have become Prime Minister when the Congress Indira Party led the coalition government that emerged from the general election of 1991. The Nehru dynasty would have continued. But she declined, and neither of these political eventualities materialized.

The first 50 years of free India's political life saw the conversion of the Congress Party from a regionally based, nationwide institution to the personal following of the Nehru dynasty and then the end of that dynasty. It also saw the rise of a Hindu fundamentalist party, the BJP, which, by 1996, had replaced the Congress Indira Party as India's strongest, measured by the number of seats in Parliament. The deepest roots of the BJP went back to the RSS, which, along with the Hindu Mahasabha, had engineered the assassination of Mahatma Gandhi. The party's leaders had continued to be active members of that militant Hindu fundamentalist organization. Despite the public disgrace which it had suffered as a result of its role in bringing about Gandhi's death, the RSS had continued in existence during the decades that followed, holding quasi-military exercises and meetings at which it honored Nathuram Vinayak Godse, the fanatical Brahmin who had shot Gandhi. Then, after 30 years as a semi-underground political organization, the RSS emerged to public view as the principal seedbed that produced the leadership of the BJP.

The BJP's rise from obscurity to political preeminence during the 1980's and 1990's had been swift and, except for a temporary set-back after the riots that followed the destruction of the Muslim mosque at Ayodhya, sure. First, the RSS had spun off a political party that espoused its ideology, the Jana Sangh (People's Voice). Because Jana · Sangh strength was confined to a few areas in North India, it was not until the late 1980's that the members of what had been regarded during the 1950's as India's political "lunatic fringe" were joined by enough more moderate Indians to form a political party that had the potential to take over the Central Government. The BJP had gotten off to a very slow start at the national level, winning only two Parliamentary seats in the 1984 General Election, but, thereafter, its strength had increased rapidly, especially in the Hindi-speaking areas of North and Northwest India. It won 88 seats in the 1989 General Election, and two years later, proclaiming that its goal for India was *Ram Rajya* (Reign of Rama), it captured 119 Parliamentary seats. In the State elections held during 1990–91, espousing an ideology of Hindu nationalism, it won control of Rajasthan, Madhya Pradesh, and Uttar Pradesh, making it the party which, at the State level, ruled almost a third of India's population.

At this point, however, the Congress Indira Party was still far stronger at the national level, with 245 Parliamentary victories, partly as a result of the public's negative reaction to the BJP's role in the destruction of the Ayodhya mosque and the bloody riots which followed. In the 1996 General Election the tables were turned when the BJP won 184 Parliamentary seats, 43 more than the Congress Indira Party. This turnabout was accounted for, in part, by the decision of BJP leaders to broaden its appeal by changing its image from that of a single-issue party advocating the cause of Hindu fundamentalism to a multi-issue party that, in addition, attacked Congress Indira Party corruption and called for nationalistic economic reforms, limitations on immigration, and strengthened national security. These additional planks in the party platform were outgrowths of its original underlying Hindu fundamentalist ideology. Its demand for limitations on foreign investments was aimed at fueling the fires of Indian nationalism. Its demand that immigration be curbed was aimed at the Muslims who were crossing over from Bangladesh into Assam. Its demand for a stronger national defense was clearly designed to remind the Indian people of the threat of aggression from Pakistan. The internal impact of these demands was to identify India's Muslims as second-class citizens who could not be trusted to stand by the motherland if external Muslim forces were to move against her. In the final analysis, the BJP's success in the 1996 General Election was accounted for by the fact that, while it went to the voters as a multi-issue rather than a single-issue party, it retained its basic commitment to make India a Hindu state that would be controlled by its Hindu majority.

Since none of the parties contesting the 1996 General Election had won an outright majority and the BJP had won more seats than any of the others, President S.D. Sharma asked Atal Bihari Vajpayee, the BJP's Parliamentary leader, to form a coalition government. Vajpayee could not deliver on this request because he could not get a majority of Parliamentarians to support a slate of ministers with himself as Prime Minister. What was startling in this political episode was not the fact that Vajpayee had failed but the fact that the politician who was asked to make the attempt to form a government had been an active member of the RSS, the organization that had helped to assassinate Mahatma Gandhi and that honored his assassin. Indian politics had been turned almost topsy turvy since the 1950's.

Just as the Congress Party had lost by 1996 its political hegemony at the national level, so too it had lost the hold it once had on the politics of the major cities. At this important local level, Congress moderation had given way to various forms of radicalism. During the early years of Independence, the Communist Party had taken control of Calcutta, but, for almost two decades thereafter, the Congress Party had maintained its dominant position in Bombay, Delhi, and Madras. By the 1990's, however, the Shiv Sena (Shiva's Army) had taken control of Bombay, the Jana Sangh had won Delhi, and Madras was in the hands of the Dravida Munnetra Kazagham (Dravidian Forward Movement). Support for these parties was rooted in regional and linguistic loyalties, with the result that they sought to promote the interests of the local population against "outsiders" who threatened to take away their jobs, their status, and their security. As for the Communists, the only "big city" party with an all-India agenda, they also did not have a nationwide following since they were confined to West Bengal and Kerala.

Nevertheless, all four parties had still played an important political role at the national level. Their strong opposition to the Congress Party in its various forms had reduced the number of Congress Party votes, and, where their ideologies coincided with those of other national parties, those votes had gone to the Congress Party's rivals. Since these "big-city" parties, localized as they were, represented millions of voters, the direction they gave to their followers in general elections had a significant impact on the outcome. The 1996 General Election provided a case in point. One of the reasons why the Congress Indira Party did so badly was that none of the four "big city" parties supported Congress Indira Party candidates. One of the reasons why the BJP did so well was that both the Shiv Sena and the Jana Sangh backed its candidates.

The opposition of "big city" parties was one of the factors which determined the outcome of the 1996 contest between the BJP and the Congress Indira Party. Another was the quality of the leadership provided by the Congress Indira Party, which, for the first time, had no Nehru at its head. Leadership of the 1991 campaign which had been fought five years earlier had fallen to Narasimha Rao following Rajiv Gandhi's assassination, but the Congress Indira Party's resounding victory at that time was the result, not of Rao's leadership, but of the outpouring of sympathy that followed the death of Indira Gandhi's son. In the final analysis, it was the assassinated Rajiv Gandhi, not Narasimha Rao, who had led the Congress Indira Party to victory in 1991. Narasimha Rao's leadership of the Congress Indira Party in the 1996 General Election campaign was leadership in name only. His bizarre and inept style was revealed even before the campaign began. He had to call for a general election in 1996 because the five-year period during which the Central Government installed after the 1991 General Election could hold office had ended that year, but he had considerable leeway in determining the exact dates. Following a political approach that would have shocked Jawaharlal Nehru, but which Nehru's daughter and contemporary Indian politicians would have understood, Rao consulted a number of astrologers as to what would be auspicious dates for the Congress Indira Party. When he was told that the heavenly bodies would be in conjunction for a Congress Indira Party victory on May 2 and May 8, those dates were made official. For Narasimha Rao, deciding the timing of the general election was not a matter of when his party would have the best chance of maximizing its support, but a matter of when the stars and planets would smile on his party's fortunes.

The Congress Indira Party campaign that was subsequently led by Narasimha Rao was also conducted in a political style very different from that of the Nehrus. Along with flying around the country to deliver lackluster speeches to crowds of party supporters, Narasimha Rao spent much of his time in meditation and visiting as many as 10 temples to secure *darshan* (blessing) from the presiding deities. When it began to appear toward the end of the campaign that the Congress Indira Party was not doing well, Narasimha Rao, instead of increasing the pace of meetings and speeches, went on a solitary pilgrimage to the temple at Tirupathi in his home state of Andhra Pradesh, hoping that a visit to a religious site that was specially efficacious for Hindus who were, like himself, natives of that state would bring the divine blessing that was needed to save the day for his party.

Despite Narasimha Rao's attempts to secure the blessing of the Hindu gods, the 1996 General Election resulted in a humiliating defeat for the Congress Indira Party. Deserted by its traditional Muslim and untouchable supporters and by the caste Hindus who were either disgusted at the corruption of Congress Indira Party leaders or won over by the BJP's attack on its "affirmative action" program, the Congress Indira Party won only 141 Parliamentary seats, compared with 245 in 1991. Since this was only a little more than half the seats needed (273) to win a Parliamentary majority and since it did not deign to attempt to form a coalition government under its leadership, its 1996 defeat marked the end of an era in which the Congress Party, in its three different manifestations, had controlled the Central Government for 45 of the 50 years since Independence

For the BJP, on the other hand, the 1996 General Election marked a great leap forward in its effort to make Hindu fundamentalism dominant in Indian politics. The party and its allies won 184 seats, far short of a Parliamentary majority, but 43 seats more than the Congress Indira Party and 182 seats more than it had won only 12 years earlier. The other major player, the National Front/Left Front, a coalition of 13 leftist and untouchable parties with the two Communist parties and the Janata Dal (People's Party) as its major components, won 111 seats. In addition to these three major players, a number of smaller parties had contested the election, winning 101 seats. These smaller parties were scattered throughout the country, but the supporters of three of them were concentrated in the southern states of Andhra Pradesh and Tamil Nadu. These three were regional parties were built upon linguistic loyalties and called for greater autonomy for their State governments. Such sentiments were particularly strong in Tamil Nadu where the Tamil Congress Party and the DMK had joined together to prevent the Congress Indira Party from winning a single seat.

National figures did not show the significant variations in degree of party support in different geographical divisions. Except in the South, seats which the Congress Indira Party won were spread evenly throughout the country, with a concentration in Rajasthan (12), Gujarat (10), Maharashtra (15), Andhra Pradesh (22), and Orissa (16). The BJP's victories, on the other hand, were centered in the North and Northwest, especially in Uttar Pradesh (52), Madhya Pradesh (27), Maharashtra (33), Gujarat (16), and Rajasthan (12). The only deviation from this pattern of concentration was the 24 seats that the BJP won in Bihar, which, although it lies in India's Eastern Division, is, like Uttar Pradesh and Madhya Pradesh, part of the country's Hindi-speaking belt. The victories of the National Front/Left Front reflected the dominant roles played by the two Communist parties and the Janata Dal Party. Thirty-seven of them were won in Bihar and Karnataka, where Janata Dal support was concentrated. Forty-one of the other 74 were won in Kerala and West Bengal, the traditional strongholds of the two Communist parties.

The brightest spot in the 1996 General Election was the way in which the election was organized and conducted. The Election Commission did a remarkable job of administering an election process that involved hundreds of millions of voters, thousands of candidates and hundreds of parties. Campaigning was quieter and less violence-prone than ever before. Voting went on with few hitches and with little or no ballot stuffing or false counting. In all these ways, 1996 represented substantial progress in the evolution of free, orderly, and honest election procedures. Unfortunately for the future of free India's elections, T.N. Seshan, the Election Commissioner who had orchestrated the smooth operation of the 1996 General Election, retired at the end of that year. Whether or not his successor will measure up to his standard remains to be seen.

This positive election scene was played out, however, only in that part of India that lies south of the 33rd Parallel. The story was quite different in Jammu and Kashmir, where, for six years, Muslim militants had been fighting for independence from India in a struggle that had cost an estimated 20,000 Kashmiri lives. In order to show the world that this struggle had come to an end and that Kashmiri Muslims had been persuaded to accept Indian rule, the Narasimha Rao government was determined to include Kashmir in the 1996 General Election even though the six seats that were at stake would make little difference in deciding which party would control Parliament. The Muslim militants refused to take part in the election and called upon all Kashmiris to boycott the election. Faced with this defiant attitude, the Indian government moved 100,000 troops and paramilitary police into Kashmir to reinforce the 350,000 who were already stationed there to maintain law and order and keep Pakistan at bay.

This force of 450,000 had two jobs to do. One was to prevent the Muslim militants from launching attacks on voting stations that would frighten people away. The second was to "get out the vote" by moving through the villages, rousting out the inhabitants, and shepherding them to the voting stations. They succeeded in accomplishing the first objective because attacks on voters by militant Muslims did not occur. But voter turnout was pushed up only to the 49% level, 6% below that achieved south of the 33rd Parallel. Nevertheless, Indian officials claimed success for the police and military's "get out the vote" campaign and argued that the 49% voter turnout was clear evidence that the Muslims of Kashmir were now ready to live under Indian rule.

By democratic standards, the Kashmir election was, as it was described by one of the U.N. observers on the scene, "a sham." Kashmiri Muslims complained that they were forced to vote at gun point and could only vote for the party supported by the Indian government because the political parties that Kashmiris backed had boycotted the election. That they were right in the latter regard was evidenced by the election results. All of Kashmir's Parliamentary seats were won by candidates supported by the Congress Indira Party. The Indian Government, on the other hand, called the Kashmir elections fair and free and maintained that the result of the polling reflected the Kashmiri people's will.

The general election was followed four months later by the first elections for the Jammu and Kashmir State Legislature since the insurgency had erupted in 1990. Even though these were State level elections, the underlying issue—whether the two-thirds of Jammu and Kashmir under Indian control should become independent or remain part of the Indian Union—was the same. The Deve Gowda government was just as anxious in September as the Narasimha Rao government had been in April that the election results would show that the Muslims of Jammu and Kashmir were content to be citizens of India and did not desire to join their co-religionists in Pakistan or to go it on their own. Accordingly, the same large force of India's paramilitary and military troops was assigned to protect voting places against attacks from insurgent groups, which had once again called on the Kashmiri people to boycott the elections, and to "encourage" voters to cast their ballots. As in the case of the general election, India's strategy succeeded in pushing the turnout at least to the 50% level, opening the way for the Indian government to make the claim that the results represented the will of the people.

In addition to generating a 50% turnout, the Jammu and Kashmir State election ballot count gave a boost to the Deve Gowda government because the National Conference Party, which had campaigned on a platform calling for greater State autonomy but within the Indian Union, captured some 66 of the 87 seats in the Legislative Assembly. This two-thirds majority gave the National Conference's leader, Farooq Abdullah, a strong hand with which to fight, in his words, "the renegades, the Pakistani infiltrators." At the same time, he expressed his willingness to talk with the insurgents and "bring them round to thinking in terms of the Constitution of India." It was hoped that this "good cop/bad cop" approach, backed by a continuing Indian military presence, would offer the possibility of taking most of the steam out of the insurgency movement.

The fact that almost half of the citizens of Jammu and Kashmir followed the militant All Party Hurriyat Conference's direction by boycotting the State elections and that the National Conference Party had won only 38% of the ballots cast showed that this was no more than a possibility. Additional evidence that the All Party Hurriyat Conference still wielded considerable political clout was the support given by almost all of Srinagar's 900,000 population to the *hartal* (general strike) which it called a fortnight later to protest the State election results. Almost as difficult for the ruling National Conference as snuffing out the insurgency would be delivering on its campaign promise to make the State autonomous within the Indian Union. The Central Government had been running Jammu and Kashmir for the past six years, and Delhi officials and those who benefited from President's Rule would not be likely to hand over their prerogatives without a fuss when the State government attempted to take over authority.

At the Central Government level, the final result of the 1996 General Election was that it produced a United Front government headed by a leader of the Janata Dal Party who had been the Chief Minister of Karnataka State, H.D. Deve Gowda. Given the failure of the two strongest parties, the Congress Indira Party and the BJP, to win a majority of Parliamentary seats, a coalition government had to be formed. President S.D. Sharma gave the first opportunity to form this government to the BJP because it had won the most seats, but the slate of ministers put together by the BJP's leader, Atal Bihari Vajpayee, could not muster enough Parliamentary support to survive. According to the number of Parliamentary seats held, the Congress Indira Party should have been given the next opportunity. It might have made the effort and might even have succeeded in forming a coalition government under its leadership, but Narasimha Rao declined to avail himself of the opportunity. The position that he took was that the Congress Indira Party would not attempt to form a coalition government and, while it would support a coalition government headed by the United Front, it would not be a part of that government.

❖

Deve Gowda's Coalition Government

After the two parties with the most Parliamentary seats had been given their chance, the task of forming a coalition government fell to the third major player in the 1996 General Election, the National Front/Left Front. This block, which had been cobbled together to fight the Congress Indira Party and the BJP, selected Deve Gowda as its Parliamentary leader. To the surprise of many, he succeeded in forming a government that managed to secure the necessary vote of confidence. He accomplished this difficult political task by adding the votes of the Congress Indira Party's 141 MP's to the votes of the 190 MP's belonging either to the Front or the small regional parties. With 331 out of a total of 545 Parliamentarians behind it, the Deve Gowda coalition had a margin of 117 seats over its opposition, led by the BJP.

The Deve Gowda coalition government, called the United Front, which took charge in May 1996 represented a sea change from the personnel who had dominated the executive branch of India's Central Government from the dawn of Independence. The Prime Minister, since he was neither a member of the Nehru family nor one of its confidantes, represented a total break with the Nehru dynasty. Nor was he, like the Nehrus and Narasimha Rao, a Brahmin. He was a member of a caste of farmers. Nor was he a university-educated urbanite. He was a ruralite who had worked as a building contractor before he entered politics. Finally, his political experience was in State government rather than ruling from Delhi, where the Prime Ministers who had gone before him had learned the governmental ropes.

The members of the new cabinet, reflecting the National Front/Left Front constituency that had prepared the way for the Deve Gowda government to assume power, were much like the Prime Minister in caste, education, and political experience. They were closer to the Indian common man than those who had directed Central Government ministries for most of the previous 50 years. Given the National Front/ Left Front constituency and the character of the Prime Minister and his cabinet, it is not surprising that the new government's program was set forth in general terms as one that would concentrate on uplifting the disadvantaged and the poor, especially those living in rural areas, by increasing their political influence and their incomes, providing better medical services and more educational opportunities, and developing the rural infrastructure.

Shortly after assuming office, the Deve Gowda government spelled out the details of that program. One-third of Parliamentary seats would be reserved for women, and all laws that discriminated against women would be repealed. A government ombudsman would be appointed to tackle the problem of political corruption and abuse of political power. India's "affirmative action" program would not only be continued but extended to include job reservations for "all sections" of the poor, not just those who belonged to "backward and scheduled castes and tribes." Regarding economic policy, the Deve Gowda government recognized both its dependence on Congress Indira Party political support and the success of the economic programs that party had instituted during the 1990's by making a commitment to continue the free market policies promulgated by Narasimha Rao. But the blockbuster came when it pledged to eliminate poverty and illiteracy *within 10 years*. Deve Gowda was not the first Prime Minister to make the pledge to eliminate poverty. Mrs. Gandhi had fought her 1971 General Election campaign using the slogan "Eradicate Poverty," but, even though she was all-powerful at the time, she did not go as far as Deve Gowda did by committing herself to accomplish this truly Herculean task within a decade.

The Deve Gowda government's program was indeed replete with lofty goals, but their very loftiness underlined the probability that they would turn out to be more statements of good intentions than plans of action. There was not a snowball's chance in hell that the Deve Gowda government, or any other government for that matter, could eliminate within a decade the poverty and illiteracy that had plagued India for centuries. While it was possible, it was not likely that Parliament and the Indian people would accept its "women's liberation" proposals. Considering that the last coalition government that had attempted to broaden India's "affirmative action" program had been brought down on that very issue, the possibility that the Deve Gowda government would carry out that part of its agenda also appeared to be remote. Given the rising tide of opposition by upper- and middle-level castes to what their members regarded as "reverse discrimination," the political battle that Deve Gowda would have to fight to accomplish this part of his government's agenda would be worse than the struggle that erupted the last time a coalition government had made a similar attempt. In 1989, the coalition government under V.P. Singh proposed to reserve an additional 17% of government jobs for the "backward castes" who are just above the "scheduled castes," in the social hierarchy. The result was riots by higher caste Hindus in several North Indian cities and the fall of the V.P. Singh government. Since Deve Gowda could hardly have forgotten what had happened only six years earlier, it is likely that including the broadening of "affirmative action" in his legislative agenda would turn out to be a gesture aimed at pleasing the lower caste constituents of the parties that had made up the National Front/Left Front rather than a serious commitment to take a major step in the direction of social reform.

But the most grandiose of Deve Gowda's schemes for changing the face of India involved, not its human resources, but its natural resources, and its unattainability stemmed from engineering and financial rather than political considerations. While receiving an Honorary Fellowship of the Institute of Engineers, apparently conferred on him because he had been a building contractor before entering politics, Deve Gowda announced that he was going to constitute a committee of India's top engineers to assess the feasibility of linking together the country's various rivers. In explaining the rationale for setting up such a committee, he pointed out that India's rainfall was distributed unevenly throughout the country, with the result that, while some areas were suffering from floods, others were suffering from drought. If India's rivers were linked together, he argued, the excess flows in one could be channeled into the rivers where flows were deficient. Thus the amount of irrigation water available for growing crops would be balanced from one region to another, and the country's harvests would be greatly increased.

Although none of the engineers who heard Deve Gowda's speech said so, because none of them would have dreamed of criticizing a scheme put forth by a Prime Minister, it is hard not to believe that most of them were thinking that this was the most preposterous proposal coming from a high level public official that they had ever heard. Engineering-wise, carrying it out would be an impossible task, and even if it were feasible from an engineering point of view, the cost would absorb so much of the Central Government's budget that little would be left for any program other than supporting the military. The members of the Institute of Engineers must have been left wondering how the committee of top engineers would go about conducting a feasibility study of a gargantuan engineering project that was, on its very face, impossible to carry out. But, if they thought that Deve Gowda was merely talking and would not pursue his idea about changing the courses of India's rivers, they were forced within six months to change their minds when the Central Government announced that such a committee had indeed been appointed and would soon begin its work. Fortunately for India, the fall of that government within less than a year prevented this preposterous engineering scheme from being implemented.

In addition to the loftiness and questionable attainability of its goals, the weakness of its political position was another good reason for doubting from the outset that the Deve Gowda government was in a position to make those goals a reality. Most of the leaders of the 13 small participating parties and of the one large supporting party had to be kept happy in order for the coalition government to stay in power. Given the conflicting ideologies of the various parties, achieving that objective over a considerable period of time was going to be very difficult and, as it turned out, impossible. Not only would the Deve Gowda government have to keep the support of the MP's who represented rival political parties in order to survive, but it would also need the backing of the Indian populace, of whom only 20% supported the National Front/Left Front.

Ramakrishna Hegde, Deve Gowda's major rival in the Janata Dal Party and the Karnataka State political arena where the new Prime Minister had first come to political prominence, had questioned his ability to function effectively at the Central Government level, saying that he would bring the ways of municipal politics to the national level. While one could charge Hegde's denigrating comment to political sour grapes, one had to wonder how a political leader of a modern state could accomplish a program of political, social, and economic reform when he was guided by astrology rather than the nature of the problems that he faced. Even more frequently than Narasimha Rao, Deve Gowda obtained the advice of an astrologer, who was with him at all times, before deciding when and how to act. Guided by his astrologer, he moved into the Prime Minister's Delhi residence at 5:00 a.m. when his predecessor was still asleep. Beginning his career as Prime Minister with a move that showed questionable manners hardly augured well for the future, whatever the stars and planets might have had to say about it.

The suspicion that the Deve Gowda government's agenda was more a statement of good intentions than a program of intended actions was confirmed when its budget for 1996–97 was presented. Although it was stated that "this budget will improve the condition of the masses" and that it "made provision for the section of society that has been totally neglected," its major benefactors were the military and the middle class. Far from reducing military expenditures to make more funds available for programs that would benefit the poor and develop the rural infrastructure, the budget increased the amount going to the armed forces, bringing it to 13% of total spending. Not only were free market economic policies continued, but the tariff on consumer goods was reduced, making it even cheaper for the middle class to purchase them from abroad. On the other hand, the percentage of total expenditures allocated for programs that would benefit the poor and address India's serious population and food supply problems were either modest, as in the case of education (1.5%), or minuscule, as in the case of health services, including family planning (0.34%), irrigation systems (0.39%), and slum housing (0.12%). Despite the fine-sounding words setting forth lofty goals for social reform and uplift of the poor, its first budget made it clear that the Deve Gowda government would not provide the funds necessary to make a serious effort in those directions but would instead follow a policy of business as usual.

Among the critics of the budget's obvious lack of seriousness regarding implementation of programs to improve the lot of India's poor were the coalition government's supporting parties with left-leaning ideologies, particularly the Communists. Responding to their criticism, Deve Gowda admitted at the end of his first six months as Prime Minister that "it is a matter of regret that after 50 years of Independence with a single and stable government at the Center we have not been able to address the basic needs of the people in the fields of drinking water, communication, and housing." To address this failure, he committed his government to allocating an additional 2,480 crores ($700 million) to implement irrigation and drinking water projects. This substantial infusion of public funds into social welfare and economic development projects might have been interpreted as the sign of a major shift in priorities away from military expenditure and toward social welfare, except for the fact that two days earlier the Ministry of Defense had announced the completion of a deal with Russia to sell India 40 high-tech fighter planes at a cost of $1.2 billion, a half a billion dollars more than the addition to the social welfare and agricultural development budgetary allocations.

As a further concession to the criticisms of his left-leaning supporters, Deve Gowda announced at the beginning of 1997 that his government would implement a program under which 66 million families living below the poverty line, defined as Rs.15,000 ($430) per annum, would be sold food grains at half the government fixed price. While the implementation of such a scheme would benefit those poor families whose income was at or just below the poverty line and who, consequently, could afford to buy half-price food grains, it would not help those families whose income was so far below the poverty line that they did not have enough money to pay even the subsidized price. By basing the subsidized price on a price fixed by the government rather than the market price, implementation of this program would place an increasingly heavy burden on the Central Government's budget as the price of the grain procured keeps going up. Given the increasing demand that will come from a burgeoning population which must be fed from a food grain supply that will be more and more difficult to continue increasing at an equal rate, it is almost inevitable that this will happen. For that reason, the Deve Gowda government deferred implementation of the program, after the Finance Minister questioned whether or not its cost could be accommodated in upcoming budgets. However the financial impact might be worked out, the fact remained that the benefit that the poor would receive would be limited by the provision that each family would be allowed to buy at the subsidized price only 22 pounds of food grains each month. Since the monthly food grains requirement of a poor family with several children is substantially higher than this amount, the program to supply cheap food for India's poor, while it would improve the diet of the higher income poor, would not go a long way toward solving the nation's overall malnutrition problem.

That the Deve Gowda government, despite its rhetoric claiming that it was dedicated to improving the lot of the poor and the ruralites, really aimed to please the elite, the middle class, and urban dwellers became even more evident when it presented its 1997–98 budget. Two of the principal changes from the previous year were cuts in both personal and corporate income taxes and in customs duties, both of which would benefit the members of the expanding consumer society. In order to please the Communist parties, the budget did increase the amount provided for subsidizing the price of food grains sold to poor families, but administration of the program was turned over to State governments which were notorious for slowing down and limiting implementation of Central Government funded social welfare projects. Finance Minister Chidambaram, who had earlier expressed his misgivings about finding more money to alleviate malnutrition among the poor, had put the increased amount in the budget but in such a way that, in the final analysis, only a part of it would be spent. The news of the fall of the Deve Gowda government before its 1997–98 budget had been adopted by Parliament was greeted with more anguish in mansions and bungalows than in tenements and huts.

❖

Major Political Issues

Just as the political parties and the other institutions that constituted India's political system of the 1990's were radically different from those of the 1950's, so too were the major issues with which those two political systems grappled. During the 1950's, language and, intertwined with language, regional autonomy, had been at the forefront. India under the British Raj was made up of a hodgepodge of three Presidencies (Bengal, Bombay, and Madras) directly ruled by the British Crown and hundreds of Princely States ostensibly ruled by a Hindu or Muslim royal family but governed in practice by a British Resident appointed by the Viceroy. These Presidencies and Princely States had come into being higgledy piggledy through conquests and agreements that had accumulated over a span of 300 years, and their boundaries bore no relation to the languages spoken by the people who lived within them. During the campaign for Independence, Indian nationalists maintained that the British had purposely drawn regional political boundaries that cut across and divided linguistic areas because they were following a policy of "divide and rule." The alleged objective of this policy was to make sure that regional political jurisdictions did not comprise people who spoke the same language because that would give a linguistic group a political platform for pursuing parochial policies that, in British eyes, were not good for the nation as a whole. Whether the result of conscious policy or historical accident, the British Raj's practice did diffuse the political power of linguistic groups because their members were split between several governmental jurisdictions.

When Independence came, these nationalist tendencies combined with traditional linguistic sentiments to put pressure on the Central Government to establish boundaries for the states that corresponded with language areas. Jawaharlal Nehru wanted to go slow with the redrawing of State boundaries along linguistic lines because he feared that giving a language group control over a state government would encourage what he called "fissiparous tendencies" that would threaten national unity. His hand was forced in 1953 and by a political action that emulated Mahatma Gandhi. A radical supporter of the principle of linguistic states fasted to death to confront the Central Government with his demand that a state be established for the Telegu-speaking people. His death led to the success of his cause, and Andhra Pradesh was created out of portions of Madras, Orissa, and the former Princely State of Hyderabad. Nehru's acquiescence in the case of Andhra Pradesh opened a Pandora's Box of demands by other linguistic groups for a state of their own. Forced against his will to respond to these demands, he established a States Reorganization Commission to work out linguistically-based state boundaries. In 1956, the States Reorganization Act was passed which went most of the way to making state boundaries coterminous with language regions.

Agitation for language-based states was the dominant issue in Indian politics during the 1950's, and nowhere was this agitation carried on more strenuously than among the Tamil speakers who lived in what was left of Madras State after the creation of Andhra Pradesh. They were proud of their language, which provided the foundation for the other Dravidian languages spoken in South India and, as such, had a history going back thousands of years. In addition, their regional consciousness had been raised since the 1920's by the Self-Respect Movement led by E.V. Ramasamy Nayaker, known to Tamils as *Periayavar* (Respected One). *Periayavar* preached that Tamil culture was far superior to the Aryan culture that had been imposed on the South by Brahmins from North India and that Tamils should free themselves from this pernicious Aryan influence. When the language state agitation of the 1950's began, E.V.R.'s lieutenant, C.N. Annadurai, welded followers of the Self-Respect Movement into a political party, the Dravida Munnetra Kazagham, popularly known as the DMK. The DMK made the most extreme demand of any political group pushing for language-based states by calling for, not only a Tamil-speaking state, but a Tamil-speaking state independent of the Indian Union.

Adding fuel to the fire of the linguistic state agitation was another language issue that had carried over from the days of the British Raj. Beginning in 1835, the East India Company had promulgated a series of enactments that had made English the language of government and higher education. These enactments led, in turn, to English becoming the language of inter-regional politics and economic activity. The end result was that, during the second half of the 19th century, English became India's national language, the language not only of government, the courts, business, and the universities but, generally speaking, the public language of India's elite, even though they also spoke one of the indigenous Indian languages at home. Ironic as it may seem in the light of later political developments, the emergence of English as a national language made a major contribution to the development of India's nationalist movement. The Indians who made up the Indian National Congress that was formed in 1885 and who led it until Mahatma Gandhi took control following World War I came from several different language areas. Because they were products of English-medium higher education, they could communicate with each other and could debate issues in a language which all could understand and speak. The important role that English played in the development of Indian nationalism was nowhere more apparent than in the case of its two greatest leaders, Mahatma Gandhi and Jawaharlal Nehru, whose command of English was better than many people for whom it is their mother tongue.

The contribution that the English language had made to the development of Indian nationalism and its usefulness as a means of communicating between India's several language areas was forgotten when Independence came. Indian nationalists then demanded that English be replaced as a national language by one of India's indigenous languages, and this provision was written into the Constitution. Since none of India's 14 major languages was spoken by a majority of the population, Hindi was selected as the language to replace English on the ground that more Indians spoke Hindi than any of the other 13. But there was a serious difficulty here because 55% of the population belonged to non-Hindi language groups. Despite this difficulty, the Central Government set out to implement the Constitutional provision by making Hindi the language of government and mandating, not only that Hindi be taught in all of India's schools, but that students show proficiency in Hindi in order to graduate.

The immediate and widespread response in the non-Hindi speaking regions was a spate of mass demonstrations and civil disobedience campaigns aimed at reversing what was seen as linguistic imperialism. Nowhere did these agitations take a more extreme form than in the Tamil region. Tamils not only thought that accepting Hindi domination would be culturally degrading but that it would also set back their efforts to win Central Government and other posts. Because proficiency in English was much more widespread among Tamils than among Hindi speakers, Tamils had a competitive advantage as long as Central Government and other civil service examinations were in English. If a switch were made to Hindi, they would be at a definite disadvantage.

These motives for opposing the Central Government's Hindi language program were widely shared by rank and file Tamils and were channeled into a well-organized program of agitations by C.N. Annadurai's political party, the DMK. Demonstrations began relatively quietly with public meetings, *hartals* (shop closings), and painting over Hindi signs at railway stations. When the police moved in to suppress what the Central and State governments regarded as threats to law and order, Tamil agitators turned violent. Police stations and government offices were attacked, and policemen were killed. The Central Government responded by sending in armed paramilitary police and later the army to quell what had become mass riots. Following "shoot to kill" orders, the paramilitary police and army units, including elite Gurkha detachments, brought peace and quiet to Tamil cities and towns, but at the price of hundreds of Tamil lives.

Military action brought the widespread and violent anti-Hindi demonstrations under control, but it was a political decision by Jawaharlal Nehru and the Congress Party that brought them to a permanent end. The Central Government saved face by continuing to maintain that Hindi was India's "official" national language so far as government and education were concerned, but that English could remain as an "ancillary" national language. This meant that government records would be maintained in English as well as Hindi and that Central Government and other civil service examinations would be in both languages. The problem in the schools was solved in a typically Indian way. Hindi continued to be taught as a compulsory subject, but students were passed no matter how poor their performance. The requirement that students show proficiency in Hindi in order to graduate was conveniently ignored by education department officials with the blessing of the governments which they represented.

The demand by Tamils that the boundaries of what was then Madras State be redrawn to correspond with their language area was also met when the States Reorganization Commission set up by Jawaharlal Nehru made its 1955 report. Still remaining, however, was the political problem created by the DMK's agitation for a state that not only followed Tamil linguistic boundaries but was independent of the rest of India. According to the Indian Constitution, no party that ran on a secessionist platform could compete for seats in Parliament and State legislatures. This provision disqualified the DMK from contesting national and State elections for almost a decade after the creation of a Tamil-speaking state. In order to overcome this long-standing obstacle to winning political power, C.N. Annadurai finally changed the party platform from secession to autonomy. Softening the party's demand in this way opened the door for the DMK to take over the Madras State government in 1967. One of its first actions was to change the State's name from Madras to Tamil Nadu.

These political maneuvers at the Central and State government levels settled the language issue and, along with it, the regional issue in Tamil Nadu, where it had generated the most heat during the 1950's. In these and similar ways, both issues were also laid to rest in the other non-Hindi speaking areas, except the Punjab. Here, language was reinforced by religion to produce in 1973 a demand for a Sikh Autonomous Region to be called Kalistan (Sikh Land). This demand by militant Sikhs sparked violence that cost the life of a Prime Minister and the lives of thousands of Sikhs and Hindus. The power of religion continued to fuel the demand for Kalistan despite the fact that the boundaries of the Punjab and Harayana had been drawn along linguistic lines in 1966 to create a state in which Sikhs could be a majority. The emergence of the turmoil over a homeland for the Sikhs foretold during the 1970's that, just as language had been the issue that dominated Indian politics during the 1950's, religion would be the issue that would more and more dominate Indian politics during the 1980's and 1990's.

To be sure, religious conflict as a political issue was not absent from the Indian scene during the early years after Independence, but it was confined to Kashmir where its origins went back to 1948. Ever since that time, a predominantly Muslim population had struggled against Hindu rule in the form of the Indian government. By the late 1980's, the conflict had evolved into an armed insurgency aimed at establishing a Kashmir State independent of both India and Pakistan. The Indian government's response had been to place the two-thirds of Kashmir which it controlled under a martial law regime enforced by the Indian Army. Clashes between Kashmiri militants and Indian troops had continued, and the result had been thousands of dead insurgents, soldiers and civilians. But Kashmir was far from the bulk of India, and the religious issue which had dominated Kashmir's politics for half a century, had come to the forefront of politics south of the 33rd Parallel only in the last two decades.

Religion's move to the political foreground outside Kashmir had begun in a small way in 1973 with the demand by Sikhs for an independent Kalistan. That agitation turned violent during the later 1970's and culminated in the 1984 occupation of the Golden Temple in Amritsar by armed Sikh militants. Prime Minister Indira Gandhi responded by ordering the Indian Army to drive them from the temple in an operation which cost hundreds of Sikh lives. She was not forgiven by Sikh extremists for desecrating their most holy place, and, within a matter of months, she was assassinated by two of her Sikh bodyguards. This reprisal enraged Hindus, just as the army's attack on the Golden Temple had enraged Sikhs. Hindu mobs rampaged through North Indian streets, killing an estimated 3,000 Sikhs and destroying their homes and shops.

The following decade, roughly the same number, but this time Hindus and Muslims rather than Sikhs, were killed when mob violence followed the destruction by Hindu militants of a Muslim mosque that had been constructed by Mogul Emperor Aurangzeb on the legendary site of the birth of Rama at Ayodhya in Uttar Pradesh. The army was finally called in to restore order, just as it had been used to quell the anti-Sikh riots that followed Mrs. Gandhi's assassination. But it was a political rather than a military solution that laid the Ayodhya mosque controversy to rest. Following the traditional Indian formula of both/ and rather than either/or, Prime Minister Narasimha Rao proposed that the mosque be rebuilt but that a Hindu temple be constructed alongside it. His proposal, since it placated the feelings of both parties, was accepted by both Hindus and Muslims as a reasonable way to cool a religious hot spot that, even though it had its origins in the 17th century, was still capable of inflaming Indian society 300 years later.

Religious conflict leading to violence had also erupted during the last decade to the east of India's heartland, in Assam. There native Assamese, who were Hindus and Animists, had attacked immigrants from West Bengal and Bangladesh, most of whom were Muslims. No doubt, economic tensions had added fuel to the fire kindled by religious conflict. West Bengali and Bangladeshi immigrants were driven into Assam by the land hunger that bedeviled one of the most overpopulated regions in the world. The native Assamese saw them as interlopers who were trying to grab land which rightfully belonged to the indigenous people. But these economic tensions would not have produced the killings that had taken place except for the animosity that Assamese Hindus and Animists felt toward the Muslims of West Bengal and Bangladesh. That animosity escalated during the 1970's, triggering deadly attacks on newly-arrived Muslim immigrants in 1983, attacks that resulted in 1,000 deaths and required the intervention of the Indian Army.

Religious conflicts between Hindus, Muslims and Sikhs were significant in and of themselves because they manifested the emergence of religion to replace language as India's major political issue. They were also significant because they contributed to the emergence of Hindu fundamentalism to seriously challenge the Congress Party's secular pluralism as India's most popular political creed. Members of religious minorities like the Muslims and Sikhs were portrayed by Hindu fundamentalists as second-class citizens who were a threat, not only to law and order, but to India's traditional way of life and even its security. Members of the Hindu religious majority, on the other hand, saw themselves as first-class citizens who were defenders of national security and preservers of the fabric of Indian society. This was precisely the ideological line that the BJP took to gain a rapidly increasing measure of support among the 82% of the population who were Hindus.

The major danger on the 1950's political horizon was that, overcome by the divisiveness stemming from language differences, India would cease to be a unified nation and become a conglomeration of more or less independent states representing its various linguistic divisions. The major danger on the 1990's political horizon was that, reacting to increasing pressure from the Hindu religious majority, India would cease to be a pluralistic secular state and become instead a state in which its religious majority would attempt tp rule its religious minorities.

❖

Westernization and Indianization

Just as the politics of free India had undergone major changes during the 50 years following Independence, so also was its society different from what it was on August 15, 1947. On the surface of Indian society, a number of changes had occurred. First and foremost, a substantial middle class had emerged, which by the 1990's constituted about 20% of the population and which reflected the consumerism and cultural style of Western middle classes. But, if one looked below the surface of Indian society, one found that the Indian way of life was much the same as it was when Nehru made his famous "tryst with destiny" speech. To the extent that change had taken place at this deeper level, the society of free India had moved in the opposite direction from its movement on the surface. On the surface, it had moved toward modernization and Westernization. Beneath the surface, it had reaffirmed its traditional ways and had moved toward Indianization.

The concurrent processes of Westernization on the surface of Indian life and Indianization at its roots clashed in a way that caught the attention of worldwide television and print news when the "Miss World" beauty contest was held in Bangalore in November 1996. An Indian company headed by a leading movie star had succeeded in securing the contest's sponsorship, an achievement which was publicized in the press as a feather in India's cap because this would be the first time in 45 years that it would take place on Indian soil. Cultural and political forces, supportive of traditional ways, took a diametrically opposed view, arguing that holding a competition between female bodies in an Indian city would be a national disgrace. Demonstrations and fierce opposition ensued, resulting in the swimsuit component of the pageant being displaced to the Seychelles.

By the time the 33 contestants arrived in Bangalore, an unusual coalition of opposition groups had formed to demand that the competition be stopped. The BJP based its opposition on the ground that the contest contaminated India's 4,000-year-old cultural tradition, women's groups on the ground that it commercialized women's bodies, and the Communist Party on the ground that it represented an exercise in Western cultural imperialism. A week before the contest's finale, an unemployed tailor from a Communist party youth group burned himself to death in protest. Although this act of self-immolation took place in Madurai, 170 miles south of Bangalore, it could have touched off protest demonstrations at the contest's site. To counter this threat, Bangalore authorities mobilized 10,000 police and paramilitary troops. Faced with such a formidable "law and order" force, the women's groups, who had planned to lead public demonstrations, appealed to the courts to issue an order putting a stop to the contest on the ground that it would be a vulgar and obscene spectacle. The courts refused to intervene. The BJP followed a political route by calling upon the citizens of Bangalore to stage a general strike that would close businesses and shut down transportation, but the response was meager.

In the end, the final events of the "Miss World" contest went on as scheduled, but under the protection of 1,500 policemen with their *lathis* (riot sticks) standing guard within the cricket stadium in which they were held and several thousand paramilitary troops on call outside. During the hours that preceded these events, life in Bangalore was disrupted by several clashes between police and hundreds of BJP-led stone-throwing demonstrators. The police used *lathis* and tear gas to break up the demonstrations, and more than 1,500 protesters were arrested. These demonstrations were not accompanied by the general strike which the BJP had called for, but one had only to look at the political situation to find the reason for its failure. Bangalore and Karnataka State were strongholds of the Janata Dal Party, one of the BJP's political foes and the party led by Prime Minister Deve Gowda. That the Janata Dal Party had endorsed the holding of the "Miss World" contest in Bangalore was publicly proclaimed by the fact that its Karnataka State Chief Minister was among the prominent spectators sitting in the stadium. The Communist Party's failure to support the BJP's call for a strike was explained by its membership in the United Front government and the two portfolios it holds.

Although the sponsors of the "Miss World" beauty contest and the Janata Dal Party had won the battle, in the eyes of the majority of Indian people, the groups that had opposed it had won the war. The strong and disparate opposition that had been aroused stemmed from the fact that, as one Indian psychologist put it, "People feel that the stability of society is being broken up." As regards its political impact, the BJP, by organizing and leading violent demonstrations opposing the contest, strengthened its image as the party that defended India's traditional culture against the inroads of the Western influences that threatened to "break it up." In contrast, Prime Minister Deve Gowda's Janata Dal Party emerged as the party encouraging these inroads and the Communists as the party that "talked the talk" of opposition but was not prepared to "walk the walk" by shedding blood and going to jail, as the BJP had, to try to prevent the contest from taking place.

However much the surface of 1990's free India displayed elements of Western cosmopolitanism, such as the staging of the "Miss World" contest in Bangalore, the reaction to that event showed that below the surface traditional social ways and institutions were still the dominant forces shaping Indian life. Supporting these traditional social ways and institutions was the caste system, which meshed with the Hindu religion to form the glue that held Indian society together. During the 1950's, some visionaries, Indian as well as Western, thought that caste would play a less and less central societal role as the years following Independence went by. In fact, the opposite had happened. Nowhere is this development better described than in one of the late 1980's *London Times* dispatches written by Trevor Fishlock:

"Although Indians had hoped for progress toward a casteless society, and there is a Constitutional commitment to one, caste plays an increasingly important role in politics and in the power structure. Caste is the enduring and resilient basis of social organization and provides politics with ready-made groups, interests, and loyalties, easily mobilized. It is through group power that people feel that they can get things done. Even voting is a contradictory, an individual action, in a society where most actions are collective. The country is committed to helping *Harijans* (untouchables), lower castes and tribal people by reserving places for them in colleges, government offices and legislatures. But this positive discrimination, a means of advancement, creates incongruities and resentments. Jobs go on quota grounds rather than merit and 'backwardness' has become a vested interest. The economics of caste, the caste block veto, and the fight for advantage among the quotas is central. It would be unrealistic to expect representative politics to develop in India except on a caste basis."

As Fishlock points out, the country is committed to helping untouchables and the low castes through legislative measures, but even those who had raised their political and economic status through this "affirmative action" program had not climbed correspondingly higher on the social ladder. In the eyes of the caste Hindu majority, they were still regarded as untouchables no matter how much they had raised their level of education or increased their incomes. As such, they still were not treated with respect. During recent decades, far from improving, their political and social position had actually worsened because of a backlash by the castes who made up the Hindu majority against what they saw as the "special privileges" that untouchables were enjoying at their expense.

It is important to note that India had never outlawed discriminatory social behavior based on caste. Only the practice of untouchability had been outlawed, and even here the effect of this change in the law had been practically nil. Almost all of the 15% of the population (approximately 150 million in 1996) who were untouchables still suffered the disabilities that they did when Independence dawned. A limited number had improved their status by winning the legislative seats and filling the government positions reserved for untouchables. A somewhat larger number had secured an education, and thereby better jobs, because of government scholarships. But the vast majority were no better off than they had been 50 years earlier.

Another minority group, whose social position had not only not improved but had actually gotten worse, was the 12% of the population (approximately 110 million in 1996) who were Muslims. The anti-Muslim feeling among Hindus that went back to Partition days, and, for some extremists, even to the Muslim invasions that had taken place centuries earlier, had been exacerbated internally by bloody communal riots and the anti-Indian agitation in Kashmir and externally by the ongoing conflict with Pakistan. Indian Muslims saw themselves as citizens of India, not of Pakistan, but in the eyes of most Hindus, they were suspect because, when push came to shove, it was expected that they would support their co-religionists across the border. Despite the Constitutional commitment to a pluralistic secular state, de facto discrimination against Muslims had been the order of the day ever since India became independent.

In the words of Indian journalist Pranay Gupta, writing in 1985:

"For the overwhelming number of India's majority Hindus, Muslims remain the ancient enemy. There is little forgiveness toward Muslims (for forcing India's Partition), much less trust and tolerance, because of real or perceived wrongs... The ordinary Muslim has been left out of India's economic and political mainstream. Most Indians consider Muslims as a fifth column for Pakistan."

Nowhere were the results of decades-old discrimination against Muslims more apparent than in the minuscule number of official positions they held. Gupta gives the following estimates of the status of Muslims during 1985:

- Indian Administrative Service: total strength 4,000—Muslims 120
- Indian Police Service: total strength 2,000—Muslims 50
- Judges: total strength 5,000—Muslims 300
- Bank Officers: total strength 120,000—Muslims 2,500

Given the crucial role which India's armed forces had played in the 50-year-old struggle with Pakistan, it was hardly surprising that, according to Gupta, very few Muslims had been admitted into the officer ranks of India's military services.

The lot of India's tiny Sikh minority (some 2% of the country's population) during the five decades since Independence had been a mixed bag. Economically speaking, most Sikhs had thrived. Sikhs had benefited most directly from the "green revolution" because many of them were farmers who grew wheat, the grain with the most dramatic yield increase. Sikhs had also done well in business and in the armed forces. On the other hand, the violent agitation which militant Sikhs had carried on for Kalistan had aroused strong anti-Sikh feeling among the Hindu majority, feeling which turned bloody in 1984 after Mrs. Gandhi was assassinated by two of her Sikh bodyguards. Even though that blood letting had taken place 10 years ago, the violent campaign for Kalistan had spilled over into the 1990's, substantiating the Hindu view that Sikhs were a trouble-making minority who were a threat to national unity and who must be treated with suspicion and kept under control.

Women's rights was another facet of Indian society that reverted to traditional ways. Not only had arranged marriages and the dowry system continued unabated, but their *modus operandi* had become more onerous. Higher dowries had been demanded from brides' families, and disputes had arisen more frequently over the way in which the terms of the dowry agreement were carried out. In extreme cases, these disputes had led to the murder of a bride whose family had been accused of failing to deliver what they had pledged in the dowry agreement.

Suttee (a widow burning herself on the funeral pyre of her husband) was almost unheard of during the first half of the 20th century because the British Raj's law banning it was rigorously enforced. But during recent decades, its practice had cropped up again, albeit still infrequently enough to make it the subject of sensational newspaper stories. Much more frequent were the instances of another practice which the British Raj had outlawed, not only *de jure* but also *de facto*: female infanticide. These instances occurred most frequently among the desperately poor and were motivated in part by the parents' inability to feed more children, but only in part. The other motivating factor was the parents' preference for boys over girls. Even the desperately poor did not kill their boy babies, however difficult it might be to bring them up. That was one of the reasons why there were approximately 50 million more men than women in today's India, whereas in Western societies it was the other way round. Parents belonging to the middle and elite classes also shared this preference for boys over girls, but, if they did not want a girl, they had enough money to take advantage of modern medical technology and identify and abort a female fetus before it was born.

All of these changes manifested the schizophrenic ways in which Indian society had moved during the 50 years since Independence—on the surface, toward the modern and the Western; below the surface, toward the traditional and the Indian. Another way of characterizing this era was to view it as a time of transition—from the days when British influence carried over into free India's life, not only in the form of leaders like Mahatma Gandhi and Jawaharlal Nehru who had had a British education and, as a result, had internalized certain British values, but also in the form of political institutions and practices which the British had left behind, to the days when that influence had almost totally evaporated. During the 1950's, Britain's imprint on Indian life, although it had already begun to dissipate, was still plain to see. During the 1990's it was conspicuous by its absence.

One place where the disappearance of Britain's imprint on Indian life was plain to see was India's contemporary maps. As soon as Independence came, the British spelling of many of India's cities were replaced by romanized transliterations of their names in the regional Indian language. The officials of the British Raj had found these "native" names too difficult to pronounce and so they had not only romanized them but simplified them. In Tamil Nadu, Tiruchirappali had become Trichinopoly, and Ramanathapuram had become Ramnad. In Kerala, Tiruvananthapuram had become Trivandram. During the 1990's a more radical form of Indianization of place names began to take over. Names of some of the major cities that had been used by the British and also by Indians for almost all of the first half-century after Independence were replaced by regional language names that predated the coming of the Europeans. Bombay became Mumbai. Madras became Chennai. When 1997 dawned, Calcutta was still Calcutta, and Delhi was still Delhi, but, once underway, there was no telling how far the process of restoring pre-European place names would go.

❖

The Environment

Changes in human life over the past 50 years had been accompanied in the realm of nature by the drastic degradation of India's environment, especially in the cities. Water and air quality had deteriorated to a shocking degree, and solid waste had accumulated to the point where the combination of these environmental problems made a city like Calcutta a human settlement on the verge of becoming uninhabitable. Here is V.S. Naipaul's description of a ride through Calcutta's streets during the early 1990's:

"After some time, the city thoroughfare appeared to shrink, to collapse in on itself from its increased human density. The roadway narrowed; roadside huts and lean-tos, without pronounced color, just a mish-mash of brown and black and gray, appearing to encroach on space meant for vehicles, had the solid, concrete buildings behind them, and gave the impression of a very long village road set in dirt, such freshness as had come with the morning already burnt up by brown traffic fumes and sun-shot traffic dust. What seemed to threaten in many places in central India appeared to have happened here; it was like witnessing the creation of a ruin: a large inhabited city was reverting to the earth."

Calcutta was the worst case, but Bombay, Delhi, and Madras were following not far behind, and even smaller cities like Madurai and Agra already suffered from severe environmental deterioration. Since the beginning of this century, India's cities had acted like sponges absorbing the rapidly increasing population that the countryside could not support and had suffered the environmental consequences of overcrowding. By the 1990's, they were approaching, if not already on the brink of, their population and environmental saturation points.

Bombay's air pollution problem was a good example. Not only had Bombay experienced a major industrial expansion during the 1980's but the number of motorized vehicles on its streets had more than doubled. The resulting deleterious impact on air quality was documented in an Urban Air Quality Management Strategy study conducted by the World Bank and the United Nations Development Program, which found that total suspended particles in Bombay's air had increased by 50% between 1981 and 1990. The principal culprit had been the thousands of additional trucks, buses, cars, and motor bikes, but the growing number of industrial and power plants had contributed a major share. The final touch had been added by the influx of migrants from the countryside whose wood-burning stoves and rubbish fires had pumped more smoke into Bombay's skies. According to the Urban Air Quality Management Strategy study:

"Long-term exposure to high levels of these pollutants results in increased susceptibility to respiratory illnesses, diminished lung function, and premature death from respiratory causes. Besides, average concentrations of lead, which have adverse effects on blood pressure, the nervous system and kidneys, have doubled from 1980 to 1987. Nitrous oxide, which also causes lung damage, has increased by roughly 25% during the same period."

The study estimated that the annual health impact on Bombay's residents was 2,800 cases of premature death, 60 million person days in which respiratory problems were experienced and 19 million person days of restricted activity. Translated into monetary terms, these annual losses amounted to 1,800 crores ($50 million).

Rural areas had also suffered severe environmental damage, especially in the form of extensive deforestation and its consequence, soil erosion and the silting up of natural waterways. An exploding population and accelerated economic development had made it necessary to increase the supply of wood for cooking and construction. Adding to the pressure on the forests was the program to put more land under the plow in order to provide food for India's rapidly increasing millions. The result had been wholesale felling of India's trees. During the 1950's, the Central Government's goal was to maintain

25% of the land as forest. By the 1990's, only 10% was still covered with trees. Nor had the environmental damage been limited to the loss of trees that provide beauty and comforting shade in a cut-over and hot country. The wholesale felling of forest trees had led to increased flooding and soil erosion during the monsoon seasons. The eroded soil, in turn, had silted up rivers and streams to the point where flows in these important parts of India's natural irrigation systems had become impeded, with the result that more of the water needed to grow crops was lost through seepage and evaporation. During the 1950's, it was estimated that 20% of India's limited supply of irrigation water disappeared into the ground and into the air before it reached the fields. During the 1990's, this loss would have become even greater.

India's tangible world of the 1990's—its population, economics, politics, society, and environment—was vastly different from the India of the 1950's. Its intangible world—its national vision—had also undergone a radical change during the first five decades of free India's history. When Independence dawned, India's leaders envisaged its future as that of a secular and pluralistic society in which there would be political equality and social and economic justice for all, where all would enjoy a decent standard of living, where conflicts would be settled by peaceful means, and where individual and community life would be guided by moral principles and mutual service. In all of these respects, free India was envisaged as being very different from the Western world from which India had detached itself when it broke free from Britain's empire. That vision had died during the 50 years that had followed. It had been replaced by the reality of an India motivated much like Western nations, where pursuit of material comforts and wealth drives most people's lives, where individuals and groups vie with each other for political, economic, and social preeminence, and where the state pursues and protects the interests of the haves over the have nots.

Politically speaking, one facet of this changed vision—the vision of India as a nation like those in the West—represented a step forward. During the 1950's India's sense of national identity was relatively weak. Indians, in addition to their caste and their religion, saw themselves as members of regional language groups. As a result, linguistic and regional loyalties were strong, and national loyalty was weak. In Tamil Nadu, those linguistic and regional loyalties were so strong that the DMK was able to muster millions to support a platform calling for secession from the Indian Union. In the India of the 1990's, regional and linguistic loyalties were still alive but, except in the Punjab and Kashmir where religion had entered into the political picture, they had taken a back seat to loyalty to the Indian nation. As a political force supporting India's unity, this strengthening of the sense of Indian nationalism made the Indian Union more stable and gave the country a common purpose which was only embryonic during its early years.

What is more, this stronger sense of Indian nationalism was not just a matter of sentiment but the product of India's 50 years' experience as an independent nation. The vast majority of Indians, whatever their linguistic and regional loyalties, had come to see by the 1990's that none of the various linguistic and regional groups could go it alone and that, if they wanted to benefit from economic development and protect themselves against what was perceived to be the threats to their national security posed by Pakistan and China, they had to stick together. During the 1950's, when the contentious issues of linguistic states and national language posed a threat to national unity, the Central Government was widely seen, especially in the non-Hindi speaking areas of the country, as an enemy of regional autonomy which should be defied. By 1997, most Indians saw the Central Government as essential to their well-being, not only to protect them from foreign invaders, but also to maintain law and order in a country rife with communal strife.

That Indian nationalism had by 1997 come into its own as a political force had been publicly displayed when a statue of Subhas Chandra Bose had been unveiled in the Parliament Building courtyard. During the early decades of Independence, Bose had been in disgrace because Gandhi had shown that the non-violent strategy that he had advocated had succeeded in ending British rule, while the strategy pursued by Bose—fighting with the Japanese to drive Britain out of India—had been a failure. Secondly, Bose had sided with the powers of fascism that sought to destroy democracy, whereas free India had committed itself to democracy. When Bose's memory had been honored by placing his statue among those of the great leaders of the struggle for Independence, India had said loud and clear that it was no longer bothered by his having advocated violence and his having allied himself with the Axis powers. It had said that all that mattered in 1997 was that, using fair means or foul, he had been an ardent patriot who had given his all to free India from British rule.

Mahatma Gandhi had taught that the end does not justify the means and that a good end cannot result from bad means. He had persuaded the Congress Party that using a bad means like violence would not produce the good end that India sought—freedom from British rule. Bose, on the other hand, had believed that the end justifies the means and had argued that the freedom movement should use every means at its disposal—including violence—to bring the British Raj to an end. When the clash between these two political philosophies had occurred, in 1939, Gandhi's had won, and his victory had been vindicated on August 15, 1947, when India became free. But on January 23, 1997, Bose's political philosophy had won out when his statue was unveiled by Prime Minister Deve Gowda. India had made it clear that it now subscribed to the kind of nationalism that characterized the nations of the West—that where India's interests were at stake, the end justified the means and every means at India's disposal should be used to further them. The force behind this about-face from Gandhian principles after 58 years was the rising tide of Indian nationalism. By 1997, this force was strong enough to bring India to the point of condoning not only the use of any means to protect and promote Indian interests, but also working with any ally that would help India achieve its goals. India was now prepared to follow the principle of "power politics" that had guided Bose—the principle that the enemy of India's enemy was India's friend and should be supported whatever the flaws in its character.

India's rehabilitation of Subhas Chandra Bose made clear the fact that its stronger sense of nationalism was a two-edged political sword that could cut negatively as well as positively. One negative direction that it might well have taken with a military force in excess of 1 million at its disposal, but did not, was to turn India into an aggressive jingoistic state that sought to expand its territory by attacking its neighbors. No doubt, India had fought three wars with its principal external enemy, Pakistan, and relations between the two countries remained bitter. But India's motive, throughout its hot wars and its cold war with Pakistan, even in Kashmir, had been to hold onto what it had rather than to acquire territory held by Pakistan. Having suffered a humiliating defeat at the hands of China in the 1962 border war, aggressive military action in that direction had been an unthinkable thought since the day that China pulled back from the approaches to Assam. Without India's support in its 1970 struggle for independence from West Pakistan, Bangladesh would not have come into existence. Since it had begun as and continued to be a client state, there was no need for India to use its military muscle to establish a dominant position vis-à-vis Bangladesh. Nor had India made any aggressive moves against Myanmar, a neighboring country that had been so locked up within itself during recent decades that interaction between the two countries had been minimal in comparison with the late 1960's when Myanmar's Tamil residents were being expelled to Tamil Nadu. After that difficult period in Indo-Myanmar relations had become a thing of the past, Myanmar no longer played a significant role in Indian foreign policy.

Other than its 1965 incursion into West Pakistan and its 1971 attack on Pakistani forces in East Pakistan, the only external direction in which India had made a significant military move had been toward the south—in Sri Lanka. That move began, interestingly enough, given Mrs. Gandhi's predilection for hinting that the CIA was behind much of the unrest that plagued India, as a CIA-style covert operation. After the Tamil Tigers had begun their insurrection against the Sri Lankan government in the late 1970's, demanding independence for the northern and eastern regions inhabited mainly by Tamil-speaking Hindus, she provided support for them by allowing them to maintain training camps in and secure arms from Tamil Nadu. Velupillai Prabakaran, the Tamil Tigers' leader, was treated by Delhi almost as a VIP government official, and he was allowed to maintain his headquarters in Madras and received the blessing of various DMK governments. Mrs. Gandhi's motives for attempting to weaken the Sri Lankan government by supporting the Tamil insurrection were both political and personal. On the foreign policy front, she felt that Sri Lanka had become so infiltrated by foreign influences that were inimical to India's interests—Britain, the United States, Israel, and China—that it was on its way to becoming a conduit through which subversion would enter India. A particular sticking point for her was that Sri Lanka had made an agreement with the United States for the building of a Voice of America station within its territory. On the domestic front, her support for the Tamil Tigers scored political points with Tamils whose votes she badly needed after her defeat in the 1977 General Election. On the personal front, Mrs. Gandhi had an intense dislike for Sri Lanka's president and wanted to see him out of office.

After her return to power in 1980, Mrs. Gandhi escalated covert support of the Tamil Tigers into overt backing by manning their Tamil Nadu training camps with Indian government personnel and supplying their weapons from Indian stocks. This policy continued under her son Rajiv and reached its zenith when Indian Air Force planes dropped supplies to a contingent of Tamil Tigers surrounded by Sri Lankan troops. This open show of India's backing for the Tamil Tigers prompted the Sri Lankan leaders to make a deal that they thought would put the Indian government on their side. They agreed to recognize Tamil as one of Sri Lanka's official languages and to give the Tamil-speaking region a high degree of autonomy. On the Indian side, Rajiv Gandhi's government agreed to send troops to Sri Lanka to disarm the Tamil Tigers and pacify the areas where fighting had taken place, provided that Sri Lanka prevented foreign military ships from fueling at its oil depots and halted construction of the Voice of America transmitter.

In 1987, the first of the Indian troops landed in Sri Lanka's Jaffna Peninsula and soon their numbers reached 70,000. Despite their presence, the insurgency dragged on. The Tamil Tigers demanded independence, not autonomy, and now they fought the Indian troops as well as the Sri Lankan army. Velupillai Prabakaran did allow himself to be persuaded by Indian authorities to fly from Delhi to Colombo and go through the motions of surrendering his forces, but, as soon as the ceremony was over, he fled to the jungle and rallied his followers to continue the struggle for Tamil independence. Since the Indian troops had little motivation to lay their lives on the line and the Tamil Tigers had a great deal of motivation to do so, superior numbers did not tip the balance in their favor. The months went by without the Indian forces achieving their objective. Frustrated by their failure to defeat the Tamil Tigers, the Indian troops took out their resentment by committing atrocities against Sri Lankan citizens. The result was an ugly and disgraceful situation which so embarrassed both the Sri Lankan and Indian governments that, within two years, the Indian forces were on their way back to India. Unfortunately, this was not the final chapter in the story of India's involvement with Sri Lanka because, two years later, Rajiv Gandhi's role in orchestrating the military fiasco cost him his life when he was blown up in a small town in Tamil Nadu by a Tamil Tiger bomb.

With the exception of Sri Lanka, aggressive action against India's neighbors had not taken a military form. On the other hand, it had certainly been felt in a non-military way by the small countries on the border with China. Here the roots of conflict went back, not just to the dawn of Indian Independence, but to the centuries that had gone before, when India and China had vied for supremacy in the Himalayan region. During the 1950's, Nehru tried to defuse this rivalry by pursuing a policy of mutual friendship. That policy ran into trouble over disagreement on the location of the Himalayan border between the two countries and crashed in 1962 when China invaded Ladakh and the Northeast Frontier Agency. That experience shook India's confidence in its ability to secure its Himalayan border and strengthened its determination to prevent China from gaining ascendancy in Sikkim, Bhutan, and Nepal, the three small countries which buffered a long stretch of the dividing line between the two Himalayan giants.

Sikkim had suffered the most from India's determination to dominate its buffer zone with China, to the point, in fact, where it lost its identity and became a part of India. During the years immediately following Indian Independence, Sikkim had the status of a protectorate that was ruled by a *chogyal* (king) who first gained notoriety because he had an American wife. As time went on, the *chogyal* showed more and more opposition to domination by India. In 1974, Mrs. Gandhi's government fomented an internal political agitation which unseated him, and a year later Sikkim was incorporated into the Indian Union. Since that time, India had kept the State of Sikkim on a tight political rein. When conflict between the Hindu majority and the Buddhist minority had led to political unrest in 1984, Sikkim's Governor, who had been appointed by the Central Government, had dismissed its Chief Minister and thus prepared the way for President's Rule. Not only had Sikkim become a part of India, but it was to be governed in a way that was acceptable to India's Central Government.

Bhutan had maintained nominal independence but at the price of accepting Indian domination. Like Sikkim, Bhutan had begun India's post-Independence era in a protectorate status, under the terms of a 1949 treaty that gave India an "advisory" role in conducting its foreign affairs. Unlike Sikkim, it had not contested Indian domination. With Sikkim's fate very much in mind, Bhutan had accepted Indian guidance in carrying on its foreign relations, Indian economic assistance in implementing development projects, Indian military training for its tiny army, and Indian education for its citizens. India had received compensation for its playing this "mothering" role in the form of Bhutan's making sure that it took actions that kept Chinese personnel and Chinese influence out of its territory.

Along with Sikkim and Bhutan, Nepal had also experienced India's tight embrace during the years following 1947. Only three years after India became independent, two treaties had been signed with Nepal. The first was a treaty of friendship that was accompanied by a letter which stated that "neither government shall tolerate any threat to the security of the other by a foreign aggressor." The second was an agreement giving Nepal, which is landlocked, trade and transit rights through Indian territory so that it would have access to the nearest port, Calcutta. Until the early 1970's, Nepal had lived quietly with its giant neighbor to the south, not only because India was much larger but also because it had a stranglehold on Nepal's external trade. That era of good feeling had come to an end when Nepal's king, had not only criticized India for annexing Sikkim, but had requested that the 1950 trade and transit agreement be amended in ways that would benefit Nepal. In 1975, he had gone even further by proposing that, rather than continuing to be treated as a satellite of India, Nepal be recognized by members of the international community as a "zone of peace." China and Pakistan, India's two principal Asian rivals, had immediately accepted his proposal; India had refused to do so. The king had repeated his proposal in 1984, but India had continued to maintain its position that it was Nepal's "big brother" and that it had a right to tell it how to behave.

In the meantime, Nepal had begun to interact more with China. Goods from China began to be sold in Nepal, and Chinese contractors began to undertake Nepalese construction projects. Nepal's government had even gone so far as to buy military equipment from China. These developments had made Delhi more and more nervous about the Chinese influence in Nepal. In 1986 Rajiv Gandhi's government had decided to crack down. The 1950 treaties had lapsed, and, when their terms had been redrafted, India had refused to sign. Since the trade and transit treaty was no longer in force, India had closed all but two border crossings and had reduced the fuel supplies which came from India and upon which Nepal depended. The severe economic dislocation which had followed flowed over into Nepal's political life when street demonstrations protesting against economic hardship forced the king to renounce much of his power and to allow elections for the first time in 30 years.

The immediate impasse had ended in 1990 when the V.P. Singh government took over from Rajiv Gandhi's administration and its foreign minister had signed the two treaties with Nepal. But the tension between India and Nepal caused by India's determination to dominate its smaller neighbor to the north has continued. No doubt, Nepal had retained its trade and transit rights, and it had continued to maintain limited economic ties with China, but it was still bound by the treaty commitment that it would not tolerate any threat to India's security from "a foreign aggressor." Since both Nepal and India took "foreign aggressor" to mean China, the events leading up to the renewal of the treaty of friendship had set a definite limit on how far Nepal could go in fostering closer relations with its giant neighbor to the north. Moreover, just as China's 1962 invasion had taught India the lesson that China would come back again if a serious dispute arose between the two, so India's 1990's "land-locking" of Nepal and reducing its fuel supplies had taught Nepal the lesson that India could play havoc with its economic life if Nepal moved too close to China for India's comfort.

India's strengthening sense of nationalism had also been the driving force behind the intransigence that it displayed when it was asked in 1996 to sign the Nuclear Test Ban Treaty (NTBT). The first proposal, made as far back as 1954, that the nations of the world stop further testing of nuclear weapons had come from none other than Jawaharlal Nehru. Forty-two years later, it had been India's refusal to sign the NTBT that had prevented it from being submitted to the United Nations for adoption. India's official reason for refusing to sign had been that the Treaty did not include a clause committing the world's existing nuclear powers to get rid of their nuclear weapons within a specified time period. India's real reason had been that it wanted to keep open the option to develop its own nuclear weapons to counter Pakistan's effort to become a nuclear power. India had become convinced that Pakistan was intent upon acquiring a nuclear capability and that, if it was successful, that nuclear capability would be used, if not to attack, at least to threaten India into giving in to Pakistani demands in Kashmir or any other point of conflict between the two hostile neighbors. Neither the Narasimha Rao nor the Deve Gowda governments had been willing to commit India to foregoing its potential for acquiring the nuclear means to prevent Pakistan from using nuclear weapons to offset India's marked superiority in conventional military force.

As these two Prime Ministers saw the NTBT situation, India signing the treaty would have meant that it was setting aside its national interests in order to conform to the wishes of other members of the world community whose national interests lay in ending the testing of nuclear weapons. On the foreign policy side, such an action would have made India more vulnerable to overt or covert aggressive actions on the part of Pakistan. On the side of domestic politics, it would also have exposed their governments to a backlash that would have been disastrous for them and their parties. The strong sense of nationalism which had emerged in India during its first 50 years of Independence would have been the driving force behind such a backlash because the Indian people would have seen signing the NTBT as a sell-out to international pressure that might result in Pakistan becoming the dominant power in South Asia. In the end, then, free India had vetoed the NTBT for nationalist reasons even though it was its first Prime Minister who had originated the idea behind it.

Countervailing the positive internal impact of India's stronger sense of nationalism was its negative political influence. Hindu fundamentalist political forces within India had been able to capitalize on the strengthening of the sense of national identity by defining the 82% of India's population who were Hindus as 100% Indians and the 18% who belonged to religious minorities as second-class citizens. This sectarian ideology had been used to back up their call for a political system in which the Hindu majority would dominate non-Hindu minorities and would see to it that all Indians followed the Hindu way of life. Because the heightened sense of national identity had taken this negative internal direction, the national vision of a pluralistic secular democracy with which free India had been born had been infiltrated and eroded by a national vision of an authoritarian Hindu state.

~ PART TWO ~

FREE INDIA'S FIRST
HALF-CENTURY DIAGNOSED

❖

Population and Politics

Put in the briefest of terms, the India of the 1950's had become lost in the India of the 1990's. Why? Any attempt to answer this question must begin with the overriding tangible development that had changed the nation during this period: an exploding population. That the population had continued to grow with little restraint (at an annual rate of just under 2% in 1996 or about 18 million per year) was the result of a complex interaction between social, political, and scientific forces. On the social side, in the absence of a social security system, children who could support their parents in old age continued to be the only "safety net" for India's masses, and the more children, the stronger the "net." Especially boys, who not only earned more money but who brought home brides with dowries. So parents who had a series of girls kept on having more children until some boys came along, whether or not they could afford to support a larger family.

On the political side, India's post-Independence governments had carried on a series of family planning programs, but the level of effort had been astonishingly low, considering the seriousness of the problem. On average, only about 1% of Gross National Product had been spent on all health services. Since this 1% had to cover the cost of running an extensive network of hospitals in the cities and clinics in the countryside, only a small portion of health services expenditures had gone into the family planning program. To exacerbate the situation, beginning in the 1980's, the annual public outlay on family planning had fallen even below the modest figure of previous decades. During the Emergency of 1975–77, the draconian methods pushed by Sanjay Gandhi, including, it was alleged, forced sterilization, discredited the government-sponsored program in the eyes of the bulk of India's population. As a result, family planning became a political "hot potato," and, since that time, no Central Government had been willing to pay the political price that would be exacted if it were to sponsor and fund a vigorous effort to slow down population growth.

On the scientific side, greater control of epidemic diseases through inoculation and more effective treatment of the sick through the use of modern medicine and technology had produced a marked increase in India's average life span. During the 1950's, life expectancy was about 40 years. By the 1990's, it had risen to 60. So India's population explosion had been fueled at both ends of the life cycle—more births and fewer deaths.

Turning from demography to India's political and social life, the first question that has to be asked is: Why did Mahatma Gandhi's vision of the new India disappear during its first half-century of life? Surprising as it may seem, the scrapping of Gandhianism was initiated by his ardent admirer and follower: Jawaharlal Nehru. Nehru rejected Gandhi's economic vision of *sarvodaya*—a traditional rural society based on mutual service—in favor of a modern industrial society based on Fabian socialism. The process of abandoning Gandhianism which Nehru began was furthered by his daughter, Indira. Her disdain for the principles of her father's mentor was displayed in a very dramatic fashion when, during the first days of her 1975–77 Emergency, she ordered the incarceration of Vinoba Bhave and Jayaprakash Narayan, the two men who were seen throughout the country as Gandhi's foremost living disciples. No doubt, they were soon released, but Mrs. Gandhi's judgment that Gandhianism was sufficiently forgotten throughout the country that she could get away with locking up its best-known contemporary practitioners was vindicated by the fact that there was no public outcry when she took what, during the 1950's, would have been a dangerous political step.

Naipaul is brutally frank in asserting that India was bound to forget Mahatma Gandhi during the decades that followed his death. Describing Gandhi as "the least Indian of India's leaders," he writes:

"He looked at India as no Indian could; his vision was direct, and this directness was revolutionary... (He) looked down to the roots of the static and decayed society and the picture of India that comes out of his writings and exhortations over more than 30 years still holds; this is the measure of his failure... Nothing remains of Gandhi in India but this: his name and the worship of his image... India undid Gandhi. He became a Mahatma. He was to be reverenced for what he was. His message was irrelevant. He remains a tragic paradox. Indian nationalism grew out of Hindu revivalism; the revivalism which he so largely encouraged made his final failure certain."

Naipaul's characterization of Mahatma Gandhi as "the least Indian of India's leaders" was anticipated by A.L. Basham who wrote much earlier, only five years after Gandhi's assassination: "Mahatma Gandhi was looked on by many, both Indian and European, as the epitome of Hindu tradition, but this is a false judgment because he was much influenced by Western ideas. Gandhi believed in the fundamentals of his ancient culture, but passionate love of the underdog...was unorthodox in the extreme and owed more to European 19th century liberalism than to anything Indian... For Gandhi's pacifism we must look to the Sermon on the Mount and to Tolstoy. His championing of women's rights is also the result of Western influence."

The connection between Hindu revivalism and what Naipaul calls his "final failure" was foreshadowed in 1948 by the circumstances of Mahatma Gandhi's death. He was murdered by Hindu revivalists. Two groups of Hindu extremists, the RSS and the Hindu Mahasabha, organized the assassination plot. It was led by two Brahmins dedicated to bringing back Bharat, the ancient India that included the Indus River valley which had gone to Pakistan when British India was partitioned. The sworn enemies of these Hindu extremists were the Muslims, who, beginning in the 8th century, had invaded Bharat, and who, during the 20th century, had caused the dismemberment of what the British had put together. In their eyes, Mahatma Gandhi was coddling the Muslims, and so he was a traitor to Hindu India who had to die.

Naipaul goes on to identify another reason why Mahatma Gandhi's philosophy could not become firmly rooted in Indian soil. He quotes one of Gandhi's fundamental teachings: "Before the throne of the Almighty, we shall be judged, not by what we have eaten or whom we have touched but by whom we have served and how. Inasmuch as we serve a single human being in distress, we shall find favor in the eyes of God." Commenting on this teaching, Naipaul points out how un-Indian an ethical idea it is:

"Hindus might try to find this ideal of service in the 'selfless action' of the *Gita*. But this is only an Indian distortion, the eternal Indian attempt to incorporate and nullify. The *Gita's* 'selfless action' is a call to self-fulfillment and at the same time a restatement of degree; it is the opposite of the service which Gandhi, the Indian revolutionary, is putting forward as a practicable day-to-day ideal... Service is not an Indian concept... In the huge Hindu ideal of self-realization...there is no idea of a contract between man and man. This was Hinduism's great flaw."

Just as Gandhianism had been a casualty of free India's first half-century, so too had Nehruism gone by the boards. Although his daughter Indira showed little respect for Gandhianism, she did honor and perpetuate the socialist principles of her father. In fact, she went him two better, when, in 1971, she nationalized India's banks and terminated the privy purses that Nehru had been willing to pay to the former rulers of princely states. A mild attack on his socialist principles did come later from within the Nehru family when his grandson, Rajiv, assumed the post of Prime Minister in 1984. Rajiv Gandhi's main aim was to accelerate economic development, and he was persuaded that the best way to accomplish this objective was to move India away from socialism and toward a free market economy. Accordingly, he reduced the scope of the "Permit Raj" system and increased the role of the private sector and the potential for foreign investment, but only to a limited degree. Perhaps the traditional respect of an Indian grandson for his grandfather was one of the considerations that held him back from launching a major assault on the socialist principles which his grandfather had held dear.

That major assault on Nehru's socialism came from Rajiv Gandhi's successor, Narasimha Rao. Although he was a long time confidante of the family, Narasimha Rao was not a Nehru and so he was not bound to follow the Indian tradition of honoring the principles of one's forebears. Following his appointment to the Prime Minister's post in 1991, Rao pushed through Parliament a number of economic reforms that constituted major steps in the direction of free enterprise capitalism. No doubt, these steps were well advised from an economic point of view because they stimulated economic development and encouraged foreign investment and foreign trade, but they sounded the death knell for Nehru's socialism as the guiding light for the Central Government's economic policy. That "death knell" is not too strong a term to use to describe the early 1990's shift away from socialism is substantiated by the fact that the Deve Gowda coalition government committed itself to carrying on Narasimha Rao's free market economic policies even though it is backed by socialist and Communist MP's and has two Communist Party leaders among its ministers.

Although it was not yet dead, another of the guiding lights of free India's founding fathers had come under serious attack by the 1990's. However much they differed on economic grounds, Mahatma Gandhi and Jawaharlal Nehru agreed that India could remain a free and peaceful nation only as a pluralistic secular society. Yet, 50 years after Independence, the overriding political question was: Will India continue as a pluralistic secular society? That there were powerful political forces at work pushing India toward Hindu fundamentalism would have surprised neither Gandhi nor Nehru. Hindu fundamentalism was abroad in their day, although it operated on the fringes rather than at the center of Indian politics. Both of these founding fathers realized that this religion-based political force posed the most serious threat to the democratic India that they sought to build, and both struggled against it during their political careers, Gandhi at the cost of his life. What would have surprised and dismayed them was the way in which their own party, the Congress Party, had contributed to the rise of Hindu fundamentalism, especially when the Congress Party's drift in this direction began during the regime of Nehru's daughter, Indira, and continued more openly under the leadership of his grandson, Rajiv.

Indira Gandhi's hawkish policies toward Pakistan which culminated in the wars of 1965 and 1971, had added fuel to the fire of the anti-Muslim feeling among Hindus. Her assassination as a result of her order to the Indian Army to clear Sikh militants from the Golden Temple in Amritsar had produced an outburst of Hindu rage against Sikhs that had led to thousands of them being murdered. Apart from these ventures into military action that heightened anti-Muslim and anti-Sikh feelings among India's Hindus, the political strategy which she followed after her disastrous defeat in the 1977 General Election also led the Congress Party away from pluralistic secularism and toward Hindu fundamentalism. Mrs. Gandhi's maneuvering to regain political power during the years following her 1975–1977 Emergency furthered the process of moving religion to the forefront of national political issues that had begun with the Sikh demand for a homeland. By pursuing a policy of holding on to office at any price, she added to the momentum of the movement that constituted a repudiation of the secularist principles of her father.

Between 1978 and 1980, Indira Gandhi had concentrated her efforts to build the Congress Indira Party out of the New Congress Party in North and Northwest India where pro-Hindu and anti-Muslim sentiments were strongest. She had lost the backing of Muslims in the 1977 General Election, and there was little likelihood that they would support her three years later because of their widespread belief that the family planning campaign that her son Sanjay had initiated during the 1975–77 Emergency had been directed at them in order to reduce their share of the population. Untouchables had also deserted her in 1977 because they saw themselves as the target of Sanjay's slum clearance program. With these two traditional pro-Congress Party groups no longer in her camp, Mrs. Gandhi had to make winning caste Hindu votes the focus of her 1980 General Election campaign. Then, having won that election, she continued her pro-Hindu policy by taking a harder line against Sikh militants and finally ordering the Indian Army to drive them from the Golden Temple, a drastic political move but one that pleased Hindus who felt that Bhindnanvale Sant Jarnail Singh and his Sikh armed followers had gone too far in using violence as their means of achieving Kalistan.

Since Mrs. Gandhi had started the Congress Indira Party in a pro-Hindu direction and since her son Rajiv, who succeeded her as Prime

Minister in 1984, was a political novice, his only political recourse, if he hoped to remain in power, was to follow his mother's strategy of wooing caste Hindu votes. Accordingly, the year after he assumed office, he had given permission to an extremist Hindu organization to raise money and to lay the foundation stone for a Hindu temple at Ayodhya, the legendary birthplace of Rama, even though it was clear that carrying out such a construction project would inevitably lead to trouble with Muslims whose mosque had stood on that site since the 17th century. Six years later, the BJP, acting as an umbrella under which members of that organization and other militant Hindu groups could gather, had organized a 50,000-strong mob action that destroyed Ayodhya's Muslim mosque. The result had been an outbreak of Hindu-Muslim riots that not only had led to more than a thousand deaths but also had added to anti-Muslim feelings among the Hindu population.

Two years after he had allowed to be set in motion the events that had led to the bloodshed following the Hindu-Muslim clash at Ayodhya, Rajiv Gandhi again followed a pro-Hindu political strategy in his handling of the Kalistan issue that had led to his mother's death. In 1985, he had taken the conciliatory step of working out an autonomy agreement that was acceptable to the Akali Dal Party that had spearheaded the drive for Sikh independence. Some of the provisions of this agreement were unacceptable to the Punjab's neighboring State of Harayana, and Harayana was part of the Hindi-speaking Hindu belt that Mrs. Gandhi earlier had made a center of support for her Congress Indira Party. In order to increase the Congress Indira Party's chances of success in the 1987 Harayana State election, Rajiv Gandhi reversed himself and refused to implement the agreement with the Akali Dal Party. To add insult to injury, he dismissed the Akali Dal government that was in power in the Punjab and replaced it with President's Rule.

These pro-Hindu actions incensed Sikh extremists; and they once again began to fortify the Golden Temple in Amritsar, which had been surrounded by paramilitary police pickets since the Indian Army had taken control in 1984. In May 1988, Sikh extremists firing from within the Golden Temple, wounded a senior police officer, and the fat was once more in the fire. The Central Government sent a commando force to Amritsar to reinforce the police pickets, and, following Rajiv Gandhi's instructions, the Golden Temple was placed under siege. Commandos and paramilitary police fired upon the Sikhs holed up in the Temple precincts but did not enter them as the Indian Army had done four years earlier. Bullets, intense summer heat, and lack of food and water eventually forced the approximately 250 Sikhs who had been defending the Golden Temple to surrender, but only after more than 30 of them had been killed or had committed suicide. Although this second violation of the sanctity of the Golden Temple did not lead to Rajiv Gandhi's death, it displayed an anti-Sikh and a pro-Hindu political bias that moved the Congress Indira Party further away from its pluralistic, secular tradition and closer to a Hindu communalist orientation.

The contention that Rajiv Gandhi had opened the door to the Ayodhya incident and to the second police action against the Sikhs' Golden Temple because of his decision to continue the pro-Hindu political strategy initiated by his mother is supported by the steps that he took during his five years in office to strengthen India's self-image as a Hindu society. One of his major public relations efforts had been to showcase India's traditional Hindu culture by ordering All-India Television to produce and broadcast a television version of the *Ramayana* and later the *Mahabharata*. Since even villagers now had access to television sets located in public places and millions of middle-class and elite families had television sets in their homes, these broadcasts were seen by hundreds of millions of Indians, who were reminded in an unforgettable way that India's traditional culture was rooted in the Hindu religion.

Mark Tully, the BBC correspondent in Delhi at the time, describes the tremendous impact which the TV broadcast of the *Ramayana* had not only throughout the country but throughout Indian society:

"An electric sub-station was burnt down by viewers enraged that a power cut had robbed them of one episode. New cabinet ministers asked for their swearing-in ceremonies to be delayed so they could watch the *Ramayana*... A bride was missing at the auspicious time for her wedding because it clashed with the *Ramayana*... A councilor in

111

Maharashtra suggested that the municipality should hold a special condolence meeting to mourn the death of Ravana (the King of Demons who had kidnapped Rama's wife Sita)... The wife of a senior Indian bureaucrat told me that one of India's great transcontinental expresses she was traveling on was delayed while passengers and crew sat on the platform at Gwalior watching the *Ramayana* on the station's television monitor... A cooperative society of women who make *pappadams* (wafers) took out half-page advertisements in the national press saying: 'For seventy-seven weeks, Sunday mornings of great many families were adorned with the atmosphere of *Ramayana*, brought alive by the glory of mythological characters, reliving the times millenniums back. Here is a day to say good-bye to that blissful nearness. Yes, the immortal world will no longer be before our eyes. But down the memory lane, this memory will accompany us with all its splendor and shine.'"

Having prepared the way with these nationwide television broadcasts, Rajiv Gandhi's political strategy then had taken a tack that went even farther than his mother's in a pro-Hindu direction. He had opened the Congress Indira Party's 1984 General Election campaign by going to Ayodhya and proclaiming that, if he became Prime Minister, his overriding goal would be to create a *Ram Rajya* in India, a kingdom of tranquillity and prosperity associated in Hindu mythology with the rule of Rama. The political irony of Rajiv Gandhi's pursuit of this openly pro-Hindu political strategy was that, while it had been intended to and did strengthen the Congress Indira Party for the time being, it is clear from the perspective of the 1996 General Election that, in the longer term, it had done more to promote the cause of Hindu fundamentalism. In an unintended way, the Congress Indira Party had contributed to the spectacular rise of the BJP which came from nowhere during the 1980's and 1990's to become its major rival. Rajiv Gandhi's showcasing of India's traditional Hindu culture for India's masses through the modern magic of television had provided powerful visual support for the BJP's ideological line that the true India was Hindu India. By adopting *Ram Rajya* as his 1989 campaign pledge, Rajiv Gandhi made it possible for the BJP to say to India's voters during the 1996 General Election campaign, and with a good deal more truth,

"You want *Ram Rajya*, but it is the BJP, not the Congress Indira Party, that you should support because the BJP is the party that adopted that goal before Rajiv Gandhi ever thought of it and the only party really committed to achieving it."

Nevertheless, even though it had facilitated the rise of the BJP, the pro-Hindu strategy pursued by the Congress Indira Party under Indira and Rajiv Gandhi was not the major factor in the BJP's emergence as a major party. Wider and deeper forces were at work during the 1980's and 1990's, strengthening the political muscle of Hindu fundamentalism. Feeding on the anti-Muslim feelings which Hindus have felt for centuries and which were exacerbated by Partition, three wars, and the continuing struggle for control of Kashmir, Hindu fundamentalism's leap forward as a political force had paralleled the growth of India's GNP under the Congress Indira Party governments that had promoted free market capitalism. Economic development had produced India's burgeoning middle class, and many of this new bourgeoisie had given their political backing, not to the Congress Indira Party, but to the BJP which had given them a sense of superiority as Hindus. Large numbers of the new middle class were caste Hindu traders, shopkeepers and small businessmen whose increased incomes convinced them that they merited a dominant role in determining how India should be governed. These and many others were members of middle or low-level castes who, because they now had more wealth, saw themselves as standing on a higher rung of the social ladder. From this higher rung they looked down on the minorities and untouchables below them, in Shakespeare's words, "scorning the base degrees by which they did ascend." Ved Mehta has encapsulated this connection between economic development and the rise of Hindu fundamentalism in one sentence: "Just as India was finally freeing its economy from Socialist shibboleths and government controls in preparation for joining the global economy, it seemed to be culturally regressing into pre-Mogul, medieval Hindu India; its response to rapid change seemed to be atavistic retreat."

Finally, and perhaps most importantly, because its influence went far beyond the middle class to include the whole of Indian society, the

BJP, more than any other party, had captured the political energy generated by the growing sense of Indian nationalism. Its jingoistic stand on foreign policy had called for giving no quarter to Pakistan, building up India's military establishment, and developing nuclear weapons and the capability to deliver them to Pakistan and China. For the domestic front, the BJP had espoused placing restrictions on economic assets that could be owned by foreigners and a hard line against minority separatists like the Muslims in Kashmir and the Sikhs in the Punjab, whom they had accused of threatening Indian unity. Both at home and abroad, the BJP had projected itself as the party of Indian patriotism, and, as more and more Indians had come to see themselves as ardent patriots, the BJP had recruited more followers to march behind its Hindu fundamentalist banner.

The other side of the coin of increased self-esteem as patriotic members of India's overwhelmingly Hindu majority was a greater feeling of disdain for members of minority groups, especially Muslims and untouchables. The feeling against untouchables focused on the Congress Party's long-standing "affirmative action" program, which elite and middle-class Hindus had come to regard as reverse discrimination—discrimination against them as members of the higher castes in favor of members of "backward and scheduled castes and tribes." Since the BJP had emerged as the party opposing this "affirmative action" program, more middle-class Indians had begun to give their votes to the BJP rather than the Congress Indira Party.

❖

The Nehru Dynasty

Just as India had moved away from pluralistic secularism and toward Hindu fundamentalism during the past 50 years, so also had it moved away from electoral republicanism and toward inherited monarchy in choosing its head of government. It is clear that Jawaharlal Nehru would have stoutly opposed the first of these two movements. It is not so clear that he would have stoutly opposed the second when it took the form of the virtual monopoly of the Prime Minister's post which his family came to hold from 1947 until 1991. Political enemies like Morarji Desai had maintained that Nehru had planned from the time he took office as India's first Prime Minister to assure a century of succession for his progeny. If Desai had been right, Nehru would have been setting aside the Parliamentary system inherited from the British and would have been going back to the tradition of the Mogul emperors who had preceded them as India's foreign rulers. While there is no firm evidence that Desai was right, it is clear that Jawaharlal Nehru helped to create the conditions that made it possible for the Nehru dynasty to come into being, even if it was not his intention to do so.

The process of handing over political power from one member of the Nehru family to another had begun long before Jawaharlal became Prime Minister. His father, Motilal, had shared leadership of the Congress Party with Mahatma Gandhi from 1920 until 1930, when he decided that Jawaharlal should succeed him as Gandhi's partner at the top. Accordingly, he handed over the post of Congress Party President which he held to his son. Jawaharlal did not have a son, but he did have a daughter, Indira. Like his father, he wanted his offspring to play a leadership role in Indian politics. So during the years that followed his assuming the Congress Party's presidency, many of which he spent in jail, he prepared Indira for her political destiny. When she was only 13, she received a letter from her father, then a prisoner of the British Raj, which contained the following passage: "If we are to be India's soldiers, we have India's honor in our keeping and that honor is a sacred trust... Goodbye, little one, and may you grow up into a brave soldier in India's service."

After Independence came, Indira took the place of her deceased mother and acted as her father's hostess in the Prime Minister's residence. She also accompanied him on his travels at home and abroad and, in the process, met the major Indian and foreign political figures with whom Nehru dealt during the heyday of his power. In 1955, she was given a top policy-making position in the Congress Party when she was made a member of its Working (Executive) Committee. Four years later, she was installed by her father as Congress Party President, just as his father had done for him.

Along with grooming his daughter for a leading role in Indian politics, Nehru prepared the way for the emergence of a Nehru family dynasty by refusing to designate a Congress Party leader as his second-in-command—one who, in the event of his death, would succeed him as party leader and, given the way that India's parliamentary system worked during the era of Congress Party dominance, as Prime Minister. Because of his silence on this important political point, Nehru was known during his lifetime as "the banyan tree." A banyan tree covers a wide area because it extends itself through a process in which its branches root themselves in the soil underneath. In this way, the banyan tree gets steadily bigger, but nothing grows underneath it. India could feel secure under Jawaharlal Nehru because he loomed so large, but there was no successor beneath him.

When he died in 1964, 18 months after India's disastrous defeat in the border war with China, there was a power vacuum not only at the top of the Congress Party but also, because India was under one-party rule, at the top of the Central Government. In the absence of a Congress Party leader whom Nehru had designated to be his successor, it fell to a group of regional Congress Party leaders, dubbed the "Syndicate" by the Indian press, to decide who should take up the

Prime Minister's reins. One of the members of the "Syndicate," Madras State's Chief Minister, Kamaraj Nadar, because he was Congress Party President, was considered to be first among equals. Consequently, he was able to take the lead in forging an agreement that Lal Bahadur Shastri would be Nehru's successor.

Lal Bahadur Shastri was by no means the most able or the most influential of the regional Congress Party bosses. Although he was a self-effacing and honest man, he was a rather lackluster politician who was a member of the "Syndicate" because he headed the Uttar Pradesh wing of the Congress Party. His only distinction was his close ties with the Nehru family. He came from the same State and spoke the same language. His political role had consisted, in the main, of carrying out minor tasks assigned him by Nehru. Significant as a forerunner of the emergence of the Nehru dynasty was the fact that, in choosing Jawaharlal Nehru's successor, the "Syndicate" selected a politician who, although he was not a family member, had functioned almost as a member of the Nehru household.

Nor was Jawaharlal's daughter, Indira, left out of the picture in forming the Shastri government. While the "Syndicate" was not about to make her Prime Minister, they did include her in the cabinet as Minister of Communications and Broadcasting. They were anxious to have a member of the Nehru family in the Shastri government in order to take advantage of the political appeal that her family name enjoyed among Indian voters, but they did not want her to play a dominant role in formulating government policy. By giving her one of the least important portfolios, they thought that they could accomplish both of their objectives and, at the same time, satisfy her political ambitions with a minor cabinet post. If they had been right in this modest estimate of how far she wanted to go in Indian politics, the "Syndicate" would have nipped the Nehru dynasty in the bud. As it turned out, they were dead wrong, and they would pay a high price for making that mistake before many years had gone by.

To begin with, it looked as though they had gauged Indira's political ambition correctly. She played a low key, almost deferential role, in cabinet proceedings during the year and a half that Lal Bahadur Shastri was Prime Minister. When, in 1966, he died suddenly of a heart attack, the "Syndicate" was once again faced with the responsibility of choosing a successor Prime Minister. The only way that they could keep the Nehru connection alive now was to turn to a member of the family itself. So this time they selected Indira Gandhi to be the leader of the Congress Party and, consequently, India's Prime Minister. This decision constituted a major step in the direction of enthroning the Nehru dynasty because it appeared to the Indian nation that the short tenure of Lal Bahadur Shastri, far from preparing the way for Prime Ministers from other families, was only an interlude during which the next Nehru in line was preparing to take over India's highest office.

In selecting Indira Gandhi to be India's next Prime Minister, the "Syndicate" certainly did not intend to recognize the Nehrus as a kind of republican "royal family." What they had in mind was to use the family name to maintain their political power now that Jawaharlal Nehru was gone but to have it carried by a Prime Minister who would be easy for them to control. In other words, they were prepared to put Indira on a republican "throne" as long as they could be the power behind that "throne." They based this strategy on the fact that this Nehru was a woman who had treated them with great respect during her apprenticeship as Minister of Communications and Broadcasting. They had no reason to think that this mild demeanor would not continue during her tenure as Prime Minister.

For the next two years, it appeared that they had been right and that installing Mrs. Gandhi had been a smart political move. She regularly consulted members of the "Syndicate" in making policy decisions and respected their views. But in 1968 it became clear that they had seriously underestimated her will to rule on her own. That truth emerged when the office of President of India fell vacant and the Congress Party had to decide whom it would support for the post. The "Syndicate" opted to put forward one of its members, Sanjiva Reddy, as the Congress Party's nominee, and they expected Mrs. Gandhi to accept their recommendation. Much to their surprise, she refused and gave her backing to a candidate of her own, V.V. Giri. Since neither side was willing to budge, the political fat was now in the fire.

The result of the clash between Mrs. Gandhi and the " Syndicate" was a split in the Congress Party, the first since its founding in 1885. The Congress Party now became two Congress parties—the Official Congress, led by members of the "Syndicate," and the New Congress, led by Mrs. Gandhi. These two Congress parties faced each other in the general election of 1971, and Mrs. Gandhi's New Congress Party soundly defeated its Official Congress Party rival. Showing for the first time her skill as a campaigner, Mrs. Gandhi had run on a populist platform which highlighted a commitment to nationalize India's banks and terminate the privy purses paid to the former rulers of the Princely States. These and other populist promises were encapsulated in the campaign slogan "Eradicate Poverty"—a goal which was bound to win the favor of India's masses, however impossible it would be to achieve during Mrs. Gandhi's coming five-year term in office.

Mrs. Gandhi's overwhelming victory in the 1971 General Election laid a solid groundwork for the establishment of the Nehru dynasty within free India's political system. The defeated Official Congress Party was now a political has-been, and the individual members of the "Syndicate" who had collectively led it had lost any chance that they had ever had of becoming Prime Minister. The New Congress, having been created by Mrs. Gandhi and then having been led by her to victory in a general election, was now her personal following rather than an organized, institutionalized political party. All members were her followers. It had no national or regional leaders under her who could challenge her for designation as Party President or Prime Minister. There was Mrs. Gandhi at the top, the rank and file strung out below, and nothing in between.

Any possibility that Mrs. Gandhi's political ascendancy could be seriously challenged by leaders of other political parties or by notables outside the political system was precluded by an event which followed within a few months of the 1971 General Election—India's victory in the Bangladesh War. From her position as Prime Minister, Mrs. Gandhi supported and provided a refuge within India for East Pakistani rebels. When the West Pakistan air force bombed rebel refugee camps set up on Indian territory, she ordered the Indian Army into East Pakistan

119

and forced the West Pakistan forces in Dacca to surrender. By these actions, she made it plain that she was a strong Prime Minister who would stoutly pursue India's national interests and, if challenged by India's principal enemy, bring Pakistan to its knees. The 1971 General Election established the Nehru dynasty within the political system. The Bangladesh War of the same year established it within the nation.

Mrs. Gandhi was not slow to recognize that she was now in an unassailable political position. Even though she continued to support republican principles in public, behind the scenes she began to prepare the way for one of her two sons, Sanjay, the younger, or Rajiv, the older, to succeed her as leader of the New Congress Party and, through this party office, to become Prime Minister. She moved both of them, with their families, into the Prime Minister's residence. Since Rajiv was not interested at the time in leaving his job as an Indian Airlines pilot, she proceeded to groom Sanjay as the first son to be in line. Even though he had almost no political experience, Mrs. Gandhi arranged for Sanjay to be appointed head of the New Congress Youth Wing and to be elected to Parliament from a safe New Congress Party constituency. More important than these official positions, however, was the unofficial position which he came to occupy as his mother's principal advisor. Like a good Indian mother, Mrs. Gandhi sought to make her son happy by letting him have his way. She gave him carte blanche to carry out during the 1975–1977 Emergency the five-point crash program which he formulated to transform the face of India within a few short years. So family planning, slum clearance, promotion of literacy, abolition of dowries, and tree planting became the order of the day during this two-year period, to be pursued by any and all means, however draconian, at the government's disposal.

She also showed her indulgence as an Indian mother by giving Sanjay her unqualified support in pursuing his personal as well as his political interests. From his youth, he had shown an interest in automobiles. Consequently, instead of sending him to an English university, Mrs. Gandhi had arranged for him to undergo mechanic's training at the Rolls-Royce factory. This experience prompted him to take the first steps to pursue what he hoped would be a career as an

Indian manufacturer of automobiles. Even though he was a complete novice in this sector of manufacturing and there were existing firms like Birla which had been producing automobiles for years, Sanjay was given a license in 1970 to build an Indian equivalent of the Volkswagen Beetle. One-fifth of Parliament's sitting members promptly requested that an investigation be conducted to ascertain how this highly-prized license came to be issued to someone like Sanjay Gandhi who had no qualifications for receiving it. Mrs. Gandhi dismissed their request without giving it a semblance of consideration. Five years later, during the 1975–77 Emergency, when she ruled as a virtual dictator, she reported to Parliament that the investigation that they had long ago requested had been carried out and that everything had been found to have been in order.

As it turned out, Sanjay did not produce a single automobile during the five years that followed the granting of the license. During the two years of the Emergency, he turned his attention to acting as an agent for foreign companies selling earth movers, trucks, road rollers, and aircraft in India. At the same time, he was learning to fly. In 1976 a London-based company purchased an American-made Pitts aircraft, designed for stunt flying and shipped it to India, ostensibly for the use of an Indian company located in Calcutta. The Pitts aircraft's arrival in India coincided with Mrs. Gandhi's defeat in the 1977 General Election, and it was impounded by India's Customs Authority. The London firm thereupon notified Customs that the aircraft had been sent to India by mistake and requested that it be released so that it could be shipped back to its point of origin. Customs refused, and the aircraft sat in a storage shed during the two and a half years that the Janata Dal coalition government was in power. Three months after Mrs. Gandhi's victory in the 1980 General Election, Customs issued an import permit allowing the Calcutta company to take possession of the aircraft, this at a time when imports were supposed to be restricted to items needed for development projects. Ownership of the Pitts stunt plane was then transferred to Sanjay Gandhi, and it was moved to Delhi. Sanjay was doing stunts in this aircraft, the only one of its kind in India, when he crashed in June 1980.

This close collaboration between Sanjay Gandhi and his mother on both the official and the personal levels might have dominated the country politically without a break from 1971 until 1980 except for a series of events that began with a political glitch which befell Mrs. Gandhi in 1975. She was found guilty of having violated a technical provision of the Electoral Law during the 1971 General Election, and a High Court ruled that she would have to give up her seat in Parliament. Since, under the Parliamentary system, the Prime Minister must be a member of Parliament, this would have meant that she could no longer be Prime Minister. If she had followed the republican course in this situation, she would have handed over the Prime Minister's post to one of her New Congress Party underlings while she appealed the High Court's decision to the Supreme Court. But she followed the dynastic course by insisting that she and no one else should be Prime Minister. She declared a State of Emergency which set aside the Constitution and the laws of the land and put India's courts out of business. The ground on which she attempted to justify this dictatorial action was that India faced a threat to its internal stability and national security, although the specific nature of this threat was not revealed and observers both at home and abroad could see no evidence that it existed. All that the public heard were rumors that foreign agents were up to mischief and that some of them were working for the CIA.

In order to make sure that there was no political agitation opposing the Emergency, she outlawed party activity and jailed leaders of opposition parties. To make sure that there was no public outcry against these dictatorial actions, she imposed censorship on India's press. Despite the fact that India had functioned as a democracy for almost 30 years, these actions were remarkably successful in inducing the country to accept the Emergency's authoritarian regime with little or no complaint. With Parliamentary opposition now emasculated, she had no difficulty pushing through a Constitutional amendment that killed the judicial proceedings against her.

Ved Mehta calls the 1975–1977 Emergency a "watershed" political event in India's movement from a Western form of electoral republicanism to an Indian form of inherited monarchy: "Sanjay's political career and the Emergency that gave rise to it are spoken of as a watershed between an Indian adoption of British democracy, with an independent civil service, an independent judiciary and an independent army, on the one hand, and a home-grown court autocracy, with personal loyalty, personal reward and personal vengeance, on the other. The two forms had more or less coexisted since Independence, but Sanjay and the Emergency seemed to have hastened the disintegration of the institutions inherited from the British."

Emboldened by the ease with which she had pressured free India into accepting virtual dictatorial rule and had reworked its Constitution to protect her political power, Mrs. Gandhi decided after two years that the time was right to go to the nation for an endorsement of her position as the person who should wield executive authority. Much to her surprise, the 1977 General Election resulted in a resounding defeat for her New Congress Party. Some observers attributed this unexpected turn in Mrs. Gandhi's political fortunes to the Indian people's reaction against the Emergency's attack on democracy. While this was undoubtedly the reason why some Indians supported Mrs. Gandhi's opponents, many more were really voting against Sanjay Gandhi and his five-point crash program. Muslims saw its family planning component as directed against them. Untouchables saw the slum clearance component as directed against them. These two minority voting blocks had supported the Congress Party from the first days of Independence, but in 1977, they turned against the New Congress Party. Faced with these defections and the desire for political revenge on the part of caste Hindus who had suffered under her iron-fisted Emergency regime, Mrs. Gandhi lost.

Mrs. Gandhi's reaction to her defeat was to pursue the same strategy that brought her victory in 1970 after she had clashed with the "Syndicate." She set out to form another Congress Party out of the New Congress Party, and one that would continue to be her personal following. During the three years between 1977 and 1980, she mended her political fences by paying her respects to prominent figures like Vinoba Bhave whom she had earlier jailed. In addition, since she had lost the backing of Muslims and untouchables, she concentrated on wooing support among caste Hindus living in India's Hindi-speaking heartland. This strategy produced the Congress Indira Party which successfully fought the 1980 General Election campaign with the slogan: "India is Indira and Indira is India." In 1971, the New Congress had won with a slogan that focused attention on eradicating poverty. In 1980, the Congress Indira Party won with a slogan that focused on Mrs. Gandhi as "Mother India." Not only was the party which Indira Gandhi led to victory in 1980 a personal following rather than a structured political organization, but the nation that put it into power did so as the personal following of the woman who led that party. In the minds of the Indian people, Mrs. Gandhi had become a "queen" even though she had been democratically elected. The Nehru dynasty had reached full flower. Mrs. Gandhi was now "Mother India," and, in her mind, she had every right to prepare one of her sons to follow her on India's "throne."

Tragically enough, the "queen's" reign was to last no more than four years, and her son Sanjay was to die within a few months of her enthronement Following her resounding victory in the 1980 General Election, Mrs. Gandhi had made it clear that it was her intention that Sanjay should succeed her as Prime Minister by installing him as General Secretary of the Congress Indira Party. Holding this post placed him only one rung below her position as its President, but he never stepped higher. Saddened but not daunted by his death, Mrs. Gandhi persuaded her older son Rajiv to resign his position as an Indian Airlines pilot and to begin his apprenticeship for the Prime Minister's post. That apprenticeship followed the same course as the one that had been used to prepare the way for Sanjay. Rajiv was made head of the Congress Indira Youth Wing and was elected an MP from the same safe constituency that had put Sanjay in Parliament. His training went further than that provided for Sanjay, however, when his mother gave him the Minister of Defense's portfolio in her new cabinet.

With Rajiv, Mrs. Gandhi did succeed in installing one of he sons as Prime Minister, but in a way which was not part of her game plan. In 1984, she ordered the Indian Army to clear Sikh extremists from the Golden Temple in Amritsar. The result was hundreds of dead Sikhs and a Golden Temple that, in Sikh eyes, had been desecrated. Mrs. Gandhi paid for this action with her life when she was assassinated by two of her Sikh bodyguards. In the general election which followed, Rajiv Gandhi, riding on a countrywide wave of outrage against Sikhs combined with sympathy for a grieving son, both of which sentiments were exploited fully in the campaign, led the Congress Indira Party to an overwhelming victory.

Rajiv Gandhi began his tenure as though he was determined to breathe new life into the Congress Indira Party by converting it from a collection of self-serving followers of the Nehru family into a principled political institution. At the celebration of the 100th anniversary of the founding of the Indian National Congress in 1985, he sounded a call for party reform. Its leaders, he maintained, "are reducing the Congress organization to a shell from which the spirit of service and sacrifice has been emptied. We talk of the high principles and lofty ideals needed to build a strong and prosperous India. But we obey no discipline, no rule, follow no principles of public morality, display no sense of social awareness, show no concern for the public weal. Corruption is not only tolerated but even regarded as the hallmark of leadership." Unfortunately, his centenary speech was little more than an exhortation based on lofty political ideals. After it was delivered, he made no serious effort to reorganize and reform the Congress Indira Party or root out the corruption that he had verbally condemned.

On the contrary, Rajiv Gandhi himself became involved in the greatest corruption scandal that had yet taken place in India. In 1986, then Defense Minister as well as Prime Minister, he authorized the signing of a contract with Bofors, a Swedish arms manufacturer, for field guns for the Indian Army costing $1.4 billion. A year later, Swedish National Radio broadcast the charge that Bofors had paid between $20 million and $25 million to senior Indian politicians and defense personnel in order to get the contract. This charge was investigated by the Swedish National Audit Bureau, which reported that these payments had indeed been made. Rajiv Gandhi's response was to send a mission to Switzerland to find out if any Indian politician or official had deposited large amounts in banks there, even though it was a foregone conclusion that such a mission would accomplish nothing because it was well known that Swiss banks did not at that time release such information.

He could have unmasked the culprits easily and quickly by demanding that Bofors reveal the names of those who had received the kickbacks. The fact that Rajiv Gandhi did not take this step convinced most Indian and some foreign observers that he was determined to shield those who had benefited from the Bofors deal. He did make a statement to Parliament that neither he nor his family had been beneficiaries, but the statement's narrow focus raised suspicions that either the Congress Indira Party or some of Rajiv Gandhi's cronies had received the Swedish money. Although the names of those who had been rewarded by Bofors were not revealed and, as a result, no evidence surfaced that he was one of them, the role that he had played in the Bofors scandal destroyed Rajiv Gandhi's "Mister Clean" image with which he had successfully fought the 1984 General Election.

So it was an unreformed Congress Indira Party, still the personal following of the Nehru family member at its head, that entered the next general election in 1989. Since the outrage and sympathy factors that had carried the day in 1984 had long since dissipated, the party failed to win a majority of Parliamentary seats and was forced to become a supporter of a coalition government that would rule India for the next two years. Rajiv Gandhi decided not to head such a coalition government and chose to put his time and energy into strengthening the Congress Indira Party so that it could win a majority of Parliamentary seats in the next general election and form a government of its own. That opportunity came within two years, when the coalition government led by the Janata Dal Party, shaky from the start, finally collapsed. But Rajiv Gandhi did not realize his goal of resuming his post as Prime Minister because he was assassinated during the course of the election campaign.

By 1991, Mrs. Gandhi and both her sons were gone from the political scene, but there was one family survivor who could have kept the Nehru dynasty alive: Rajiv Gandhi's widow, Sonia. Congress Indira Party leaders were quick to make a last ditch effort to perpetuate the Nehru dynasty by offering her the party's presidency. Only when she refused their offer did they face the fact that no member of the Nehru family was available to take Rajiv Gandhi's place and that they would have to look elsewhere for a party leader and candidate for the Prime Minister's post.

Ved Mehta summarizes the legacy of the Nehru dynasty as one of failure: "Even if India did not disintegrate, the fact that, for 45 years, the governments of Jawaharlal Nehru, Indira Gandhi, and Rajiv Gandhi did not succeed in getting their priorities straight—(if they) had not maximized expenditure on defense to concentrate instead on hygiene and sanitation, or controlling the population...and the spread of pollution and, at the same time, extirpating illiteracy, liberating the Indian economy and opening up to foreign capital—meant that the country had forfeited a singular opportunity to modernize itself and to develop countervailing forces to religious extremism and Hindu chauvinism."

Considering the honor and veneration that free India bestowed on the Nehru dynasty during 45 of the first 50 years of its life, Mehta's negative evaluation of the results of their reign may sound unduly harsh. But his assertion that they "did not succeed in getting their priorities straight" is borne out by the way that India's resources were allocated in the Five-Year Plans that they approved and which their governments followed. The 1969–74 plan that Mrs. Gandhi promulgated during her first term as Prime Minister provided a good example of how they ranked the country's needs. A total of $9.2 billion was to be spent to support the armed forces and to develop a "nuclear device." Family planning and housing were to receive $370 million and $200 million respectively. Making these Five-Year Plan allocations resulted in military expenditures that were 16 times as great as those for family planning and housing combined. Given the magnitude of India's population and housing problems and the fact that, after the border war with China, India did not face a serious external threat to its national security, it is difficult to argue that Mehta is being unfair when he faults the Nehru dynasty's priorities.

As if the Mehta characterization of the Nehru dynasty as a failure were not enough, the unraveling of the Bofors gun scandal which occurred five years after Rajiv Gandhi's death provided evidence that, while the dynasty began on an honorable note with a great-grandfather and a grandfather, it neared its end on a note of dishonor with a grandson. In February 1997, 10 years after the Swiss banks which had received the Bofors payoffs had initially refused to reveal the names of the holders of the accounts to which the money had been credited, they began to hand over this information to the Central Bureau of Investigation. There were five names on the first list of account holders. Three were those of Bofors' Indian agent, his wife, and his son. The other two were those of Ottavio Quattrocchi and his wife. Quattrocchi was the head of the Indian branch of an Italian multinational company who had lived and done business in India for 20 years. His company had nothing to do with armaments, and he had not played any official role, as had Bofors' Indian agent, in arranging the gun purchase. The only connection he had with any of the players in the transaction was that he and his wife were close friends of Rajiv and Sonia Gandhi.

Four years before the Swiss banks gave his name to the CBI, Quattrocchi had been identified as one of the depositors who had requested that they refuse to tell Indian authorities that their accounts had received money from Bofors. That information had been passed on to the CBI, which was under the direction of Prime Minister Narasimha Rao. Despite the fact that the Prime Minister's Office claimed that it had been trying since 1988 to obtain a lead on who had received Bofors payments, the CBI did not question Quattrocchi before he was allowed to leave for Malaysia to continue his business activities.

At the same time that the CBI received the first list of recipients of Bofors money, the Indian generals who had been involved in purchasing the guns began to give TV and press interviews. The general who had been responsible for selecting the best artillery piece for the Indian Army stated that he had not recommended Bofors guns and that the choice would ordinarily have been made between guns manufactured in France or Austria. Then, out of the blue, word came from the Prime Minister's Office that Bofors was to receive the contract.

His testimony was supplemented by the words of the Army Chief of Staff at the time, who revealed that, when reports surfaced during

1987 that Bofors had made payments to Indian parties in order to receive the gun contract, he had recommended to the Prime Minister's Office that the contract be canceled. The reply that he received was that he should withdraw his recommendation and, instead, write a memorandum stating that India's national security would be damaged if the Bofors contract were not honored. Refusing to comply, he responded by stating that India's national security would not be damaged. His position was seconded by his civilian counterpart, the Minister of State for Defense. Despite the fact that neither the military nor the civilian official responsible for advising the Prime Minister provided support for honoring the Bofors contract which had become tainted with scandal, the purchase went ahead.

According to the former Army Chief of Staff's statement to the BBC TV, both he and the Minister of State for Defense were convinced that Prime Minister Rajiv Gandhi was determined that, whatever the army might think, its artillery pieces should be purchased from Bofors and that its contract should not be canceled even when it was revealed that Bofors had bribed its way to the deal. Being a good soldier, the Chief of Staff continued to serve in his post, but the Minister of State for Defense resigned in disgust. Neither the information which had been given to the CBI nor the generals' testimony made Rajiv Gandhi's role in the Bofors gun scandal transparently clear. But, at the very least, they provided evidence that he had pushed the Swedish guns on the army when they were considering purchasing artillery pieces from either France or Austria and that he was determined that the deal should go through even when it began to be enveloped in scandal. His failure to take decisive action to find out who had received Bofors money when the Swedish National Audit confirmed that it had indeed been deposited in Swiss banks showed that he did not want the beneficiaries' names to become known. His motive for orchestrating this cover-up came to light 10 years after it was staged when the names of his close friends, Mr. and Mrs. Quattrocchi, showed up in the list of recipients of Bofors money.

It was not clear what role the Quattrocchis had played in securing the business for Bofors, but, whatever it was, Bofors' action in depositing money in their Swiss Bank accounts showed that Bofors was indebted to them—to the tune of $7 million, according to the *Indian Express*. Following the Swiss banks' release of the five names, a company spokesperson stated, "We had a contractual obligation to our agents who were helping us in securing the Indian order. After the contract was finalized, we had to pay them the money and what was paid was a final settlement and not a bribe." Apparently, Quattrocchi was regarded by Bofors as an honorary "agent" because he was never identified as an official company representative.

The Swiss banks also informed the CBI that Quattrocchi had subsequently closed his account with them and transferred his funds to banks in several other countries. Since they had no way of knowing whether he had retained the money or passed it on to others, it could not be determined whether he was the ultimate beneficiary or had simply acted as a conduit to pass the Bofors payments on to others. The fact that Rajiv Gandhi's name did not appear on the Swiss banks' list of recipients and his statement to Parliament that neither he nor any member of his family had benefited from the Bofors gun deal provide pretty conclusive evidence that he was not a direct recipient, but they do not rule out the possibility that the Bofors funds that the Quattrocchis received ended up in the hands of a person or persons in whom the Gandhis had a political or personal interest.

❖

Resurgence of Indian India

The easy, almost natural, way that India, in selecting its head of government, converted modern democratic election into traditional dynastic rule was a political manifestation of the general process by which it became less British and more Indian during its first half-century. There were other manifestations, and Ved Mehta points out their pervasive operation in unequivocal terms: "The British are credited even by their critics of having unified India and imposed law and order upon it. The 'Indianization' of India that has been going on since Independence is becoming a kind of regression to the days before the (British) Raj."

The rule of law to which Mehta refers was begun by the East India Company when its Governors General came to realize after 1818 that they had to rule as well as trade with the parts of India that they now controlled. It was reinforced and extended by the British Crown after it took over from the Company 40 years later. This British legal tradition was passed on to India when Independence came in 1947. It was based on the notion that laws were established to be enforced, and they were to be enforced in a way that provided equal treatment for all Indians regardless of their economic status, caste, or creed. This inherited legal principle had gradually gone by the boards during the first half-century of India's Independence, in two respects. In the first place, India's laws had become more statements of good intentions than standards of behavior with which all citizens had to comply. Secondly, India's citizens were not treated equally under its laws. Short of heinous crimes like murder, a member of the elite and middle class of the 1990's was not likely to feel the weight of the law, provided, of course, that he was not in the way of a powerful politician or official who wished to do him in. If he did violate one of its provisions, a word or a bribe in the right place would set things right. In sharp contrast, members of the working class and the poor were vigorously prosecuted if they fell afoul of the law, and the Indian police often used "third degree" methods to extract confessions from members of the lower orders who had been arrested.

Intertwined with economic status but, from a social point of view, a separate factor determining the degree to which citizens of free India were made to abide by the law was caste. Generally speaking, the higher the caste to which a person belonged the less likely it was that the law would be rigorously applied to him. The lower the caste to which a person belonged, the more the obverse was true. Untouchables who violated the law were punished more harshly than any other group in Indian society. A striking instance of the latter form of discrimination was the death sentence handed down in September 1996 in a case involving an untouchable butcher who had been convicted of killing two Sikh boys during the riots which followed Mrs. Gandhi's assassination. Although there were hundreds of caste Hindus who had committed similar murders, it took the Central Government over 10 years to prosecute any of the culprits and, not surprisingly, the first to be convicted and condemned to die was an untouchable.

The important role that caste played in the law enforcement process pointed to a general change that had taken place in the last 50 years. As free India became more Indianized, it was governed more and more by tradition and less and less by law. When a law was passed that flew in the face of tradition—for example, the law forbidding the practice of untouchability—tradition prevailed over law. During the days of the British Raj, it was the other way round. Where a traditional Indian practice, like *suttee* or *thuggee* (ritual murder by devotees of the Goddess Kali), clashed with a law forbidding that practice, law prevailed over tradition even though a cost was paid by the British rulers. One of the sources of popular support for the Bengal Army when it mutinied in 1857 was the feeling among both Muslims and Hindus that the East India Company's outlawing of those and other traditional practices were steps in a program aimed at destroying their religion and way of life. That the British priority of law over tradition would be reversed when India came into its own following Independence was hardly surprising when one remembers that one of India's scriptures, the *Laws of Manu*, taught that "immemorial tradition is transcendental law." What happened when tradition began to take precedence over law was simply that India was returning to its ancient roots.

A striking case of tradition taking precedence over law was reported by the BBC's Mark Tully. In September 1987, a young widow living in a village in Rajasthan committed *suttee* by climbing on her husband's funeral pyre and was burned to ashes along with his body. India's law books included legislation which made aiding and abetting a suicide a punishable offense. Accordingly, the police set out to investigate the incident but soon gave up because none of the witnesses was willing to give evidence. Outraged because of what they saw as an attack on the rights of women, representatives of three women's organizations confronted Rajasthan's Chief Minister and demanded that action be taken against those who had encouraged and assisted the young widow. His reply was: "It is a matter of religion. I will do the needful." His definition of "the needful" was to do nothing to enforce the law.

Twelve days after the *suttee* incident, a community ceremony was held at the site where it had taken place. The *Times of India* described what happened: "Now the devotees came in teeming hordes, squatting atop jeeps and buses and spilling out of camel carts. They came from as far as Delhi and Jaipur to this remote village to propitiate the goddess of *Sati*... Meanwhile the village economy has got a shot in the arm with an average of 10,000 pilgrims streaming in every day."

The Rajasthan government had not taken steps to prevent the commemorative ceremony from taking place. The only order given to the local police official was to keep the crowd small. Faced with the thousands who flocked to the scene, it proved to be impossible for him to carry out his order. "What can we do? " he asked. "Thousands and thousands of people had already arrived and buses were pouring in from Delhi and other states and from Rajasthan itself. There would have been a riot."

When India's liberals and women's organizations objected to the government's inaction, a number of Rajasthan's political leaders organized a Committee for the Protection of Religion. The committee held a rally in the capital of Jaipur, attended by 100,000 men, to defend the traditions of Hinduism which had supposedly come under attack from India's Westernized elite and "independent" women. One of the speeches made at the rally characterized *suttee* as "a supreme example of a woman's duty to worship her husband." "Independent" women's organizations responded by organizing a counter demonstration objecting to the use of religion and caste as weapons to oppress women. Only 3,000 women attended the counter demonstration, and the speeches received little notice from the press and public.

Along with the rule of law, the British style of public administration, which India had inherited in 1947, had also gone by the boards during the decades that followed. That style was based on the principle that administrators served the people and that those who sought their services should be treated alike, whatever their socio-economic or religious status. The 1980's and 1990's style of public administration was based on the opposite principle, that the public served the administrators and the treatment that was meted out by the administrators depended either upon the status of their clients and/or their clients' willingness to pay for the service that they received. The pay-back that the administrators received sometimes took the form of a future benefit that the administrator could derive from doing a favor for a client. More often, however, it took the form of money or some other tangible item of value.

It is important to understand that the contemporary style of administration was not invented by free India but was a reversion to traditional governmental and business practices.

Trevor Fishlock has described 1990's public administration in words that make it clear that it is part and parcel of traditional practices that have been followed for centuries. He writes that what British administrators would have seen as "corruption" has been:

"...part of political and commercial dealings in India since ancient times and retains its place in society with the considerable element of the feudal in its culture. Patronage and the using of office for profit and for granting favors have the sanction of long custom... Fixing of routine necessities like licenses, allowances, tickets, and permissions is often done in response to family and group loyalties. These commitments are much more important than loyalty to some abstract ideology. Fixing is also done for material gain, of course, and the receiving of money for such services is not condemned, for public office has always been regarded as a way toward the noble goal of enrichment, part of one's duty in life. Positions not only have status, they also have the envied 'over and above' that enables people to earn an above average living."

In some respects, however, public administration in India of the 1990's differed from its British predecessor in ways that did not enjoy general acceptance. Recruitment to administrative posts during the days of the British Raj was by competitive examination. Although competitive examinations were still held, the results of these examinations were regularly skewed by appointments that were the products of nepotism and influence peddling rather than the candidate's performance. While contemporary Indians did not condemn nepotism and influence peddling in and of themselves, they objected when these practices gave others a competitive advantage in the struggle for highly-prized administrative posts. In addition, while the British administrative system drew a sharp line between public and private funds, this line tended to be fuzzy or non-existent in the post-Independence administrative system. The result was that public funds frequently found their way into Indian administrators' private pockets. In most cases, the amounts involved were modest, but when they reached scandalous proportions, as in the scandals involving the former Chief Minister of Tamil Nadu, the former Minister and Deputy Minister of Telecommunications, the Jain brothers, and the Bihari rural administration, a loud outcry went up against what was considered to be an outrageous degree of corruption that should be punished.

The withering away within 50 years of the British tradition of a rule of law administered by officials committed to do their duty as servants of the public would have surprised and dismayed Mahatma Gandhi and Jawaharlal Nehru and many ordinary Indians who belonged to the generation that had heard the "tryst with destiny" speech. For Indians of the 1990's, while it might still be dismaying, it was hardly surprising. Trevor Fishlock makes this point using these very words:

"The spread of corruption in politics may be dismaying but should not be surprising. There is much anger and shame felt by those whose education, idealist outlook, and experience led them to hope for a certain rectitude in the public life of free India. There is, especially, disappointment among those who lived through the independence period and hoped that British principles of public service would remain preeminent. That time has seen corrosion of such ideals is part of the pain of modern India. There is a feeling of betrayal and indignation. The British brought ideas of fairness, equality, impartiality, and independence in such institutions as the judiciary and the press. Many of those who took part in the independence struggle and later in the government of free India were profoundly influenced by these ideas. In Nehru's time many Indians exulted in their democracy, Parliament, and courts. Standards of public life were good. Moreover, during the independence struggle many discovered the exhilaration of a cause in which they could see themselves as a great and united people, free of feudal restraints and pettiness, unchained. Today, it may be easy to romanticize that period but it was heady and noble, a reason for pride, and many look back on it now with great wistfulness, not least when fresh reports of graft and greed in public life are added to the pile."

It was not surprising that the political tradition that the British passed on to free India would have eroded and disappeared during the decades following Independence for the simple reason that, during the more than 300 years of the British Raj, these traditions had not penetrated below the surface of Indian life. The British had not come to India to convert and acculturate the Indians whom they ruled, as the Portuguese had done in Goa. The East India Company was originally interested only in trade and, far from seeking to Christianize those who came under its control, it barred missionaries from entering its territories. As time went on, the Company, almost willy nilly, used military force to extend its domain and assumed political control over more and more of India, but the primary aim of these military and political excursions remained that of extending its trading operations. In 1813, Parliament, responding to pressure from William Wilberforce and other influential English Evangelicals, withstood the opposition of the East India Company and enacted an amended Company Charter that included a statement that Britain's interest in ruling India went beyond making money—that it included care for the well-being of its Indian subjects: "It is the duty of this country to promote the interest and happiness of the native inhabitants of the British dominions in India and such measures ought to be adopted as may tend to the introduction among them of useful knowledge and religious and social improvements." As the first steps in carrying out this "duty," the East Indian Company Act of 1813 provided that an Anglican Bishopric should be established in India, that missionaries should be allowed to enter and work in the Company's domain, and that the Company should set aside £10,000 to promote Indian education.

Having suffered a Parliamentary setback, the Company, still convinced that taking steps "to promote the interest and happiness of the native inhabitants" would interfere with trade, responded by doing next to nothing for the next 15 years to carry out the Act's provisions. It was not until Lord Bentrick became Governor General in 1828 that any of India's traditional social and religious practices were changed in ways that Company officials believed to be "religious and moral improvements." Even then, the changes that were made during the 1830's and thereafter were narrow in scope and consisted of putting a stop only to those practices that the Governors General considered to be the most inhumane: human sacrifice, *suttee*, *thuggee*, female infanticide, and slavery. With these exceptions, it remained Company policy to avoid interfering with the traditional ways of Indian society because it feared that doing so would stir up a hornet's nest of opposition that would be bad for business. Twenty-five years later, when the Mutiny of 1857 began to brew, it became clear that the Company had good reason to harbor that fear.

When, following the Mutiny of 1857, the Crown took over from the Company responsibility for law and order within Company territories, Britain's principal focus shifted from trade to governance. For the next 90 years, although economic considerations remained important, the major British concern was ruling the empire's "Jewel in the Crown," not only because they believed that it was Britain's destiny to do so, but because, more than any other single colony, holding India made Britain the world's preeminent imperial power. Rudyard Kipling expressed the destiny justification when he wrote: "The responsibility for governing India has been placed by the inscrutable design of providence on the shoulders of the British race." Winston Churchill used the political prestige justification in a 1931 speech to Parliament, echoing the words used 30 years earlier by Lord Curzon, India's Viceroy at the time: "The loss of India would be found out fatal to us. It could not fail to be part of a process that would reduce us to the scale of a minor power."

The Britishers who came to rule India, unlike the Moguls who preceded them, did not intend to become a part of Indian life. They did, like the Moguls, build some imposing structures, like the Victoria Memorial in Calcutta and the Gateway to India in Bombay, but these were buildings which reflected their roles as the governors of India, not members of Indian society. The Moguls too built imposing structures, but, along with their forts and palaces and mosques, they also built mausoleums. The mausoleums of the Mogul emperors were constructed to hold the bones which they purposed to lay in India— Humayun's in Delhi, Akbar's in Sikandra, Jehangir's in Lahore, Shah Jahan's in Agra, and Aurangzeb's in Aurangabad. Nowhere on any of the British-built edifices was a sentiment enshrined anything like the words that were carved on the stone lintel over the entrance to the Hall of Private Audience in Shah Jahan's Red Fort in Delhi: "If there is a paradise on earth, it is this, it is this, it is only this."

Unlike the Moguls, who came to India for life, the British rulers, if they survived long enough, completed their terms of service and then returned to Britain to enjoy their wealth, like Robert Clive in the real world, or like Jos Sedley of Thackeray's *Vanity Fair*, if they had traded for the Company, or to retire on a pension if they had worked for the Crown. Those who had children sent them "home" to England at an early age to begin their education. As much as possible, they followed a British lifestyle during their years in India and anyone who took on Indian ways was looked at askance by their fellows, a fate suffered fictionally by Principal Fielding in E.M. Forster's *A Passage to India*. They kept their social distance from Indians even when, during the last half-century of British rule, Britishers and Indians served together as colleagues in the Indian Civil Service and Indian Army.

As A.L. Basham points out, the social standoffishness exhibited by the British rulers was reciprocated by the high-caste Hindus whom they ruled:

"Hindu society reacted at first to the British rulers as it had done to the Muslims, tending to withdraw itself even more into the closed circle of its ancient traditions and there was no realization of a fundamental break with the past. From the orthodox point of view the British rulers of India constituted a caste, low in the social scale, which had succeeded in gaining political power. This caste had its own rules and customs which were not those of the Hindus...and should therefore not be imitated. The British readily accepted this position and, after the 18th century, made few attempts at social contact. Any real friendship between Englishman and Indian became more and more difficult as the century progressed. In fact, the Englishman in India unconsciously tended to adopt the ideas of social stratification of the Indians whom he ruled, and to look upon his own people as members of a class so exalted above the Indians that any close association with them was taboo."

High-caste Hindus looked on their British rulers as a caste "low in the social scale," because, like India's untouchables, they ate beef and, as a result, had to hire untouchables to cook their food. But this British "caste" had succeeded in gaining political power so high-caste Hindus, especially Brahmins, while maintaining their social distance, changed their ways to the extent required to obtain a share of that political power. Just as they had learned Persian in order to become a part of the Mogul administration, they learned English and adopted British dress in public so that they could become clerks and administrators under the British Raj.

139

Writing in 1948, T.S. Eliot is scathing in his criticism of the superior, almost arrogant, manner in which the British came to rule India: "Into this confused world [of India] came the British with their assurance that their own culture was the best in the world, their ignorance of the relation between culture and religion and their belief (at least since the nineteenth century) that religion is a secondary matter." Because of their "ignorance of the relation between culture and religion," these British rulers thought they could give India the benefits of Western civilization by imposing elements of a culture rooted in the religion of Christendom on a culture which was rooted in the Hindu religion. In Eliot's view, this policy could not work, and so he makes a statement in 1948 which, considering its timing, was prophetic indeed: "The benefits of British rule will soon be lost."

Just how prophetic Eliot's words were can be seen when they are compared with those written 10 years later for the *Oxford History of India* by an English historian who was commenting on Britain's withdrawal from India on August 14, 1947:

"Thus the British period came to an end after nearly three and a half centuries of trading, two centuries of political power, and a hundred and thirty years of general supremacy. The dream of Macaulay, Elphinstone and their contemporaries came true in a way that they would not have expected. They might have disapproved in part, but on the whole they would have felt that their prescience had been justified. For the India which the British left in 1947 differed greatly from the anarchic country which their diplomacy and arms had mastered over a century and a half before. If there was not 'a class of Indians in blood and colour but Englishmen in taste, in morals, and in intellect' as Macaulay and Munro had hoped for, a radical transformation had in fact taken place. Not only the external conditions of life but the soil of India itself had been greatly changed... While the superstructure of Indian society remained impervious to the casual observer, ideas and ideals from the West, new values along with new institutions had taken root in the country.

"The ideological skin of traditional Hinduism which had covered Hindu society for so long was wearing thin among the Westernized and forward-looking section of the people. Over village life it still stretched firm and largely intact. But while rural India forms the weight of Indian society, it is weight in the form of ballast. In the longer run and provided the run is long enough, it will follow the leaders in the towns... To the majority of Hindus, Hinduism meant Gandhi.

"In every branch of activity, India was standing on its own feet and making her own decisions. She was increasingly ready to face the West on its own terms, to learn to absorb and to teach in turn. In the realm of the spirit as well as in that of politics India was pressing to shape its own future. And whatever form that future might take, it would certainly contain a large element of the West. So it is at least arguable that in dying politically the West in India bids fair to triumph spiritually."

Reading these contrasting prognoses of the future of British influence in independent India from the perspective of 1997, one is struck by the degree to which developments during free India's first half-century showed that Eliot's was right and the Oxford History of India's wrong. Eliot was a poet, essayist, and literary and social critic, but his understanding of the fused nature of the relationship between Hinduism and the Indian way of life gave him a basis for assessing the degree to which the British had or had not changed India that was sounder than the observations of the surface of the Indian scene made by a later historian.

The gulf that existed between British and Indian cultures prevented British values and traditions from penetrating below the surface of Indian life. British ways remained a veneer. In V.S. Naipaul's words: "The British refused to be absorbed into India... While dominating India, they expressed their contempt for it and projected England; and Indians were forced into a nationalism which in the beginning was like a mimicry of the British. To look at themselves, to measure themselves against the new positive standards of the conqueror, Indians had to slip out of themselves. Indians floundered about in a new world whose forms they could see but whose spirit eluded them."

Naipaul's description of the beginnings of Indian nationalism as a "mimicry of the British" is based on the historical fact that the Indian

141

National Congress began in 1885 as a coalition of Britishers and members of the Indian elite who were the product of Macaulay's famous Minute of 1835 establishing English as the medium of higher education and government. Its first secretary was a retired English civil servant and, during its first 15 years, three of its presidents were Englishmen. To make it more British, its original platform did not call for Independence but for continuation of the British Raj. The only request made to the Crown was that Indians be allowed to play a larger role in India's governance. It was only after Mahatma Gandhi took over leadership of the Congress after World War I that the party began to demand *swaraj* (Independence).

British values and traditions could never become more than a surface veneer, even though the British influenced India for over 300 years, because they were rooted in the British way of life. While they could cover the surface of Indian life to some degree, they could not reach down to the heart and soul of its social system and religious beliefs. To use Naipaul's words, Indian "mimicry" of the British was that of "an old country that has been a native aristocracy for a thousand years and has learned to make room for outsiders, but only at the top. The mimicry changes, the inner world remains constant. That is the secret of [India's] survival."

❖

The Military Establishment

By a strange quirk of history, given Mahatma Gandhi's unfailing commitment to non-violence, it was the armed forces that had done best since Independence. They had not only retained their effectiveness but had grown in size. At the same time, they have maintained the British tradition of operating under civilian authority and staying out of politics. Mahatma Gandhi envisaged an India which would gradually reduce and ultimately do away with its military establishment. In fact, India's defense expenditures have gone in the opposite direction, with rapid budgetary increases under Jawaharlal Nehru following the debacle of the border war with China and an even greater escalation during the 1980's when Rajiv Gandhi was Defense Minister. The result of these increases is that the current level of defense expenditure averages 3.5% of Gross National Product, against less than 2% before 1962.

India's conversion from a country inspired by Mahatma Gandhi's vision of *ahimsa* to a major military power was a reaction not only to internal unrest but to external forces not foreseen by its founding fathers. When the British left, the army numbered approximately 280,000 men. Gandhi's idea was that this modest military establishment could be disbanded because a country that followed his principle of non-violence would not need it. Nehru did not agree that free India needed no armed forces, but he was ready to keep their numbers at the point where they would be sufficient for maintaining internal security. By 1948, Indian and Pakistani forces were fighting in Kashmir, and the continuation of the conflict with Pakistan made it clear that India's armed forces had to be built up in order to counter the Pakistani threat. So, five years later, the armed forces numbered 350,000.

Had Pakistan remained India's only external antagonist, this limited force might still be the military establishment of the 1990's. But China entered the national security picture. India's large neighbor to the north, far from being seen as a threat when Nehru delivered his "tryst with destiny" speech, was looked on by him as an Asian "blood brother." As far back as 1942, Nehru had written: "The future of which I dream is inextricably interwoven with close friendship and something almost approaching union with China." He welcomed the coming to power in 1949 of the Chinese Communist regime and remained silent a year later when that regime used force to take control of Tibet. In April 1954, India and China signed a treaty containing the five principles (*pancha sheel*) of mutual respect for each other's sovereignty, mutual non-aggression, non-interference in each other's internal affairs, equality and mutual benefit in trade, and peaceful co-existence. For the remainder of the 1950's, "Hindi-Chini bhai-bhai" (India and China are brothers) became the slogan chanted by schoolchildren all over India.

During free India's first decade the surface of Indo-Chinese relations was all sweetness and light. But under the surface lurked a problem that would soon bring the two countries to blows. When India became independent in 1947 and China came under centralized control in 1949, both the western and the eastern ends of their Himalayan border were disputed territories. The dividing line at the western end, in Ladakh, had been drawn on maps prepared by the British Raj, and China refused to recognize this "colonial" cartographic authority. At the eastern end, in the Northeast Frontier Agency (NEFA), India recognized the McMahon line which had been surveyed by the British in 1914, but the Chinese maintained that they had never accepted it. The appropriate time to bring the border dispute problem into the open and begin discussions to resolve it would have been in 1954 during the days when the *pancha sheel* treaty was being negotiated. But neither China nor India wanted to bring up a contentious matter at a time when they were seeking to cement their friendship.

India's silence was prompted by a number of additional factors. One was Nehru's romantic vision of Indo-Chinese brotherhood, which led him to believe that disagreement about their Himalayan borders could never become a source of serious conflict between them. Another was his legalistic view of the boundary problem. In his mind, the historical maps made it clear that the border was as it was defined by India. Finally, Nehru and India's other political leaders saw themselves as inheritors of Britain's dominant role in the Himalayan region.

According to Neville Maxwell, this reading of the overall political situation was unrealistic in the extreme:

"For the previous one hundred years and longer, the dominant influence in the Himalayan belt had been the British Raj. Not only did the British have a local preponderance of power, she could also bring vast economic and military resources to bear outside the sub-continent when necessary and these had been repeatedly deployed against China. The withdrawal of British power from the sub-continent in 1947 prepared the way for a reversal of the balance that had existed across the Himalayas: the emergence in China of a strong central authority with the establishment of the People's Republic in 1949, confirmed the shift. Henceforth, the advantage would be north of the Himalayas, not south."

It took Nehru eight years to recognize the reality of India's Himalayan position. Not only did he not attempt to resolve the border disagreement during the course of negotiating the 1954 *pancha sheel* treaty, but he followed its signing by taking the first step in the direction of solving the border problem by military rather than diplomatic means. India's army was ordered to set up and man check-points in the disputed areas. This inevitably brought Indian troops into contact with Chinese forces. Contact first escalated into conflict at the western end of the Himalayan line, in Ladakh. The part of Ladakh claimed by both countries was known as Aksai Chin. In 1956, China began building a road through Aksai Chin to connect Tibet with Sinjiang. Aksai Chin was an area so remote from India that Indian authorities did not know that the road had been built until a year later when its construction was reported in Beijing newspapers. When India's ambassador cabled this news to Delhi, an Indian Army patrol was sent into Aksai Chin to investigate. Chinese authorities arrested the members of the patrol on the ground that they had invaded Chinese territory.

For another year, until 1959, Nehru kept the border dispute with China a secret, not only from the Indian people but also from Parliament, because it ran counter to his publicly proclaimed policy of mutual friendship and cooperation. When he finally brought the dispute out into the open, Nehru loudly protested China's building the road through Indian territory and arresting the investigating patrol, calling them acts of "aggression." At this point the level of conflict intensified because the people of Tibet had revolted against Chinese authority, and the Dalai Lama had been given asylum in India. China showed its anger at what it considered to be a hostile act on India's part by ordering its troops to return fire when they were confronted by Indian patrols at Long Ju in NEFA and Kongka Pass in Aksai Chin. In response, Nehru accused China of trying to "bully" India.

While these military moves were taking place, China had been trying to persuade India to take the diplomatic route to a solution of the border conflict. Zhou Enlai had proposed that China and India maintain the military "status quo" while negotiations went forward aiming at a settlement. Nehru appeared to agree, but then went on to insist that maintaining the "status quo" should mean that China would withdraw her troops from the disputed areas, while Indian military personnel remained where they were because they were on Indian soil. China refused to agree to this one-sided arrangement but countered with a proposal that each country's forces withdraw 20 kilometers from the McMahon line in NEFA and from the line of actual control in Aksai Chin. Once again India refused to accept this step toward defusing an increasingly serious military confrontation. In December 1959, Zhou EnLai reiterated the proposal and suggested that he and Nehru hold a summit meeting to negotiate a settlement. Nehru expressed his willingness to hold the meeting but made it clear that he would do no more than "talk" with Zhou EnLai. In his mind, "negotiation" was out of the question since India was clearly in the right, and there was nothing to "negotiate."

Four months later, the two Prime Ministers did meet. Zhou Enlai offered Nehru a political compromise. China would give up its claim to territory in NEFA if India would recognize China's claim in Aksai

Chin. Nehru turned the compromise down on the ground that India could not give up any of its territory whatever the quid pro quo that China offered. Zhou also proposed that both sides stop sending patrols into the disputed areas in order to avoid further armed clashes. Again Nehru refused to agree. On the contrary, following the failed summit meeting, Indian troops were ordered to patrol more aggressively.

By 1961 India had become even more aggressive by instituting what it called a "forward policy." Nehru made a statement to Parliament explaining this policy: "A certain aggression has taken place in our territory. How do we deal with it? First of all, what is the objective? Obviously, our objective can only be to get that aggression vacated. How do we get the aggression vacated? By diplomatic means, by various means, and ultimately if you like by war... We go on to strengthen our position to deal with the situation whenever we feel that it is strong enough to be dealt with by us, and not from a weak position." In a later speech, he escalated his bellicose talk: "If war is thrust upon us, we shall fight and fight with all our strength... There are some things a nation cannot tolerate...any attack on its honor, on its integrity, on the integrity of its territory, no nation tolerates, and it takes risks, grave risks even, to protect all that."

On the ground, in the disputed territories, this "forward policy" took the form of Indian troops setting up posts overlooking Chinese positions and athwart Chinese lines of communications. China warned that such provocative military moves could lead to "grave consequences," but Nehru, confident that China would not use military force to settle the border dispute, responded with words that, while they sounded reassuring to India, sounded pugnacious to China: "There is nothing to be alarmed at, although the Chinese note threatens all kinds of steps they might take. If they do take those steps, we shall be ready for them." His words regarding India's readiness were backed up in July 1962 by a change in the Indian Army's rules of engagement. Up to this point, their rules of engagement had been that Indian troops should fire on the Chinese only if the Chinese fired on them. The rules change was that Indian troops should fire "if Chinese troops press dangerously close to your positions."

In early October 1962, India took a further step in the direction of a military solution by shifting from the defensive to the offensive. Indian troops in brigade strength (2,000) were ordered to move forward to push the Chinese troops facing them from their positions. Chinese troops responded by vigorously defending their posts. When this first round of open warfare was reported to Delhi, the Central Government's response was that the Indian troops should hold their ground. In Nehru's words: "Our instructions (to our troops) are to free our territory." He promised the Indian nation that its army would carry out these instructions and would "clear Indian territory of Chinese aggression."

Faced with India's refusal to desist from continuing its aggressive moves, China ordered its troops on October 20 to attack in division strength (12,000). Within a month, Chinese troops had occupied strategic points in Ladakh in the west and, in the east, had driven the Indian forces in NEFA south to within 48 kilometers of the Assamese plains. Indian defenses had been overrun, and Indian troops had retreated in disarray. Indian casualties totaled approximately 7,000 in killed, missing, and captured. A month later, China declared a unilateral cease-fire and announced that it would withdraw its forces to a point 20 kilometers north of its line of control. After this withdrawal had been carried out, China once again proposed that negotiations begin to settle the border dispute but, once again, India refused.

Most democratically elected governments that had led a nation into such a disastrous military and political defeat would have paid the price by losing office, but not one headed by the undisputed leader of the Indian nation, Jawaharlal Nehru. Krishna Menon, the Defense Minister, was forced to resign, but otherwise the Central Government remained intact. What did change as a result of the war with China was India's defense policy. In Neville Maxwell's words: "Stinted for years, the armed services, and especially, of course, the Army, was now given almost a blank check. In the next two years defense expenditures more than doubled." That the expansion of the Indian Army was directly the result of its disastrous defeat in the border war was attested to by the fact that the first six of the new divisions added were mountain troops.

The increase in defense expenditures, which began in 1962–63 when budget figures rose almost 60%, was followed by a further increase of well over 60% in 1963–64 and then continued at a slower pace for the next two decades. During the late 1980's, mainly due to purchases of expensive high-tech weapons from abroad, the rate of increase shot up to a point that topped even that of the mid-1960's. Between 1988 and 1992, India imported more arms than any other developing country. The result was that, within 25 years of the border war with China, India's military establishment had become a formidably equipped force of well over 1 million, a number exceeded only by the armed forces of China, the Soviet Union, and the United States. By 1990, India's expenditure for military equipment was the third highest in the developing world, and India ranked first in the amount of military equipment produced domestically, accounting for 31% of the developing world's total.

Despite this rapid and extensive buildup of its armed forces, India did not revert to the "forward policy" of 1961 and 1962 as a means of settling the Himalayan border dispute with China. Both sides were content to let stand the actual situation that existed on the ground after the Chinese withdrawal. India was in no mood to take military action against China after the humiliating defeat it had suffered. China had taken control of the disputed areas which were important for security reasons, particularly the portion of Aksai Chin through which the road from Tibet to Sinjiang ran. While all remained quiet at the military level, a situation of hostility continued at the diplomatic level for the next 14 years, ending only in 1976 when the two countries exchanged ambassadors.

Although the border dispute had drifted into the background, India and China remained politically estranged for the next 20 years, until 1996 when significant developments took place that changed their political relationship. The first of these developments was the visit which China's President Ziang Zemin paid to India. Although this visit was part of a tour which also included a stop in Pakistan, India's political leaders took his coming to Delhi rather than insisting that they go to Beijing as a sign that China's leaders now wanted to restore the good relations that had been destroyed by the border war. While he was in Rawalpindi, Ziang Zemin had announced that China would continue to assist Pakistan in carrying out its program to develop nuclear power, the ultimate aim of which, India was convinced, was to produce nuclear weapons. Nevertheless, China's gesture in arranging for its President to stop first in Delhi was seen by India's political leadership as evidence that China was not taking sides with Pakistan against India and could be expected to restrain Pakistan if it developed nuclear weapons as anything more than a deterrent to prevent India from launching a nuclear attack on Pakistan.

The Deve Gowda government decided to reciprocate this friendly gesture by making some friendly moves of its own. In the first place, it finally accepted the proposal made 35 years earlier by Zhou EnLai that the two parties withdraw their troops 20 kilometers from their lines of control and thereby avoid any further military clashes. Secondly, a week after the Chinese President's departure, the Defense Ministry announced that India would suspend further work on a research and development project that had been underway for several years to produce a missile with a range of 1,500 miles, one that would be capable of carrying nuclear warheads to Beijing and Shanghai from India's eastern border. The first stage of the project had been completed in 1995 when the Defense Research and Development Corporation had demonstrated that the re-entry technology that they had tested would work. The second phase would have consisted of building and testing a missile based on this re-entry technology to see whether it would actually fly. By announcing that this second stage would not be undertaken until such time as India's security situation warranted such a move, Deve Gowda's government said to China that it was India's intention to bury the hostility that had grown out of the 1962 border war and to return to the friendly relations that had characterized the first decade after Independence. Deve Gowda gave no indication, however, that the money that would be saved by shelving the 1,500-mile missile program would be used to step up social welfare programs. On the contrary, if the equipment requests of India's military commanders were to be met, these savings would have to be used to purchase the additional high-tech conventional weapons that the armed forces maintained they needed.

Conflict with Pakistan and China had resulted in India having had to bear the cost of four wars, to which must be added the expense of maintaining an expeditionary force of 70,000 troops in Sri Lanka's Jaffna Peninsula between 1989 and 1991. Externally-oriented military operations were not the only factors, however, that pushed up military expenditures. The army had been used extensively to secure territory and maintain law and order within India's domain—in Kashmir and Hyderabad in 1948, during the 1950's language agitation, in Goa in 1961, in Assam in 1983, in the Punjab in 1984, and in North India during the riots that followed Mrs. Gandhi's assassination and the Ayodhya incident. The downside of these numerous military operations has been a level of defense expenditures that has been disproportionately high, considering the seriousness of the economic and social problems that also needed to be addressed with Central Government funds. The upside was that India's armed forces had been kept busy doing what its military establishment was supposed to do rather than getting involved in politics because it had nothing better to occupy its time.

This was one of the factors that help to explain India's impressive record, unmatched by many of the other former colonial countries, of preserving continuous civilian rule during the decades following Independence. Several other factors had combined with this high level of operational activity to keep India's military from becoming a player in the political system. Rapid and steadily increasing defense expenditure meant that the military had remained relatively satisfied with what it received from the civilian sector. The supply of manpower, equipment, pay, and living quarters had met the basic needs of officers and enlisted men. Equally important was the respect which had been paid to military personnel because their record of continuous military activity had convinced the Indian people that India's security both at home and abroad depended, in the final analysis, on the members of the armed forces. This conviction was clearly reflected in the Central Government's budget for 1997–1998 and the defense policy decision that went into its formulation. Not only was the allocation for defense increased by 11%, but the Defense Minister announced that this substantial increase was the first step in a five-year program aimed at putting India's armed forces on a par with those of China. Speaking for the Deve Gowda government, he asserted that China commanded worldwide respect because of its military strength and stated that India would not be able to pursue an "independent" foreign policy without "self-reliance in defense."

Finally, credit must be given to the fact that the British tradition remained alive in India's armed forces more than it had in any other of free India's political institutions. Following this tradition, the military had seen itself as an army, navy, and air force under civilian control whose job it was to fight wars and insurrections, not run the government. This ideology had been accompanied by a recruiting practice carried over from British days that were peculiar to India. The British Crown, when it took control of India in 1858, following the Bengal Army's mutiny, had taken steps to ensure that another mutiny did not take place. They had introduced what might be called a "divide and control" policy in recruiting for the Indian Army. Soldiers were enrolled from several ethnic groups that, far from being traditional allies, had usually been at odds with each other—Rajputs, Marathas, Jats, and Sikhs from India and Gurkhas from Nepal. With such a multiethnic and mutually distrustful rank and file, it was all but impossible for the enlisted men to organize a conspiracy. Later on, when Indians became eligible for officer rank, they too were recruited on the basis of the "divide and control policy." A special wrinkle of this strategy was to give preference to Sikhs in recruiting both officers and enlisted men. The Sikhs had provided the bulk of the Indian force that joined with British troops to put down the 1857 Mutiny and had thus proved their loyalty to the British Crown. Moreover, since they were members of a communal group who were looked at askance by both Hindus and Muslims, it was unlikely that Sikh officers and enlisted men could obtain the support of their Hindu and Muslim counterparts for a Sikh-led mutiny against the British authorities.

This "divide and control" recruiting policy was an important ingredient in the British tradition which the Indian military inherited in 1947 and which they have perpetuated since then. It explains in part the non-political role which India's armed forces have played. Along with the fact that they have a centuries-old reputation as good soldiers, it also explains why Sikhs are the largest ethnic contingent in the armed forces of the 1990's. They account for approximately 15% to 20% of service personnel, compared with only 2% of India's population. With such a small Sikh population, it would be impossible for Sikhs, were they to lead a military coup, to get the civilian backing that they would need to hang on to power. Realization of this demographic fact has reinforced the loyalty of Sikh officers and men to the British tradition, with the result that Sikh military personnel limit their activities to the military realm and do not attempt to use their strong position in the military to seize political power.

This fact of Indian military life was dramatically displayed in 1984 at the time of Mrs. Gandhi's assassination. True, she was killed by two Sikh bodyguards, but these two were the exceptions to the rule that Sikh military personnel do not get involved in politics. In fact, she had other Sikh bodyguards who did not take part in the assassination plot. More importantly, the more than 200,000 Sikhs in India's armed forces at that time did not mutiny even when thousands of their co-religionists were slaughtered by Hindu mobs, and the Central Government did little or nothing to bring the mobs under control until most of the killing was over. Except for a few local incidents in which Sikh troops defied the authorities, Sikh military personnel remained under discipline and carried out the instructions given them by the civilian government. When army personnel were finally sent in to restore order, these loyal Sikh officers and enlisted men were among them.

❖

Culture and Religion

Since Independence, India has experienced a resurgence in its traditional ways. These traditional ways had remained largely intact during the more than 300 years of British influence and 200 years of British rule because they were highly resistant to change by outside forces. In the words of Trevor Fishlock: "The unique nature of India, its conservatism, massiveness, passivity, opaqueness, apathy, and nearly sanctified privileges and rivalries make it resistant to change... The struggle between castes, the rule of hosts of petty tyrants, the repression of the weak, the fight for a meager existence, and the intimate knowledge of poverty are the enduring lot of most people and this has not changed much in many hundreds of years. The tyranny of the land and rulers and invaders have produced in this ancient civilization a willingness to bend reed-like before oppression and evil; the people's obeisance to power, their readiness to compromise, their resistance to change, their suspicion of those not their kin are elements in the survival of the Hindus. They have bent and, like their religion, have accommodated."

Using Fishlock's terminology, India's traditional ways "bent" and "accommodated" in response to the institutions and practices which the British brought with them, but sprang back, reasserted themselves, once the British were gone. V.S. Naipaul describes how this process worked in the political realm:

"The freedom that came to independent India with the institutions it gave itself were alien freedoms, better suited to another civilization: in India they remained separate from the internal organization of the country, its beliefs and antique restrictions. In the beginning it did not matter. There were development plans. India industrialized, more effectively than is generally supposed; it more than doubled its

154

production of food... The population grew; the landless fled from the tyranny of villages; the towns choked; the rebelliousness created in the beginnings of economic development in a land immemorially abject expressed itself in the streets in various ways. In this very triumph of democracy lay its destruction."

Naipaul does not expand on this passage by explaining why the British practices and institutions were "alien freedoms, better suited to another civilization." Elsewhere in his writings, however, he makes it plain that he finds the answer in India's traditional society and way of life. That traditional society and way of life constituted India's culture and, according to T.S. Eliot's *Notes Toward a Definition of Culture*, India's culture was the incarnation of India's religion. Eliot used the word "incarnation" because he wanted to avoid the word "related," which separates culture from religion, and the word "identity," which makes them the same. In his view, culture and religion are different, but they are fused with each other to the point where one cannot exist without the other. Another way that Eliot makes his point is to say that religion and culture are different aspects of the way of life of a people. That is to say, looked at from the top down, from the level of the supernatural, "the whole way of life of a people from birth to the grave, from morning to night and even in sleep" is its religion. Looked at from the bottom up, from the level of the natural, that "whole way of life" is its culture.

Eliot's *Notes* is couched in general terms, but there are convincing reasons to see India as a striking case in point. India's culture is so infused with Hinduism that the concept of "religion" as distinct from culture is nowhere to be found in its philosophical or theological lexicon. The orthodox name for Hinduism is *Santana Dharma* (Eternal Duty), a term that covers both the social code that guides day-to-day behavior and the cosmic law that shapes a person's ultimate destiny. A Westerner, looking at this name, would say, with Eliot, that India's way of life is a fusion of India's culture and religion, or that India's religion and India's culture are different aspects of the same thing. A Hindu, looking at this name, would say that there is no sense in making a distinction between the two because there is no difference between them.

From either the Western or the Hindu point of view, it is clear that India's culture—its way of life, its practices, and traditions—are rooted in its dominant religion, Hinduism. In other words, India's way of life grows out of and is shaped by Hinduism just as a plant grows out of and is shaped by the soil in which it is planted. So, if one is to understand that way of life, and what happened to it during and after the days of the British Raj, one must view it in terms of, to use Eliot's word, its "incarnational" relationship with Hinduism.

As Eliot saw clearly in 1948, the ethical standards for society and politics that the British brought into India had failed to take lasting root because the soil of Indian culture into which they had tried to plant them, permeated as it was by the Hindu religion, did not nurture ethical standards that grew out of the religion of Britain. As Mrs. Gandhi has put it, "The secret of India is the acceptance of life in all its fullness, the good and the evil." India is equally accepting of good and evil because Hinduism holds that, in the final analysis, the distinction between them disappears. India believes this because, according to Hindu theology, ultimate reality is beyond good and evil.

From this amoral theological position stems the fact that Hindu gods and goddesses are neither morally good nor morally bad. Their actions are a mixture of the two—sometimes good and sometimes bad, depending on their feelings and their situation at the moment. Nor are they concerned about the moral conduct of their devotees. Hindu gods and goddesses have the power to help those who please them and to harm those who displease them, not the power to redeem and sanctify their followers. As one student of Hinduism has put it, "The function of the gods is not the direction of morals but the distribution of blessings and, if not duly propitiated, punishments... The gods are offended not by sin but by neglect. They are pleased by offerings and ceremonies, rather than by repentance and a new life."

Some of the actions of Rama prove this. His triumph over Ravana, the King of Demons, is recounted in the *Ramayana* and celebrated in Hinduism's most popular festival, *Diwali*. Rama's wife, Sita, is kidnapped by Ravana and carried off to Sri Lanka. Rama sets out to punish Ravana for committing a deed that has greatly tarnished the god's honor. On his way to Sri Lanka, he encounters an ape who has usurped the throne from its rightful ape ruler, but, in the process has lost his wife to that rightful ruler. The usurper ape offers to help Rama find Sita if Rama will help him recover his wife. Rama agrees to become his ally. When the two apes fight for the kingdom and the usurper's wife, Rama shoots the rightful king in the back from a thicket in which he is hiding. Before he dies, the rightful king asks Rama why he has shot him when he has done nothing to harm Rama. Rama replies that the rightful king has dishonored the usurper by carrying off his wife. Even though he was the rightful king, he deserves to die so that the usurper can recover his honor.

With the help of the usurper ape, and thousands of monkeys mustered by the monkey god Hanuman who provide a bridge for Rama to cross the Palk Strait into Sri Lanka, Rama finally corners Ravana. In the meantime, Sita has refused to marry Ravana and has remained faithful to Rama. Even though he is the King of Demons, Ravana has not forced himself on Sita, but, in a very civilized and gentlemanly manner, has proposed marriage to her and has given her one year to make up her mind. Before that year has elapsed, Rama arrives and kills Ravana. Sita thereupon rushes to Rama, thinking that he will welcome her with open arms. But, much to her dismay, he spurns her, saying that he has not come to Sri Lanka and killed Ravana for her sake but to avenge the insult which Ravana has inflicted upon him by stealing his wife. Shouting that her sight is unbearable to him because she has been the bride of the King of Demons, he orders Sita to go as far away from him as possible. Crushed by Rama's rejection, Sita asks that a funeral pyre be built and, when the flames are lit, she walks into them and is consumed. Having gone through this ordeal of fire, Sita reappears and is vindicated when the god of fire assures Rama that she has not been touched by Ravana. Rama, knowing now that his honor will not be tarnished by taking back a woman who has been used by another man, accepts Sita as his wife and takes her back to his home in Ayodhya.

As the actions of both Rama and Ravana make clear, when Hindus celebrate *Diwali*, they are not celebrating the triumph of good over evil. Rama is not the personification of good as he pursues Ravana to Sri Lanka and kills him in order to avenge the dishonor done to him. Nor is Ravana the personification of evil as he proposes to Sita and patiently awaits her reply. Rather, Hindus are celebrating the superior power of a warrior hero who is an earthly appearance of the god Vishnu over the chief practitioner of the black arts who had the effrontery to kidnap the hero's wife. They react with joy at Rama's victory much as American boxing fans cheered in 1935 when Joe Lewis knocked out Max Schmelling, the German fighter who had defeated him in an earlier match and was regarded by Americans as an exemplar of the arrogance of Nazi Germany. Joe Louis' victory had restored America's honor and had put the strutting Nazis in their place.

The ethical standards imported into India by officials of the British Raj were a part of the culture of their homeland and, again following Eliot, that culture was an outgrowth of Britain's religion. Britain's religion was not peculiar to its islands but a religion shared by Europe and the Americas, that part of the world which has been called Christendom. Few of these British officials were deeply religious, nor did the British Raj seek to Christianize its subjects as the Portuguese tried to do in Goa. But most of them shared Christendom's traditional belief that good and evil are essentially different and that good should be nurtured and evil suppressed. The best of them lived up to their ethical standards and carried out their duties following the principle that their governance of India, along with maintaining law and order and collecting revenue, should promote what they saw to be good and get rid of what they saw to be evil. Traditional practices like *thuggee*, *suttee*, female infanticide, slavery, and human sacrifice, which were followed in some parts of India and which they considered to be evil, they outlawed. Principles, projects, and programs that they considered to be good for India's people and, in the long run, for the British Empire, they made a part of their governance: famine relief, education, medical services, irrigation, transportation and communication facilities, honest administration, and equal treatment under the law.

Nineteenth-century Indian reformers like the Hindu Ram Mohan Roy and the Muslim Syed Ahmed Khan internalized and espoused much of Christendom's ethics, as did 20th-century political leaders like Jawaharlal Nehru and, especially, Mahatma Gandhi. The result was that the ethical standards of the British Raj were a significant part of the social and political vision with which free India began its life. During the decades that followed, however, the amoralism of Hinduism gradually took over. Although the ethical standards espoused by free India's founding fathers were still honored in speech, daily life went on following the traditional Hindu belief that, in the final analysis, the difference between good and evil disappears. Using Mrs. Gandhi's simple language, free India became more and more accepting of both good and evil because it more and more saw good and evil as distinctions that belonged to the illusory material world but were not a part of the world of ultimate reality.

Just as Hinduism is an amoral religion, so too is it an individualistic religion. Hindus do not worship together in congregational gatherings, but as individuals. To those who have witnessed or seen pictures of the thousands of Hindus who participate in temple festivals and *yatras* (pilgrimages) and the millions who take part in *melas* (ritual bathing in rivers which Hindus consider to be holy, on days that they consider to be particularly auspicious), this may sound like a ridiculous statement. But the observers of such scenes should not make the mistake of failing to distinguish between a congregational gathering and a gathering of individual devotees. A congregational gathering is composed of persons who share in each other's worship and benefit spiritually as members of a group. A gathering of individual devotees is made up of persons who come together, as at a temple festival, to express their individual devotion to a deity and to derive individual spiritual benefit from his or her act of devotion or, as at a *mela*, to undertake a religious exercise that will give each individual spiritual merit (*poonyam*) that will improve his or her destiny (*karma*). The difference between a religious congregation and a religious gathering is not a matter of numbers but a matter of whether those who gather act together for their mutual spiritual benefit or act individually for their individual spiritual gain.

Taking part in festivals, *yatras*, and *melas*, however much they involve great numbers of devotees and display great excitement, is not the way that Hindus worship, in the strict sense of that word. When they worship, each one comes to the temple, as an individual, even if he or she comes as part of a family group, to receive his or her own *darshan* (blessing) from the god or goddess enshrined there. As they do their *pujas* (worship rituals) and make their offerings, they pray for their own souls, not for the souls of others. Put simply, Hinduism believes, in the final analysis, that each individual must achieve salvation on his or her own. Christendom's notion that men and women can bear one another's spiritual burdens and that individual salvation is found in relationship with others is foreign to Hinduism.

Reinforcing the individualism of Hinduism is its belief that the world is an illusion and that the individual must seek, not to redeem it, but to make his or her escape (*moksha*) from it. According to the Hindu view, not only is there no salvation in community but also no salvation for the community. Given Hinduism's individualism and the lack of concern for the life of the community as a whole, it is not surprising that independent India gradually lost its founding fathers' commitment to the common good, their belief that all Indians should concern themselves, not only with their individual physical and spiritual well-being, but also with the physical and spiritual well-being of the community in which they lived. This commitment on the part of the founding fathers was accompanied by a commitment to a standard of social intercourse in which all who lived in the community were to be treated with respect and decency regardless of the caste or religious group to which they belonged.

As founding fathers like Mahatma Gandhi and Jawaharlal Nehru died and their influence faded, free India abandoned those commitments and reverted to Hinduism's traditional lack of interest in the common good. Hinduism offered the individual a passing kind of happiness in the illusory material world. That happiness came through fulfilling the *dharma* defined by his or her caste. In the daily round of the "here and now," the individual found his or her identity and achieved the degree of well-being ordained by his or her *karma*, not as an individual, but as a member of the caste into which he or she has been born. But the happiness which did not pass away was available only in the spiritual world of ultimate reality. Every man and woman had to enter that world, not as part of a caste group but on his or her own.

Thus, at both eternal and temporal levels, Hindu theology undermined interest in and action for the common good. At the eternal level, its focus was on the individual. At the temporal level, its focus was on the parochial group. At neither level did the Hindu way of life encompass the commonality of persons, the larger community to which everyone belonged simply by virtue of being a human being. As the broad vision and social perspective of India's founding fathers declined and as the Hindu outlook and way of life reasserted themselves, the common good more and more ceased to be a goal of public policy and private endeavor. More and more, as the years went by, the degree of respect and humane treatment that the individual received came to be a product of his or her place in the socio-economic hierarchy rather than his or her membership in the human race.

Reacting to a statement by William Russell, an English newspaper correspondent who, in reporting on the Mutiny of 1857, wrote that he was impressed by "the high delight of the Indian camp followers who were pouring toward Lucknow to aid the [British] foreigners to overcome their brethren," V.S. Naipaul observes:

"The idea of brethren—an idea so simple to Russell that the word is used with clear irony—was very far from the people to whom he applies it. The Muslims would have had some idea of the unity of their faith; but that idea would always be qualified by the disposition of their rulers, and the Muslims would have had no obligation to anyone outside their faith. The Hindus would have had no loyalty except to their clan; they would have had no higher idea of human association, no general idea of the responsibility of man to his fellow. And because of this missing large area of human association, the country works blindly on, and all the bravery and skill of its people lead to nothing."

India's relative indifference to the well-being of the "other fellow" and lack of concern for the common good have been destructive of harmonious and mutually supportive political and social relationships. They have also been destructive of its man-made and natural environments, especially in its cities where the pressures of a booming population and rapid economic development have been heaviest. The environment is the common space in which all individuals live and, if it is not protected and nurtured out of a sense of mutual responsibility and commitment to the common good, it will be trashed and all segments of the population will suffer from its destruction. Unfortunately, this is exactly what has happened in India during the 50 years since it became independent. Water, air, and open spaces have been polluted to the point where the countryside has been damaged and the cities are on the brink of becoming unlivable. In comparing the environment of India's cities in the 1950's with their present state, the striking difference is, not only that the degree of its degradation is so much greater, but that the urban elite and middle class have joined the poor among the residents who suffer the deleterious consequences.

A parallel taken from American history would be the "destruction of the Common." In colonial New England, each town had a Common which was owned by the community and which was used for purposes which its residents had in common. One of these common purposes was grazing their cows and sheep. As long as these animals were few in number, the environmental cost, the cost of making good the damage caused by their grazing on the Common, was low. The grass had time to grow back. As more cows and sheep were put out to pasture, the environmental cost of each additional animal that joined the flock went up because it was now more difficult for the grass to recover. If no limit was placed on the number of animals grazing on the Common, the environmental cost of adding the last animal would be infinitely high. At that point, the Common would have been destroyed.

Although India's contemporary cities are far removed from the towns of colonial New England, the environmental process that had taken place there can be analyzed in terms of "the destruction of the Common." There were differences between the two. Colonial New England's Commons were only a part of the town, set aside from the dwellings of its inhabitants, and sheep and cattle grazed there. The typical Indian city does not have a common area separated from its residential quarters, but it does have streets and open spaces that all of its citizens use. As each new immigrant was added to the city's population, the environmental cost of one more person using those common spaces went up, just as the environmental cost went up as one more sheep or cow was turned loose on the colonial New England Common. If no limit was placed on the number of additional immigrants that moved into the city, the environmental cost of the last additional immigrant would become infinitely high—the common areas which all residents of the city use would become uninhabitable. During the 50 years following Independence, unlimited urban immigration had been the order of the day, and India's urban environment had approached destruction as a decent human habitation.

Exacerbating this destructive process was the fact that the allocation of resources to offset rapidly rising environmental costs had been grossly inadequate. To be sure, India had many pressing needs and limited resources to meet them, but making good the damage to its urban environment should have been placed higher on the priority list. One reason why it has not been given a higher place is that Indian culture, rooted as it is in Hinduism, does not promote a sense of the "common," the environmental dimension of community life for which all are responsible and within which all suffer if that responsibility is not discharged. Traditional Hindu culture holds that Indians are responsible only for their private space—their households and their compounds—and not for what lies outside. So they sweep their households and their yards and throw the sweepings into the street.

India's lack of concern for the "common," the absence of a sense of responsibility for the common space and the common good, has been graphically described by Trevor Fishlock:

"So it is when a new building is erected, its staircases are soon covered with red *pan* (betel leaf) spittle, the paint peels, and the cement crumbles, and no one cleans or minds. But homes are neat and clean. The gap between private cleanliness and public squalor is one of the notable paradoxes of India. Buses run you off the road. Electricity junction boxes lie broken open in a tangle of fuses and scrap wire. Bodies lie for hours on railway lines or roads, a public spectacle until someone makes a decision to move them. People flee from road accidents, rather than help the injured, for fear of becoming involved. Concern, altruism, and reform are not the attributes of the new politics."

Not surprisingly, public policy has reflected this lack of concern for the "common" represented by the natural environment. Neither by regulating pollution in any effective way nor by investing significant resources to make good the environmental damage that has been caused by economic development and population growth have the Central or State governments taken serious action to deal with the rapid destruction of healthy and comfortable living spaces. Central Government environmental protection policy has been little more than tokenism, and at one political point, was treated almost as a joke. When a coalition government took over from Rajiv Gandhi in 1989, Manicka Gandhi was appointed Minister of Environment and Forests. She was the widow of Sanjay Gandhi and was heartily disliked by Indira Gandhi, so much so that, after Sanjay's death, she and her children were forced to move out of the Prime Minister's residence. Given the background of dissension in the Nehru family household, it was clear that giving Manicka Gandhi a cabinet office was intended as a slur on the memory of Indira Gandhi and as a slap at Rajiv Gandhi who had replaced Sanjay as his mother's heir. It was equally clear that giving the post of Minister of Environment and Forests to an inexperienced member of the Congress Indira Party opposition who had no political influence as a means of insulting the Nehru family meant that the Central Government did not consider protection of the environment as an area of public policy which it intended to vigorously pursue.

❖

Contrasting World Views

India's relative indifference to the "common" in the form of the environment was supported theologically by the traditional Hindu belief that the material world is *maya* (illusion). Translating this belief into the words that Shakespeare put in Hamlet's mouth, the material world is "a tale told by an idiot, full of sound and fury, signifying nothing." Holding such a belief fosters the feeling that what goes on in the material world does not really matter, for it makes no sense to take care of, much less improve, something that is only a dream. It tells the Hindu believer that, rather than work hard to preserve and improve the material world and make it a better place in which to live, the way of wisdom is to endure its sufferings and escape from it as soon as possible. Escape, not redemption, is the way to deal with a world that is *maya*.

By way of contrast, officials of the British Raj had believed, not only that the Indian world which they ruled was real, but also that it could and should be improved. Lord Curzon, India's quintessential Viceroy, was preeminent among them in this respect. He was a consummate imperialist who justified Britain's rule over India, not in terms of what it meant for India but for what it meant for Britain, by stating in almost the same words that Winston Churchill used 30 years later: "As long as we rule India we are the greatest power in the world. If we lose it, we shall drop straight-away to a third rate power." But Curzon believed that the best way for Britain to hang on to its prominent place in the imperial world was to direct its rule toward improving India so that it would come closer to being a real "Jewel in the Crown" which Queen Victoria wore as ruler of the British empire. This he set out to do with all the enormous energy at his disposal.

As described by Geoffrey Morehouse:

"[Curzon] set himself energetically to improve the Indian economy by attracting more investment from Britain, and all the relevant statistics rose sharply during his six years in Government House. He extended the irrigation of the land even more extensively than his predecessors had done... He galvanized the educationalists to pay more attention to primary and secondary schooling on the ground that there was little point in filling universities 'unless we attack, permeate, and elevate the vast amorphous, unlettered substratum of the population'... More than any other ruler of India, Curzon cared for the visible reminders of her history and under him the conservation of ancient buildings and monuments (including the Taj Mahal) became a high priority... Curzon adhered strictly to his own ideal of British rule and he summarized its principles in one of the last speeches he made before leaving for home in 1905. To be an Englishman in India, he declared must be: 'To fight for the right, to abhor the imperfect, the unjust or the mean.'"

That escape rather than redemption is Hinduism's traditional answer to *maya* is evidenced by the linguistic fact that, in all of India's major languages, the word that has to be to used to express Christendom's concept of "redemption" is one that means "escape." Escape in its ultimate form is the state of *nirvana* (enlightenment) when the Hindu is freed from the wheel of reincarnation and is merged with the ultimate reality which is the antithesis of *maya*. But short of ultimate escape, during his stay in the material world of *maya*, if he is a traditionally religious Hindu, he can go into the forest or to a mountain top, leaving behind his worldly desires and difficulties, and meditate upon the spiritual world of reality. Or, if he is a modern, not very religious Hindu, he can escape into the cinema and watch either an entertaining movie full of beauty and glamour in the form of song and dance or a serious movie portraying the struggle of idealism against the corrupt ways of the world, either of which will make him forget for a few hours the ugly and unjust world of *maya* which awaits him in the street outside.

During his travels through India in the early 1990's, Jonah Blank encountered many of these "modern, not very religious" Hindus and saw them flocking into the cinema as an escape from the illusory world

166

of *maya* into the illusory world of film. He reacted with this comment on India's hundreds of millions of movie-goers: "Film is the ultimate form of illusion. It is blatant untruth blatantly confessed. Audiences flock to the movie houses and crowd around television sets anxiously hoping to be well deceived. They revel in the deception, if it is skillful enough, for it lets them live briefly in a world far more exciting, glamorous, fair, and pleasurable than the one they inhabit."

V.S. Naipaul calls this escapist mind set, stemming from the Hindu concept of *maya*, the "Indian ability to retreat, the ability genuinely not to see what was obvious." He goes on to say that, in other societies, it would be "the foundation for neurosis, but with Indians it is only a part of a greater philosophy of despair, leading to passivity, detachment, and acceptance." One result of this ability is a disconnection between lofty ideals and concrete actions to achieve them. No doubt, there is a gap in every society between lofty ideals and the degree to which they are achieved. In some of them, however, people are painfully aware of this gap, are greatly troubled by it, and make a serious effort to close it. In India not only is the gap wide indeed, but people do not pay attention to it, do not seem to be bothered that it exists, and do not exert themselves to make the ideal a reality.

The result is laws which incorporate good intentions but are not enforced and speeches that express lofty ideals but to which the hearers respond by lauding the eloquence of the speaker rather than by committing themselves to take action. A sign along a Madurai curbside identifies it as a "Clean Area," but the gutter below is overflowing with trash. No one bothers to clear the trash or take down the sign. Prominent above the squalid shelters of the pavement dwellers who live along the road leading to Bombay's airport is a billboard reading: "Make Mumbai (Bombay) a Garden City." Nothing is being done to move toward this goal by getting these pavement dwellers out of their miserable shelters and into decent housing, but the billboard remains.

A striking instance of this tendency to make public gestures which proclaim an intention to improve India's living conditions but which will not materialize in any tangible form occurred in December 1996 when the Supreme Court ruled that 292 coal-fired industrial plants located in the Agra area and whose smokestack emissions threatened the marble of the Taj Mahal, must either switch to another energy source by April 30, 1997, or close down. As a means of making sure that conversion to other energy sources took place within this four-month period, the Court further ruled that these industrial plants were to receive no coal supplies after the April deadline. No doubt, the Supreme Court was to be commended for expressing an interest in preserving the beauty and durability of India's most treasured building, but the measures that it had prescribed to accomplish this commendable end were so draconian that it was clear from the outset that they would not be implemented. Given India's continuing drive for industrial development, neither the Uttar Pradesh government nor the Central Government was going to allow 292 industrial plants to be shut down. Given the energy supply problems, not to mention the technical and fiscal problems that would have to be overcome to switch these industrial plants to electricity or gas within four months, it was also clear that it was impossible for their owners to comply with the Supreme Court's order. The result of these two considerations was that the order would inevitably remain on the books while political maneuvering and legal proceedings were dragged on to make sure that it was not enforced. In the end, then, the Supreme Court's order would turn out to be another expression of good intentions that had no positive impact on the real world.

That the Supreme Court was prone to making these gestures of good intention that had no possibility of becoming reality was indicated earlier in 1996 when it ruled that the use of child labor was a violation of the Constitution and that any business that continued this illegal practice would be fined Rs. 20,000 ($600) per day. While the Supreme Court was again to be commended for taking a stand against the human and social cost of using children as a labor source, India's economy would be staggered if this traditional practice were to be stopped on the ground that it is illegal. No doubt, under the Supreme Court's ruling, a business could continue with child workers if it paid the Rs. 20,000 per day fine, but, since most businesses that depend on child labor are family enterprises or small operations, this substantial additional cost would be more than most of them could bear. Collecting this fine, then, would put thousands of these businesses out of business, with the result that millions would be added to the already swelling ranks of the underemployed and the unemployed. Given this harsh economic reality, the Supreme Court's earlier ruling on child labor was no more likely to be enforced than its ruling on the Agra area's 292 industrial plants.

Even more pervasive than Hinduism's traditional concept of *maya* in influencing India's way of thinking and acting is the popular Hindu belief that what happens in an individual's life is ultimately determined by the movement of the stars and planets, not by his or her own will. Believing as they do in reincarnation, Hindus see themselves as entering each life with a *karma* (destiny) that is the product of the quality of the life that they have lived in previous existences. The alignment of the heavenly bodies at the time of their birth reveals the characteristics of their *karma*. As they work out their *karma* during the course of their life, they must precede each action by taking into account the positions of the stars and planets at the time if things are going to work out well for them. In day-to-day living, this is done by consulting an astrologer who studies his charts and tells his client when the heavenly bodies will be aligned in a manner that will be auspicious for accomplishing what he or she has in mind.

The advice of the astrologer is sought in major as well as minor affairs. Mrs. Gandhi was the first Prime Minister to consult an astrologer before making political and governmental moves, a practice that would have horrified her father who was a scientifically minded humanist with little use for the practices of Hinduism or any other religion. Narasimha Rao was the next Prime Minister to seek astrological advice before making a political decision when he set the dates for the 1996 General Election only after ascertaining from his astrologer what voting dates would ensure a Congress Indira Party victory. The results of the election made it clear that he had received bad advice. Nothing daunted, his successor, Deve Gowda, took it one step farther. He not only wanted to install himself in the Prime Minister's residence on the auspicious day but at the auspicious hour. Since his astrologer had told him that the hour would be 5:00 a.m., his arrival awoke Narasimha Rao who was asleep in bed at the time.

Popular Hinduism's pervasive belief in the power of the stars and planets to determine what happens to human beings stands in sharp contrast to the belief that the officials of the British Raj brought with them. They had been brought up to believe that a man's will and actions, not the movements of the stars and planets, ultimately determine the outcome of what he sought to do. They had been educated reading Shakespeare, and nowhere is this belief better stated than in the words which Cassius directed to Brutus in *Julius Caesar*: "Men at times are masters of their fate. The fault, dear Brutus, is not in our stars, but in ourselves that we are underlings."

The sharp difference between these contrasting beliefs helps to explain the attenuation in vigor of actions taken to reform Indian society that had characterized the first 50 years after Independence. As Hinduism's traditional belief that what happened to the people of India depended upon the movements of the stars and planets took over from the belief imported by the British and shared by free India's founding fathers that human will and human action were the decisive factors, the drive to undertake programs and projects to reform Indian society lost the power that it had had when Independence dawned. Free India began with leaders like Mahatma Gandhi and Jawaharlal Nehru who believed that human will and action were the forces which would make India what they wanted it to be. It is ending the first 50 years of its history led by politicians like Narasimha Rao and Deve Gowda who believe that India's destiny lies more in the stars and planets than in what they and the rest of the Indian people determine should be done.

Another area of belief in which the view of Christendom brought into India by officials of the East India Company and the British Crown contrasts with traditional Hindu view is the way in which they understand history. British officials, reflecting the culture from which they came, saw history as a line which was not only going somewhere but going up. They were a product of 18th- and 19th-century Christendom's belief in progress and, not just progress, but the steady, almost inevitable progress that provided the ideological background

170

for Charles Darwin's theory of evolution. Moreover, since they did not believe that the material world was *maya*, they saw India's history, including its ancient language, as something that mattered and, therefore, something that should be studied and recorded. Thus it was Britishers who wrote the first modern histories of India and undertook the first grammatical analysis of India's ancient and then unspoken language, Sanskrit.

For traditional Hinduism, history is not a line that goes somewhere but a wheel that keeps turning but never moves in any direction, up or down. To borrow a contemporary American colloquialism, Hinduism believes that "what goes around, comes around." In terms of traditional Hindu theology, the history of the material world is a never-ending cycle of creation and destruction, a belief that is incorporated in the figure of its greatest god, Shiva, who is the god of both creation and destruction. When he dances in the form of Natarajan, he holds in one hand the drum that symbolizes the beat of creation and in another the flame that symbolizes the fire of destruction. Belief in this cyclical view of history filters down into everyday life in the popular view that there is nothing new under the sun, that everything that happens that is supposed to be new is really the same old thing in a different form, and that things are going nowhere. Most contemporary Indians, even though they do not understand the language, would agree with the French proverb: *Plus ça change, plus c'est la même chose.* (The more things change, the more they are the same.) Such a popular belief inevitably fosters inertia in the spirit, saps the drive to make life different, and destroys the vision of a better society. Just as the climate of South India has not given the Tamil language a word for "snow," the Hindu religion has not given it a word for "hope."

When this traditional Hindu view that history is a wheel that goes nowhere takes the place of the view imported from Britain that history is a line that is going onward and upward, Indian writers like V. S. Naipaul are forced to lament that "the saddening element in Indian history is the absence of growth and development. It is a history whose only lesson is that life goes on. There is only a series of beginnings, no final creation . . . All creation in India hints of the

171

imminence of interruption and destruction." As the minds of India's leaders have become more and more conditioned by the belief that "all creation in India hints of the immanence of interruption and destruction," their dedication to creating something new and better has become more and more conspicuous by its absence.

Among contemporary Indians, only a Hindu *guru* (teacher) would articulate this set of traditional Hindu beliefs, and only a Hindu *saddhu* (holy man) would follow them explicitly as a rigorous guide for living. But the Indian people as a whole have been taught them for centuries by the attitudes that they have heard expressed in daily conversations and the day-to-day actions that they have observed going on around them. They are articulated only by the few, but they are the unexamined assumptions of the many. The philosophy and theology of traditional Hinduism is not on the lips of the average member of the Hindu citizenry. One does not often hear them openly expressed. They are in the back of minds and in the marrow of bones, molding thoughts and guiding actions in an almost instinctive way. In this virtually silent and unobtrusive way, the traditional Hindu way of looking at the world and the lot of the men and women who live in it has exerted a more and more decisive influence on India's life as the 50 years following Independence have gone by, not on its surface but in its underlying content and direction.

❖

Caste

Last but by no means least, because it is the most important point at which Hinduism gives shape to Indian society, the 50 years following Independence had seen a resurgence of the overriding power of the caste system. To say that the caste system is the most important point at which Hinduism impacts Indian society is to say something which is true but, at the same time, does not accurately express the relationship between the two because neither Hinduism nor the caste system could exist without the other. In Eliot's terms, the caste system is a cultural "incarnation" of the Hindu religion. That they cannot be separated is attested to by the fact that one way that a Hindu can be described in simple terms is to say that he or she is a person who belongs to a caste. Trevor Fishlock notes the totally interdependent, almost fused, relationship that exists between "the central dynamic of Hinduism, its pervasive religious power and code for living, and the mesh of caste" and goes on to say: "These forces are inseparable. Caste and religion grind together like gears... Caste is in India's fiber, inextricably bound up with Hindu ideas of life, rebirth, and predestination."

Caste is such a dominant force in Indian society that it permeates the lives of communities that are not made up of caste Hindus. Outcaste Hindus have their caste divisions and caste hierarchy. Parayens differentiate themselves from pallars and each vies for a superior position. Valluvas are accorded the status of "outcaste Brahmins" because they preside over religious ceremonies. Vettiyans are shunned by members of other untouchable castes because they tend the grounds where bodies are burned or buried. Most followers of religions other than Hinduism whose doctrines reject the caste system identify and organize themselves into groups according to their caste origins.

Factional disputes within the Christian community more often than not can be traced to conflicts between groups that trace their antecedent roots to different castes. Muslims differentiate themselves between those who are descendants of Muslim invaders and those who are descendants of converts from Hinduism, but members of the latter segment are grouped according to the caste from which their ancestors came. Most marriages within the Christian and the Muslim convert communities take the form of an alliance between a bride and a groom whose forebears were converted from the same caste.

The forms in which the caste system manifests itself as free India's first half-century comes to a close have changed in some superficial ways from the caste practices which were the order of the day when Independence dawned. These changes in outward form have been more apparent in the cities because rural areas have tended to cling more closely to traditional caste practices. The very nature of the urban scene in which many more Indians live today makes it almost impossible for high-caste Hindus to avoid pollution by being overshadowed by or coming in bodily contact with a fellow urbanite who belongs to a lower caste or who is an untouchable. Nor can the high-caste patrons of city restaurants be sure that the food that they are served is prepared by a Brahmin cook. Nor can an urbanite be sure that the person who works next to him or her in the office or factory belongs to his or her caste because their work is not identified with a particular caste.

Nevertheless, as Indian city dwellers move from public places and work places to their homes, their observance of caste practices has changed little from what it was 50 years ago. Neighborhoods occupied by elite, middle class, and working class urbanites still tend to be differentiated by caste, and the city's untouchables are still segregated in the slum areas that are scattered throughout the city. Guests who are invited into city homes for dinner, with few exceptions, belong to the caste of the householders with whom they eat. What is most important, marriages between the urban young, no matter how Westernized their dress and the music and films they enjoy, are still almost invariably arranged by their families within the caste to which the families of both the bride and groom belong.

Given the imperviousness of the caste system to foreign influences, either Muslim or European, and its amazing staying power, it is no wonder that what V.S. Naipaul calls the "veneer" of British values that carried over into free India was so thin where it touched the caste system as to be almost invisible. Nor is it any wonder that even this thin "veneer" quickly disappeared as the process of Indianization advanced during free India's first 50 years. Neither the East India Company nor the British Crown made any attempt to interfere with or change the caste system. What is even more striking was the support given to the caste system by a radical Indian reformer like Mahatma Gandhi for whom British values were much more than a "veneer." Not only did Gandhi not call for the abolition of caste, but his program for alleviating the wretched lot of untouchables was, in effect, to bring them within the caste system. When Dr. B.M. Ambedkar, the most prestigious of India's untouchables because he played a major role in drafting its Constitution, advised untouchables to embrace Buddhism, Gandhi opposed him on the grounds that changing their religion would put them outside the Hindu caste fold. According to Gandhi, that was where they belonged.

The position that Gandhi took in this conflict with Dr. Ambedkar was based on the traditional Hindu belief that a Hindu should accept the caste into which he or she is born, not switch to another caste or religion which is more to his or her liking or offers a better life in the here and now. Here he was following the words of the *Bhagavad-Gita*: "Do thy duty, even if it be humble, rather than another's, even if it be great. To die in one's duty is life: to live in another's is death." The good life, for Gandhi, was to be faithful to the precepts and practices of the caste and religion of one's birth, a view that was squarely in line with one of Hinduism's principal theological underpinnings—the doctrine of *dharma*. Accordingly, Gandhi formulated the argument that the solution for the plight of the untouchables was not to convert to Islam or Buddhism or Christianity, but to remain Hindus. Gandhi appealed to caste Hindus, on their side, to give up their tradition of considering untouchables "unclean" and, instead, treat them with decency and respect. In this way, the problem of the untouchables would be solved, not by their finding a place in another religion, but by being given a place in the Hindu caste family.

When even modern India's greatest reformer, Mahatma Gandhi, supported the caste system, it was to be expected that it would undergo only cosmetic changes when Independence came. Backed by Dr. Ambedkar, a commitment to work toward a casteless society was included in India's Constitution, but no substantial legislative action was subsequently taken to move the country toward that goal. India's citizens were no longer obliged to identify for census enumerators the caste to which they belonged and it became unfashionable in enlightened quarters to append a caste label to one's name. In Tamil Nadu, for example, some Brahmins ceased to use the traditional caste appellation "Iyer" and "Iyengar." But underneath these surface changes, the caste system remained as alive and well as it had been for centuries. Even at the official level, where it was not supposed to be recognized, caste was made the basis for participating in the Central Government's "affirmative action" program. As a result, there was a scramble by members of some of the lower castes to take advantage of their depressed status and get themselves on the eligibility list for reserved legislative seats, government posts, and scholarships, even at the price of labeling themselves as one of the groups that were on the lower rungs of India's social ladder.

During the 50 years that followed Independence, the limited changes wrought in the outward appearance of the caste system by exposure to British influence completely disappeared. By the 1990's, caste was back to business as usual, with an influence on Indian society that was powerful and pervasive. It was the dominant force in the political arena, where candidates ran and voters voted, first and foremost, on the basis of their caste. Since it was difficult to form political coalitions because of caste factionalism, no strong opposition party had been formed to check the dominant Congress Party until the 1980's when the BJP burst on the political scene. It had taken India over 40 years to evolve a strong opposition party that could challenge the dominance of the Congress Party, and it remained to be seen in 1997 whether or not the rise of the BJP represented a step in the direction of the emergence of a sustainable two-party political system that a healthy democracy requires.

The nationalist fervor to free India from British rule had been a powerful enough political force to overcome caste factionalism and make it possible to form the Congress Party. The attraction of Hindu fundamentalism has played a similar role in bringing a number of castes together to create the BJP. Still, caste factionalism remains very much alive within both of the major parties, opening the way to rapid shifts in intra-party alliances. These shifts had already played a part in two relatively rapid and drastic reorganizations of the Congress Party under Indira Gandhi. They might lead to similar changes in the BJP that would give it a different shape and produce political consequences as significant as those which followed the conversion of the Congress Party into the New Congress Party and the conversion of the New Congress Party into the Congress Indira Party.

~ PART THREE ~

FREE INDIA'S FIRST
HALF-CENTURY PROJECTED

❖

Population and Food Supply

When one contemplates a milestone in the life of a nation, one is prompted to adopt a forward looking as well as backward looking perspective. Taking India's 50th anniversary year as such a milestone, what does the state of the nation in 1997 have to say about what its state is likely to be during the years to come? Writing during the late 1980's, Trevor Fishlock provides the somber highlights of what is still the current picture of the Indian scene:

"The new Indian today takes up his inheritance of a country where dreams that bubbled in the wake of independence have remained to a large extent unfulfilled. The unity and sense of purpose that fueled the push for freedom and made the years of struggle and transition seem like a golden age have faded. The fizz has flattened. All the good intentions of Nehru's 'tryst with destiny,' of making the people literate, better housed, bigger consumers, better fed and watered, less victims of their own fecundity, of mitigating the cruelties so many endure, have been corroded...

"Mahatma Gandhi's moral force and Nehru's ambition for the country combined in what seemed an unquenchable flame. Nehru suffered setbacks, but did not live to see widespread disillusion. Since his death, Indians have been ambushed by shadows, confronting with increasing dismay the realities and harsh paradoxes of their land, the sordidness of politics, the rule of greedy and endomorphic satraps, the spreading fingers of corruption, and inherited cruelty and brutality which persist unabated. The hopes of Gandhi and Nehru have been swiftly overwhelmed and a generation after midnight there is profound disappointment that so much appears ill ordered: politics, policy, poverty, and population...

"The green revolution can produce more grain and feed more people, but it cannot build the schools, hospitals, and roads which the new millions will need. Such failings as there have been in, for example, industrialization, production, communications, and power supply, might not be the basis for grave threats in ordinary circumstances. But India lies under the shadow of a phenomenal population growth, about which little has been done. This will increase economic pressures and intensify social rivalries and antagonisms in a future time when political authority may not be as complete and unchallenged as it is now."

Like all informed observers of the contemporary Indian scene, Fishlock points to the "phenomenal population growth, about which little has been done" as the "shadow" that casts a pall over India's future. Population growth in the mid-1990's was running at the rate of almost 2% per annum, and there were no indications that this rate would decrease during the years to come. As the population base gets larger, the continuation during the next decade of the current annual rate of increase will boost the annual increase in absolute numbers from the present figure of approximately 18 million to more than 20 million. If this upward trend continues unabated during the remaining years of the 20th century and on into the 21st century, India's population will reach 1 billion by the year 2000 and 1.25 billion by 2025. It is estimated that India will overtake China at the 1.5 billion level sometime between 2035 and 2040 to become the world's most populous country, a dismaying prognosis when one considers that India's land area is only one-third that of China. Whether or not India will be able to support a 30% increase in its already huge population during the coming quarter century will depend upon whether or not it can muster the will and the resources to provide the food, clothing, and shelter that hundreds of millions more men, women, and children will need to keep alive.

The pressure of adding that many more bodies to an already bulging population will be felt everywhere, but especially in the cities. Trevor Fishlock provides a glimpse of what India's future urban environment would look like in his description of the urban scene as it was before this major increase in population had taken place:

181

"The true Indian motif is not the Taj Mahal, the elephant, or the patient peasant behind the ox-drawn plow. It is the crowd, the ocean of faces in the land of multitudes, endlessly striving, pushing, moving. It is in this human circulation that one sees India's color, variety, and hive-like busyness, and senses its power, vitality, and grandeur, its near-inertia, its remorseless glacial movement, as imperceptible and irrevocable as continental drift... Indians have learned to cram, to take a deep communal breath, to admit just one more, to hang by their nails, to sit on one buttock, to stretch the seams of their streets, houses and vehicles."

With India's present urban population almost bursting the cities' seams, its future urban environment will become ever more problem plagued as the national population continues to grow. Increased population pressure will be felt especially in the cities because natural increase among city residents will be augmented by the rising tide of rural people who will migrate into the cities in response to growing population pressure in the countryside. During free India's first half-century, the pressure of increased rural population had been relieved by migration into urban areas, but this demographic safety valve will have greater difficulty playing its relieving role as the cities become more and more saturated with people. To use Fishlock's words, "stretching," "admitting just one more" cannot go on forever. Some idea of the magnitude of the numbers of people that would be involved as India's major cities continue to grow can be gleaned from the United Nations' estimate that the population of Bombay will increase from 15.1 million to 27.4 million in the 20 years between 1995 and 2015 and the population of Calcutta from 11.7 million to 17.6 million. What this will produce in the way of the worst cases of future urban population density can be projected from Bombay's present 150,000 per square mile and Calcutta's present 55,000 per square mile.

Faced with a non-stop population explosion, India would encounter an even more formidable task during the coming decades in feeding hundreds of millions more of its citizens. During the first 50 years of its existence, free India had managed to increase food production at a pace that kept up with population growth. This remarkable feat was achieved by exploiting the "green revolution," increasing the supply of irrigation water, and bringing more land under cultivation. But all of these resources for boosting food production have their limits, and, if the population increase goes on unabated during the next half-century, there will be the real possibility that the increases in food production that can be achieved during this period will not match the rate of population growth.

Because food grain production fluctuates to a significant degree from year to year depending upon the volume of monsoon rain, figures for the long term have more meaning than those for the short term. Nevertheless, recent production data cannot be ignored, and they are disquieting. According to the Economic Survey of 1996–97, output of food grains had increased substantially during the 1970's and 1980's, but the 1990's saw the rate of increase slow down. The result was that the average annual rate of population increase began to exceed the average annual rate of increase in food grain production. Although the difference was small (population up 1.9% and food grain production up 1.7%), what is troubling is the possibility that population will continue to increase at a more rapid rate than the increase in food grain output and that the gap between the two will widen. There are experts who would say that this is a probability rather than a possibility. One of them is Lester Brown, president of World Food Watch, who predicts that the shortfall in the supply of food grains will continue and increase in the coming years, to the point where, by 2030, India will have to import 48 million tons per year. Foreign exchange reserves are now at a record high, but they would have to be drawn down rapidly to pay for food grain imports of this magnitude.

A serious shortfall in the supply of food grains, if it develops during the near future, would be unlikely to bring on famine conditions. At the current level of population, food grains held in reserve are sufficient to tide the country over several years of deficient monsoon rains. But, as the population increases, a larger and larger food grain reserve will be required to counter a series of monsoon shortfalls. Before India's population matches that of China, the point could be reached where food grain production would not be high enough to feed its growing population and still set aside enough of the harvest to provide additions to the food grain reserves that would be needed to protect that many more people against food shortages caused by vagaries of the weather.

Even without famine conditions, a shortfall in the additional supply of food needed to feed a rapidly increasing population would produce more widespread and more serious malnutrition. At the 1997 level of population, continuing endemic poverty prevented the 50% who lived on the lower rungs of the socio-economic ladder from getting enough to eat. As the population goes up, there will be hundreds of millions more people in this condition unless food production is augmented at a rate which keeps pace with population growth and the additional food is distributed in a way that allows the poor to receive the share that they need to maintain their present caloric intake.

Discussing the possibility of a food shortage developing in the face of India's population boom inevitably brings to mind Thomas Malthus, whose 1798 "Essay on the Principle of Population" caused his readers to label economics "the dismal science" and who, coincidentally enough, taught at Haileybury College where the East India Company's recruits for service in India were trained. Malthus argued that there is an "iron law" which holds that when the food supply increases, the population increases more rapidly. Unless wars and disease reduce the population or families limit the number of their children, the population is brought back into balance with the food supply by famine and starvation. During its first 50 years, free India had avoided Malthus' "iron law" by increasing the food supply at a pace that matched the increase in population. Whether or not it has the will and the resources to succeed in carrying out this Herculean task during the coming decades is a real question. If it does not, it may well be that the "iron law" would not be enforced in its most severe form of famine or starvation, but it would still be enforced on the Indian people in the form of population reduction caused by deaths from diseases brought on by increasingly severe malnutrition.

❖

Government under Gowda and Gujral

In the world of politics, free India began its 50th anniversary year under a coalition government headed by H.D. Deve Gowda. The Deve Gowda government was backed by the leftist and low caste parties which fought the 1996 General Election as the National Front/Left Front, as well as by the Congress Indira Party. In order to keep Congress Indira Party support, the coalition government had continued to promote the free market economic policies instituted by Deve Gowda's predecessor as Prime Minister, Narasimha Rao. On paper, the ruling coalition was also committed to fostering programs that would improve the lot of India's poor and disadvantaged and develop the countryside by providing more drinking water, better communications, more educational opportunities, and improved housing.

Given the number of different parties with different ideologies, different agendas, different constituencies, and different leaders that formed the National Front/Left Front, it was difficult from the outset to see how the Deve Gowda government could implement a program that would keep all of these core backers behind it for very long. In order to accommodate at least a few of the 13 parties' leaders, the Prime Minister had already appointed a 37-member Council of Ministers and was planning to add even more to this unwieldy number. Increasing its fragility was the fact that the coalition government also needed the support of the Congress Indira Party to maintain its Parliamentary majority, and that support was contingent *upon* its continuing to encourage the development of India's free market and the private sector of its economy. Pursuing that goal in order to keep the support of Congress Indira Party MP's brought its economic policy into conflict with the ideology of the two Communist parties that were members of the National Front/Left Front. Walking a socio-economic policy fine line that was acceptable to both the Congress Indira Party and the two Communist parties might work for a time, but it seemed likely that, sooner or later, a misstep would occur. If the coalition government veered too far in the direction of free market capitalism that benefited mainly the elite and middle classes, it would offend the Communist parties. If it veered to far in the direction of a government-controlled economy that benefited mainly the working class and the poor, it would offend the Congress Indira Party. Losing the backing of either would mean the end of the coalition government.

Conflict over economic policy was only one of the issues that had a bearing on the question of how long the Congress Indira Party would continue to support the United Front government. Another was the working relationship between party leaders. Deve Gowda and Narasimha Rao had gotten on well together, even though they belonged to different castes as well as different parties. Perhaps the fact that they both came from South India—Deve Gowda from Karnataka and Narasimha Rao from Andhra Pradesh—gave them a common ground of regional origin that made it easier for them to forget their caste differences. (Next to being members of the same caste, being born and raised in the same place is the strongest bond that ties Indians together.) This positive personal chemistry disappeared at the end of 1996 when Narasimha Rao was ousted from the leadership of the Congress Indira Party and was replaced by Sitaram Kesri. Kesri was not only a hard driving politician anxious to replace Deve Gowda and become Prime Minister, but he was from Bihar, a part of Hindi-speaking India. On both political and personal grounds, then, Deve Gowda and Kesri were destined to have a conflict-ridden relationship.

The fat was thrown into the fire when, a fortnight following Kesri's takeover of the leadership of the Congress Indira Party, the Central Bureau of Investigation, which was under the administrative control of the Prime Minister, began to interrogate him. The explanation that was given to the press was that Kesri's assets appeared to be larger than could be accounted for by his legal income and that an investigation had been undertaken to ascertain whether or not he had received any ill-gotten gains. Congress Indira Party leaders immediately raised a howl of protest, arguing that the absence of a specific charge of corruption showed that the CBI was engaged in a clear case of political harassment and that Deve Gowda was behind it. The Prime Minister's Office denied that this was the case, but Kesri's supporters were not convinced and, for the first time, began to discuss whether or not the Congress Indira Party should withdraw its support from the United Front government. The stage was now set for the two leaders to engage in open warfare.

The clash between the two came on March 30, 1997, when Kesri presented a letter to President Shanker Dayal Sharma stating that the Congress Indira Party was withdrawing its support from the 10-month-old Deve Gowda United Front coalition government:

"The Congress Working Committee extended its support to 13-party coalition-United Front to form government at the Centre by a resolution dated 12th of May, 1996. The Congress Working Committee reviewed its decision on two subsequent occasions on 4th November, 1996 and 16th February 1997.

"In these two meetings, Congress Working Committee reviewed the performance of United Front Government headed by Mr H D Deve Gowda. CWC expressed its concern over the deteriorating law and order situation, drift in the economy leading to rising prices and unemployment, growing communal menace and lack of cohesive functioning of the government. The principle of collective responsibility of the Cabinet was completely ignored which is imperative for any parliamentary form of government.

"The very basis of the support of the Congress Party to the United Front Government led by Mr H D Deve Gowda was to contain the communal forces and consolidate the secular forces. This objective was reiterated in the resolution of the Congress Working Committee dated 16th February, 1997. It appealed to the United Front Government to critically review its own performance.

...It was stated in the same resolution inter alia—'CWC is constrained to note that the UF has failed to provide the leadership necessary to consolidate the forces of secularism and to confront the forces of communalism. In UP, Punjab and series of by-elections, the UF failed to work together with the Congress to contain the forces of communalism. On the other hand the anti-Congressism which was the main objective of non Congress political parties is still dominant in the constituent units of the UF. They have not come out of their old mooring.'

"I myself expressed our concern to constituent parties of the United Front and requested them to take corrective measures but unfortunately nothing happened. It appears that the efforts of the United Front Government headed by Mr H D Deve Gowda are determined to marginalise Congress and to allow the urgent national issues to take a back seat. The law and order situation of the country today has completely collapsed. In the state of Uttar Pradesh where the Central Government was directly responsible for its administration, the Union Home Minister was constrained to observe that the situation there was heading towards anarchy, chaos and destruction.

"The sensitive defense issues and security requirement of the country have not been properly addressed. There is an overall demoralizing effect in the civic services and in various organs of the government.

"Lack of coordination, direction and will to govern have created a situation of drift. Communal, divisive and separatist forces are raising their heads in almost every part of the country and there is no serious effort to arrest this. I am enclosing copies of two resolutions dated 4th of November, 1996 and 16th of February, 1997 for your kind perusal and ready reference.

"In view of the changed situation, the Congress Party is compelled to withdraw its support from the United Front Government headed by Mr H D Deve Gowda with immediate effect. I take this opportunity of requesting you to take such steps as you consider necessary."

That this momentous decision had been arrived at by Kesri and his hand-picked followers within the Congress Indira Party was made clear when the Party's Working Committee met after rather than before the submission of the letter to the President. Some of the committee members were caught by surprise and were not even in Delhi. Only 11 of the full complement of 18 attended. These 11 voted a resolution that stated that "the Congress Working Committee welcomes the decisions of the Congress President and leader of the Congress Parliamentary Party to withdraw support from the United Front Government led by Shri H D Deve Gowda. While appreciating the move already taken by the Congress President for staking claim to form government at the Centre, this meeting authorizes the Congress President and leader of the CPP to take appropriate steps for formally stating the claim to form government."

Upon receipt of the Congress Indira Party's letter and resolution, the President set April 11 as the day when Deve Gowda would have to win a vote of confidence in Parliament. After first insisting that they stood solidly behind him, leaders of the United Front changed their tune and tried to persuade Deve Gowda to resign. He refused and, in an embattled mood, faced Parliament. During the course of a 90-minute speech, he not only defended his government but attacked Sitaram Kesri for trying to engineer his downfall for no other reason than that "that old man" wanted to become Prime Minister. He expressed his determination to "rise from the dust and come back here" and defied the Congress Indira Party to meet the United Front once again at the polls where "a final judgment will come from 950 million people." His brave front was to no avail, and the motion of confidence failed by a wide margin—292 nays against 158 yeas.

Following the motion's defeat, Deve Gowda drove to the President's residence and tendered the resignation of the Cabinet of Ministers which he led as Prime Minister. Out of deference to the other United Front leaders whom he knew did not want to face an immediate general election, he did not recommend that the President dissolve Parliament. The President accepted his resignation but asked him to stay on as head of a caretaker Central Government until a new Cabinet of Ministers was installed. This was part of a stop-gap arrangement that had to be made in order for the Central Government to continue to function, especially in a situation where the 1997 budget had not yet been passed. The other part was an agreement among Parliamentary leaders that a special three-day session should be held beginning on April 21 to debate and pass that budget.

The April 11 defeat of the motion of confidence and the fall of the Deve Gowda government that followed appeared to be the beginning of what would become a sharp and continuing clash between the United Front and the Congress Indira Party, particularly when Deve Gowda defended himself with a vigorous attack on Sitaram Kesri, labeling him "that old man." But, in Indian politics, outward appearance and underlying reality are often very different, and that proved to be the case during the following days. The very next day Kesri contacted United Front leaders and told them that, if they would select a replacement for Deve Gowda, the Congress Indira Party would withdraw its letter to the President stating that it was abandoning the United Front government. On April 14 this position was made official through a resolution passed by the party's Working Committee. Neither Kesri's communication nor the Working Committee's resolution mentioned the party's claim to form a government under its leadership.

The United Front's first reaction was to state unequivocally that it stood by Deve Gowda as its leader and would not elect anyone to replace him. Before long, however, a split began to appear when leaders of its regional parties argued that, in order to avoid the danger of facing the electorate, the Front should accede to the Congress Indira Party's request. This split widened to the point where, by April 15, the United Front was ready to replace Deve Gowda, provided that the Congress Indira Party withdrew its claim to form a new government under its leadership. Although Kesri and the other Congress Indira Party leaders made it clear unofficially that they did not intend to push for such a government and were prepared to support but not participate in a United Front government, they refused to make the position official until a new United Front leader had been chosen.

What had emerged was a situation in which neither the United Front nor the Congress Indira Party was willing to budge, each waiting for the other to make a move. That stalemate was broken three days later when Kesri sent a letter to the President to the effect that the Congress Indira Party was willing to support a United Front coalition government provided the Front chose a new leader. Since the letter made no mention of the party's earlier claim to form a coalition government under its leadership, the United Front took this silence to mean that this claim had been abandoned and, accordingly, that it could now go ahead and elect a new leader.

Electing its new leader proved to be a contentious affair that tested the United Front's unity. The early front runner was G.K. Moopanar, the leader of the Tamil Maanila Congress (TMC) that had broken away from the Congress Indira Party at the time of the 1996 General Election. Prior to that time Moopanar had been a loyal Congress Party member for 40 years and had become a friend of Sonia Gandhi. It was this close connection with the Congress Party and the adult survivor of the Nehru dynasty that proved his undoing. The Communist parties, whose representatives, together with their allies, filled almost half of the United Front's seats in Parliament, were dead set against choosing a new leader who was so well disposed toward the party that had been their political enemy almost from the dawn of Independence. They also used as an argument against Moopanar's candidacy the fact that, as a Tamil, he was identified with South India, whereas the United Front needed a leader from North India where the BJP, the Front's communal enemy, had the greatest number of followers.

When the United Front could not agree on whether it should be led by a South Indian or a North Indian, it turned to a member of the Janata Dal Party who was identified with neither region but who had been born and had grown up in a city of British India, which, after Partition, had become a part of Pakistan. As a young man, I.K. Gujral had been forced to take refuge in India and had settled in Delhi, where he began a political career. He had been elected first to the Delhi Municipal Council and had served as a Member of Parliament from 1964 to 1976. He was Mrs. Gandhi's Minister of Information when she declared her Emergency but was ousted from that post when he refused to allow Sanjay to censor news programs on All-India Radio. From 1976 to 1980 he had represented India as its ambassador to the Soviet Union, and subsequently, for two terms, as its Foreign Minister. Having switched his party membership from the Congress Indira Party to the Janata Dal Party, his second stint as Foreign Minister had been under the recently deceased Deve Gowda government.

The day following his April 20 selection as the United Front's new leader, Gujral was sworn in as acting Prime Minister and was asked by the President to show that he had the Parliamentary votes needed to form a coalition government under his leadership. Gujral responded to his elevation to India's highest executive post by pledging to exercise that office for the benefit of the country where he had taken refuge when British India was divided:

"I bow my head in all humility before the people of India and I promise them one thing, that I will to the best of my ability give them a clean Government, a Government that serves them, and attends to the problems of India, which are poverty, backwardness, and the need for social justice."

The immediate political crisis caused by the sudden fall of the Deve Gowda government was now over, and it looked as though India would have a functioning Central Government when it celebrates its 50th anniversary of Independence on August 15. Looking back, it was clear that, despite the long litany of charges of malfeasance, misfeasance, and nonfeasance made against the Deve Gowda government in the Congress Indira Party's letter to the President, the fatal rupture was caused, not by a policy clash nor by a party clash, but by a personal clash between Deve Gowda and Sitaram Kesri. Kesri was determined that Deve Gowda should go as Prime Minister, and, when a United Front replacement had been chosen, he was ready to sign the Congress Indira Party on again as a supporter of a United Front-led coalition government that would be essentially the same as the one he had just scuttled. Although the March 30 letter had been followed by a Congress Indira Party Working Committee resolution staking a claim to forming a coalition government under its leadership, that claim had been quickly abandoned once it became clear that Deve Gowda was on his way out. As long as it had a new head, Kesri and his followers were content to carry on with Central Government "business as usual" because the alternative that frightened them was another general election in which their party would fare worse than it had in 1996.

That is not to say that the attitude of all Congress Indira Party leaders toward the Gujral government was the same as it had been toward its predecessor. Kesri had greeted Gujral's selection as United Front leader with positive words: "Mr. Gujral is an old Congressman, he is not anti-Congress. I am very happy with his election and hope he will be a successful Prime Minister." But some leaders below him in the party ranks were bitter toward the United Front parties for having refused to select the TMC's Moopanar, their preferred candidate. Their wrath was particularly strong because of the words that had been used by the Communist Party (Marxist) spokesman who had attacked Moopanar on the ground that he would be too friendly toward the Congress Indira Party, which the spokesman maintained was controlled by "an irresponsible leader lacking in commitment to the country and to Parliament." When he went on to say that "no one can trust Congress," a Congress Indira Party spokesman responded with strong words, accusing the Communist of indulging in "filthy, malicious propaganda."

Given the bitter feelings against the Communist constituents of the United Front and the uncertainty about the way in which Prime Minister Gujral would treat its outside supporter, the Congress Indira Party adopted a "wait and see" policy regarding the ultimate shape that its relationship with his government would take. The party had pledged to support the Gujral government but whether or not it would eventually become a participant would depend upon whether or not the demeaning treatment that it had received from Deve Gowda was converted into friendly collaboration. A first step in that direction was taken immediately following his accession to the Prime Minister's post when Gujral agreed with Kesri to form a coordination group, made up of five United Front members and five Congress Indira Party members, that would meet regularly to discuss and work out policy positions that were acceptable to both sides. Whether or not a second step would be taken was still unclear two months after Gujral's installation. As July dawned, neither the United Front Steering Committe nor the Congress Indira Party had appointed its members of the collaboration group, even though Kesri continued to affirm Congress Indira Party support for the coalition government.

The creation of this mechanism for furthering collaboration between the United Front and the Congress Indira Party, if eventually created, was one way that the Gujral government might function more effectively and last longer than the Deve Gowda government. Another was the different make-up of the new Prime Minister. He represented a reversion to the kind of political leader who had occupied that post in almost unbroken succession prior to Deve Gowda's accession. A member of a Keshatriya (warrior) caste from pre-Partition Punjab, he was not, like the Nehrus, a Brahmin, but his social background was closer to the top of Indian society than that of his predecessor. He was highly educated (a Ph.D.), urbane, and Delhi-trained, rather than a self-described "farmer" who had earned his political spurs at the state level. In addition, Gujral's long and successful career in diplomacy, although it might tempt him to spend an inordinate amount of time on foreign policy (he had said that one of his "burning ambitions is to sort out the problems with Pakistan"), has given him more of the people skills needed to hold together the numerous conflicting political parties upon whose continuing support his government will depend.

Despite these changes that augured for the possibility of a more stable coalition government, the bottom line is that the regime that will be making preparations for celebrating free India's 50th anniversary will be almost as fragile as the one it replaced, but for a different reason. The fragility of both grew out of their fragmented nature—a coalition made up of more than a dozen small political parties in the lead, supported from the outside by a single large party. Coalition governments of this nature can fall either because the leading coalition breaks up or because the supporting party pulls the rug out from under it. The downfall of the Deve Gowda government came when the latter happened. The greater danger for the Gujral government appears to be that it will fall victim to the former. Although some Congress Indira Party leaders emerged from the events of April 1997 bitter toward the United Front's Communist constituents, this negative feeling was not shared by the Party President and was not widespread enough to provide, in itself, grounds for a repetition of the fate that befell Deve Gowda.

What was more likely was that the collapse of the Gujral government, if and when it occurs, would result from a fallout among the numerous parties that constitute the United Front. Sharp conflict first emerged within its ranks during the battle over selecting Deve Gowda's successor, particularly between the Communist parties and the parties that supported Moopanar's candidacy. This conflict led in turn to the first open crack when Moopanar ended his TMC Party's role as a participating member and, in so doing, took with him four of Deve Gowda's ministers. No doubt, his party had only 20 representatives in Parliament and would have continued to support the Gujral government from outside, but this open crack in the solid front could have turned out to be the first of a series of rifts that would widen to the point where the United Front government fell. This was precisely the scenario that A.B. Vajpayee, the BJP Parliamentary leader, predicted would be played out during the months ahead. He forecast that the Gujral coalition government would soon reveal its true colors as the same old Deve Gowda coalition government led by a different standard bearer and that, like its predecessor, it would fall in short order. In making this forecast, he had quoted the aphorism that history unfolds as tragedy and repeats itself as farce.

A short time after Gujral's inauguration, it began to look as though Vajpayee's negative prognosis for the future of the new coalition government would prove to be wrong. The first small crack in the United Front unity was healed when Moopanar was persuaded to bring his 20 TMC MP's and four Cabinet Ministers back into the coalition fold. Since one of the four was Finance Minister P. Chidambaram, the 1997–98 budget was passed without difficulty and without amendment by Communist MP's who were critical of the special benefits which it conferred on the well-to-do. The following month, however, events took a decided turn in the direction that Vajpayee had predicted, but not for the reason that he had identified. He had expected that the stability of the Gujral government would be tested by a falling out among the disparate parties that made up the coalition. As it turned out, the test of its stability was triggered by a clash between leaders of the Janata Dal Party to which the Prime Minister himself belonged.

The trouble began when the CBI requested permission from Bihar's Governor to charge Laloo Prasad Yadav, Bihar's Chief Minister and the president of the Janata Dal Party, with complicity in the

$270-million "fodder" scandal. At the same time, the CBI reported that it was prepared to prosecute the Union Minister of State for Rural Affairs, a Janata Dal MP, for his participation in the scam but could not do so until his immunity was terminated by the Prime Minister's dropping him from the Cabinet. A chorus of demands followed immediately that Yadav should resign from his governmental and party posts and that the Prime Minister should dismiss the Minister of State. Loudest among these were the voices of leaders of the Communist parties which either participated in or supported the coalition government. Yadav turned a deaf ear to these demands, asserting that he was the innocent victim of a political conspiracy and that, backed by the Janata Dal Party and the people of Bihar, he would defy the Central Government to take action against him.

Despite this challenge to the authority of the Prime Minister's office and the assurance that he had given at the time of his inauguration, that he would insist upon "clean" government and would demand high standards of moral conduct from public officials, Gujral did nothing and said nothing to pressure Yadav into resigning either his governmental or his party post. Nor did he dismiss from his Cabinet the Union Minister of State facing prosecution. His only response was to say that the fate of those two public officials was a legal rather than a political matter and that he would not enter the fray on either side but would let the law take its course. Referring to the political fray arising out of the Bihar "fodder" scandal during the course of a speech he made on May 25, Gujral explained that, while he was against corruption, he was also against witch hunting, in particular "publicity-oriented investigations." His refusal to take action and his characterization of the CBI's actions as a "publicity-oriented investigation" elicited scathing criticism from both Indian press and politicians. An editorial in *The Hindu* asserted that "Mr. Gujral has not only exposed himself to serious ridicule but more important experienced the mortification of the office of Prime Minister losing its political relevance. His commitment on the floor of the Lok Sabha (lower House of Parliament) that his government would not protect the guilty and none would be spared may well come to naught." *The*

Hindu's questioning of Prime Minister Gujral's commitment to give no quarter to political corruption was strengthened a month later when he replaced the CBI director who had led the "fodder" scandal investigation, presumably on the ground that the director was too "publicity-oriented."

While the controversy over those involved in the Bihar "fodder" controversy continued at its height, the Gujral government decided to deliver on the Janata Dal Party's commitment to introduce legislation mandating that 33% of all legislative seats be reserved for women candidates. The result was an uproar in Parliament, the likes of which had not been seen for years. The Minister who attempted to introduce the bill was physically attacked and the Prime Minister was shouted down when he tried to open debate on the legislation. What was even more striking than the unprecedented uproar was the fact that the opposition was led by Janata Dal MP's. According to their speeches, they based their objections on the ground that the bill was deficient in that it did not contain within the overall 33% reservation specific quotas for women belonging to Other Backward Classes (untouchables and tribals) and minorities (Muslims). Since the Janata Dal Party's commitment to a 33% legislative reservation for women candidates went back to its 1996 General Election platform and the Janata Dal MP's now opposing the bill had said nothing up to this point about its deficiencies, it was hard to believe that their real political agenda was not a hidden one. Further evidence that this was the case was provided by the fact that these Janata Dal MP's were followers of Party President Laloo Prasad Yadav. Putting these two pieces of evidence together, it became clear that their undisciplined and disruptive tactics were a way of saying to the Gujral government: "Go easy on Yadav or we will see to it that your legislative program is stalled in Parliament and, even worse, that your government will fall because the Janata Dal Party will cease to support it."

The storm stirred up by the introduction of the bill calling for a 33% legislative reservation for women was weathered when the Prime Minister assured Members of Parliament that his government had no intention of rushing its approval and would allow sufficient time for the issue to be debated throughout the country. But its political repercussion lingered on, and they were serious. Not only did the Parliamentary incident provide further evidence of a growing lack of respect for the Prime Minister's office and generate more questions about Gujral's ability, not only to govern the nation but to lead his own party, but it also heightened the level of conflict that existed within his coalition government. The Janata Dal Party, which was its keystone, ended up at the throats of both the Communist Party of India, which was a member, and the Communist Party (Marxist), which supported it. The two Communist Parties had not only been most vociferous in their demands that Yadav resign and that he be prosecuted for his involvement in the "fodder" scandal but had also voiced strong support for a 33% legislative reservation for women. Both of these positions and the strength with which they had maintained them made them direct opponents of the Prime Minister's Janata Dal Party. Thus far, both Communist parties had kept this political bad blood under wraps in the interest of continuing the Gujral coalition government's life, but maintaining this truce will become more and more difficult as time goes on and the contentious political issues that produced such a high degree of conflict do not go away. Given the less than masterful role which he had played in dealing with the uproars that had occurred over Yadav and in Parliament, it had become more doubtful that Gujral would have the governmental stature and political presence to deal effectively with a "no-holds barred" clash among the components of his coalition government if it came. There was every hope at the end of June that the Gujral government would still be in power when free India celebrated its 50th anniversary on August 15, but how long it would last after that historic day remained an open question.

❖

The Congress Indira Party's Decline

When the Deve Gowda government fell in April 1997, the Congress Indira Party, which precipitated its demise, was not in a strong enough political position to win the number of Parliamentary seats required to form a Central Government on its own. The party had been in disarray since its defeat in the 1996 General Election and the resignation of seven of Narasimha Rao's Cabinet Ministers in the wake of the Jain brothers scandal. Narasimha Rao had managed to hang on to his position as Party President during the months immediately following the general election debacle despite his role in helping to bring that defeat about through his inept leadership. In July 1996, however, he was indicted as a co-accused in a criminal case that involved defrauding Lakhubhai Pathak, the major marketer of Indian pickles, to the tune of $100,000. This indictment came on top of two other cases of political corruption in which it was charged that Narasimha Rao had had a hand. In 1989, he had allegedly used his position as Foreign Minister in Rajiv Gandhi's government to order the Indian Consulate in New York to authenticate fake documents that would have proved that the son of one of the Congress Indira Party's political opponents was operating an illegal foreign bank account. He had also been accused of having participated in the bribing of four Members of Parliament to support his government when it faced a 1993 vote of no confidence.

Now personally accused in several political corruption scandals, Narasimha Rao had become more vulnerable to attack from those within the Congress Indira Party who felt that the party needed new leadership. These critics included six members of the party's Working (Executive) Committee who had gone so far as to demand his resignation. Narasimha Rao had responded by refusing to resign and by petitioning the court to discharge him from the Pathak case. When the judge refused to grant his petition, it became clear that Narasimha Rao would have to stand trial. A fortnight later, he was arrested and released on bail, awaiting the first hearing of the first of his cases. His political problem now compounded by a series of legal problems, Narasimha Rao had then followed the example of the BJP president, whom, ironically enough, he had earlier helped to undo, by resigning as president of the Congress Indira Party.

His resignation statement asserted that he was quitting as party president, not because he was a guilty party in the criminal cases, but for the good of the party: "The learned sessions judge has, by an order passed today, rejected my plea that the process issued against me in a criminal case be withdrawn. Even though the case is yet to be heard on merits, I have decided to relinquish the office of the Congress president. I am totally innocent and the allegations leveled against me are false, frivolous and baseless, and are intended to cause harm to my reputation. During the period I was in positions of power, including that of Prime Minister, I have not done anything violative of law nor have I done anything which might bring discredit to my Party or to my government. I have taken the above decision in the interests of the Congress Party and to avoid tension and confusion in the ranks. I have full faith in the rule of law and I am confident that all the allegations made against me will be proven false and without any substance."

The end of Narasimha Rao's tenure as Party President did not mean that his career as a Congress Indira Party leader was over, but it was approaching its end. He continued as the party's leader in Parliament until December 1996 when that last vestige of political power was wrested from him. Shortly after Narasimha Rao resigned, his successor, Sitaram Kesri, who had formerly held the office of Party Treasurer, had begun replacing Party General Secretaries who had been appointed by Narasimha Rao with General Secretaries who had left the party because of their opposition to Narasimha Rao's leadership. Since these General Secretaries also held seats on the party's Working Committee, these changes had not only weakened Narasimha Rao's position in the Party Secretariat but, more importantly, in its Working Committee. Kesri's strategy to also divest Narasimha Rao of the party's leadership in Parliament had come to a head in two meetings held in December 1996. The first was a morning meeting of the Executive Committee of the Congress Parliamentary group which passed a no-confidence motion calling upon Narasimha Rao to resign as leader of the Parliamentary party. Not surprisingly, Narasimha Rao had refused. In the afternoon a meeting of the party's Working Committee was held, which Narasimha Rao, although a member, had not attended. The Working Committee directed Kesri to take "appropriate action" to see to it that Narasimha Rao relinquished leadership of the Parliamentary group. When confronted by Kesri, Narasimha Rao had reluctantly agreed to resign his remaining party leadership post.

The death knell of Narasimha Rao's 70 years of leadership in the Congress Party and later the Congress Indira Party sounded on January 4, 1997, when the Parliamentary group elected Kesri as their future head. Although this political development received no attention in the foreign press, Indian newspapers gave it wide coverage, and for a very good reason. Narasimha Rao's total loss of leadership in both the government and in the Congress Indira Party marked, not only the end of his political career and the increased possibility that he would end up in jail, but also the driving of the final nail into the coffin of the Nehru dynasty. Narasimha Rao was the last confidante of the Nehrus who had exercised leadership in the Central Government and the Congress Party. He had been a faithful follower of Jawaharlal Nehru from pre-Independence days and had supported Mrs. Gandhi during her restructurings of the Congress Party. As a result, he had been given the important post of Foreign Minister in Rajiv Gandhi's government and had been installed both as Prime Minister and Congress Indira Party President when Gandhi's widow refused to continue the Nehru dynasty by assuming these offices following her husband's assassination. His close ties with the Nehru family were maintained during his days as Prime Minister in the form of social contacts with Sonia Gandhi that were so frequent that his political enemies accused him of getting Nehru family political advice behind the scenes. With Narasimha Rao's total demise, Congress Party leadership passed into the hands of men like Sitaram Kesri whose political influence was not based on membership in or close connection with the Nehru family.

On a personal rather than a political note, the chances that Narasimha Rao's political demise would be followed by his demise as a free citizen of India were greatly increased two months later by the confession of one of the participants in a 1993 bribery scheme. In July of that year, Narasimha Rao's government was faced with a no-confidence motion that it knew it would lose if it was not backed by four MP's belonging to a splinter party. In order to obtain their support, leaders of the Congress Indira Party agreed to pay each of the four 50 lakhs (approximately $160,000) for their votes. The bribe recipient who later confessed made it clear that Narasimha Rao was an active participant in the bribery scheme, quoting the Prime Minister as saying, "You please help us and I will also help you." After the four MP's had voted against the no-confidence motion and saved the Narasimha Rao government, they were escorted to a South Delhi bank where the bribe money was deposited in their accounts. The bribe recipient who confessed was told that the 50 lakhs which he had been paid "had been sent by the Prime Minister."

Although Kesri's strategy of purging Narasimha Rao's followers from positions of power in the Congress Indira Party and ultimately destroying Narasimha Rao as a party leader was carried out in the name of restoring party unity, its immediate result was to deepen factional divisions. No doubt, a number of disaffected leaders who had left the party during Narasimha Rao's days in power were brought back by Kesri's anti-Narasimha Rao moves and some of them brought with them splinter groups that were now ready to rejoin the main body. But the fact remained that the members of the party's pro-Narasimha Rao's faction were embittered by the ruthless way in which he had been ousted from the party's leadership. Their reaction was expressed in the words of one of the General Secretaries who had been dismissed: "Kesri has gone mad; in the name of unifying the party, he is bent on splitting the party."

The chances of the Congress Indira Party's overcoming these

handicaps during the remaining years of this century and taking control again at the Center appear slim. By 1997, the party had lost the idealistic vision that was imparted to it by founding fathers like Mahatma Gandhi and Jawaharlal Nehru. It had lost the mystique of the Nehru dynasty that had provided its leadership for 38 years and, in the process, had transformed it from a political organization into a personal following that had won overwhelming victories in the general elections of 1971, 1980, and 1984, and had kept it in power at the Center from 1991 to 1996. Last, but by no means least, it has lost the confidence of the Indian people who had come to see it as a party motivated by greed and the lust for power rather than by the commitment to pursue the nation's well-being with which it had taken up the reins of government when India became independent.

As the 1990's drew to a close, the best that the party could hope for at the national level was to become the leading party in a coalition Central Government. It had appeared that Sitaram Kesri was prepared to seize the opportunity to bid for this second-tier form of national political power when he led the April 1997 move that unseated the Deve Gowda government. Not only did this move succeed in putting the party in a prominent political position after 10 months of playing "second fiddle" to the United Front, but it also helped to heal some of the wounds that had been created when Kesri and his clique purged Narasimha Rao and his followers from party leadership positions. To the surprise of many foreign and domestic political observers, given the rift that had developed between the two factions, Congress Indira MP's on both sides, encouraged by the prospect of once again playing a prominent role in the national political scene, rallied behind their President in demanding that Deve Gowda must go as United Front leader and Prime Minister and that his government must be replaced by a Congress Indira Party-led coalition.

As it turned out, the Congress Indira Party's bid to lead a coalition Central Government was quickly withdrawn. Instead, Kesri and his followers contented themselves with continuing the role which the party had played during the short lived Deve Gowda regime—that of a supporter of a United Front-led coalition government. The fear of pushing its claim to the point of destroying its alliance with the United Front and opening the door to a general election overcame the party's impatience to rule once more in Delhi. That fear was well founded as was evidenced by the results of a public opinion poll taken at the time which showed that the party would win fewer Parliamentary seats in 1997 than it had won in 1996. Whether its fortunes at the national polls will continue to decline or will improve as a result of the more prominent political role that it played in bringing about the fall of the Deve Gowda government will depend upon the way it continues in its role as the indispensable supporter of a United Front-led coalition government and upon how successful it is in maintaining the unity within its ranks that it displayed in April 1997.

At the State level, 1997 brought no signs that the Congress Indira Party's political fortunes were likely to take a turn for the better in the near future. In the February election held in Punjab State, the party suffered its worst defeat ever in that State. Despite the animosity felt by many Sikhs against Indira and Rajiv Gandhi, the party which they had led succeeded in winning a sizable majority of 87 seats in the 117-member State Assembly when the previous election had been held in 1992. Five years later, the party, hoping to continue its control of the Punjab State Government, fielded 105 candidates. Only 14 won Assembly seats. Making its defeat all the more bitter was the political complexion of the alliance that had crushed them by capturing a majority of 93 seats. It was bad enough that the senior partner was the Akali Dal Party which had led the charge against mother and son Gandhi. Adding insult to injury was the presence of the BJP, the Congress Indira Party's principal political enemy, as the junior partner.

The Congress Indira Party's humiliating defeat in the Punjab State election was followed a month later by the loss of both its political voice and its party ally in Uttar Pradesh. The party's failure to persuade the United Front to back Mayawati for the Chief Minister's position in a coalition government, caused the Bahujan Samaj Party (BSP), which she led, to work out a "power-sharing agreement" with the BJP that produced a coalition government replacing President's Rule. Here again the Congress Indira Party suffered a "double barreled" blow. Not only had it been shut out from having any influence in Uttar Pradesh's coalition government, but the BSP, which had been its ally in the State election held in October 1966, had now joined forces with its arch enemy.

Further dimming the future prospects of the Congress Indira Party was its loss in the eyes of India's minorities of the political virtue upon which it based its claim for support against the BJP in the 1996 General Election—its claim that it was a champion of political secularism. This loss was well expressed in an article published in the April 11, 1997, issue of *The Hindu*:

"The Congress (Indira) is notionally secular but, functionally, it no longer qualifies to be a secular party. In the eyes of the minorities and the secular minded, it has lost its credentials. Mr. S.B. Chavan's disclosure of the complete inaction on the part of the then Prime Minister, Mr. P.V. Narasimha Rao, in saving the Babri Masjid (the mosque at Ayodhya) further compromised the Congress (Indira) secular credentials. In fact the Congress (Indira) commitment to secularism at least functionally, if not notionally, came under a cloud much before the Babri Masjid episode. From the early Eighties, Indira Gandhi had subtly inclined towards Hindus for their votes as she became unsure of the minority and Dalit votes. In the 1983 elections in Jammu and Delhi she was openly supported by the RSS, which considered her a Hindu leader. The RSS leadership preferred her to the BJP as she was thought to be representing the Hindu interests. This was the first serious compromise the top Congress leadership made to weaken the secular forces. Since then, Congress secularism never recovered and the minorities became more and more alienated."

Although the ousting of Narasimha Rao from the leadership of both the Congress Indira Party and its Parliamentary Committee had constituted "the final nail in the coffin of the Nehru dynasty," much to the surprise of most observers of the Indian political scene, that coffin showed a hint of life in the early days of May 1997. That hint took the form of the announcement that Rajiv Gandhi's widow, Sonia, had become a primary member of the Congress Indira Party. It caused a considerable political stir for several reasons:

- It came as a surprise because Sonia Gandhi had heretofore shown no interest in playing a role in the Indian political scene. Questions arose. Why had she chosen that particular time to become a party member? How far did she intend to go in making herself a force in the Congress Indira Party?
- It offered hope for a reversal of the Congress Indira Party's fortunes at a time when they had fallen to an all time low—with only 26.3% of Parliament's seats held by Congress Indira MP's and only 12.5% of India's population living in states with Congress Indira governments.
- It had an impact on the factional struggle within the Congress Indira Party between the Kesri and Narasimha Rao cliques.

There appeared to be a possible answer to the question raised by its timing. Since the announcement came a fortnight before the sixth anniversary of Rajiv Gandhi's assassination, his widow may have taken the step in preparation for observing that anniversary in a new and more political way. But that answer was brought into question when Sonia Gandhi did not attend the meeting which the Congress Indira Party's Youth Wing had organized to observe the occasion. The answer to the question regarding the extent to which she proposed to participate in party affairs remained even more of a mystery. She had become a primary party member, of whom there are approximately 2 million, rather than an active party member, of whom there are some 750,000. She could, of course, go on to become an active party member, and thus become eligible to occupy a party post and run for public office. But, given her Italian ancestry, her inexperience in Indian politics, and her lack of the language and oratorical skills, it was difficult to believe that she intended to play the part of an active party member. For the time being, it looked as though any influence that she might have envisaged for herself in party affairs would take the form of "behind-the-scenes" discussions with party leaders.

The only immediate impact of Sonia Gandhi's taking up party membership that was plain to see was the repercussions it had on the struggle between the Kesri faction and Rao factions. Kesri, who was now on friendly terms with Sonia Gandhi, welcomed it with glowing words: "The future of the Congress Indira is safely in the hands of the Nehru-Gandhi family." According to Kesri, the missing link between the party and the Nehru dynasty had been restored when Sonia Gandhi became a primary member.

Narasimha Rao's reaction was as negative as Kesri's was positive. His ties with Sonia Gandhi had been broken at the time that he had ceased to be Prime Minister. He saw her membership in the party as an asset for the Kesri faction and a threat to whatever influence was left to him and his followers. In order to counter that threat, he took the drastic step of trying to tarnish her image by tarnishing the reputation of her assassinated husband. A few days before the observance of the sixth anniversary of Rajiv Gandhi's death, Narasimha Rao gave a court deposition in one of the criminal cases in which he faced charges that accused Rajiv Gandhi of having ordered him to carry out the act of forgery for which he had been arraigned. In this way, Narasimha Rao sought to neutralize the political benefit that would accrue to Sitaram Kesri through his association with Rajiv Gandhi's widow.

Kesri's followers responded by castigating Narasimha Rao for his "dastardly attack" on the memory of one of the party's venerated leaders and a member of India's most illustrious family. As a result, the split between the Kesri and Rao camps widened, and the unity of the Congress Indira Party that had been strengthened for the time being by Kesri's successful ouster of the Deve Gowda government was once again threatened. It was impossible to predict as August 15, 1997, approached what the future impact of Sonia Gandhi's membership in the Congress Indira Party would be. Perhaps it would lead in the long run, as Sitaram Kesri had predicted, to a strengthening of the party organization. But this much, at least, was clear. Its short-run impact had heightened the degree of factionalism from which the party suffered, and this intensification of factionalism would be a source of weakness rather than strength if the party had to face a general election before the decade of the 1990's had come to a close.

This intensified factionalism did rear its ugly head a few weeks after Sonia Gandhi joined the Congress Indira Party, when the time came to elect a regular party president. (Sitaram Kesri had been filling that office since December 1996 on a provisional basis following Narasimha Rao's resignation.) For 47 years, the Congress Party had been able to choose its president by arriving at a consensus among party leaders because there were no factions within the party backing competitors for the post. But when nomination papers were filed on May 28, two party leaders, Sharad Pawar and Rajesh Pilot, precipitated a contest by stepping forth as opponents of Sitaram Kesri. Their actions meant that the days of party consensus were over and the days of party elections had begun.

Pawar was backed by the Narasimha Rao forces. Pilot did not have an organized following but, based on the fact that he was much younger than Kesri, he appealed to newer, "up-and-coming" leaders as a reform candidate. Kesri relied on the support of the party organization, which he had succeeded in bringing under his control during his four months as general secretary followed by five months as provisional president. When the voting took place on June 9, it became abundantly clear that this institutional backing was all that he needed to win an overwhelming victory. Pawar could muster only 888 votes and Pilot only 354 votes against Kesri's 6,224. Not only had Kesri won, but he had won by a margin that made it clear that the party strongly endorsed the actions that he had taken as provisional president, particularly his move to unseat the Deve Gowda government.

The outcome of the Congress Indira Party's first contested presidential election in almost 50 years showed that, as of June 1997, Kesri had a firm grip on the party's helm and that opposition forces had the backing of no more than a modest share of its leaders. But looking forward to the years ahead, that election takes on a significance that makes it much more than a routine party exercise in which the provisional president became the regular president. So far as the post of party president was concerned, two younger leaders had put themselves forward as potential replacements when the 82-year-old Kesri was no longer capable of leading the party. So far as the party was concerned, the election ushered in a new era in which its presidents would be chosen by a process of election rather than by a process of consensus. Future contests for the party's top position could not help but generate a degree of conflict and dissension among leaders and members that was not there during the days when consensus prevailed. The result could not help but be a further weakening of the party's unity and institutional strength. One could safely predict that, in the long run, the June 1997 election of the Congress Indira Party's President would turn out to be important, not because of its result, but because it was held at all.

❖

The BJP and the Specter of Hindu Fundamentalism

In contrast to the Congress Indira Party, the Bharatiya Janata Party was in a position by 1997 to increase its political strength during the rest of the 1990's and beyond. It not only had the momentum of a strong party on the rise but the image of a party which was committed to protecting India's integrity and sovereignty against insurgents at home and enemies abroad. As the party that had taken a hard line against Pakistan and pushed for increased defense spending and the development of nuclear weapons, the BJP was and would continue to be the loudest voice of Indian nationalism. Like the BJP, the strength of Indian nationalism was on the rise and, even at its pre-1997 level, had been strong enough to produce the hard line stand on India's part that prevented the nations of the world from adopting the Nuclear Non-Proliferation Treaty. During future years, the BJP's image as India's strong defender against internal and external threats would stand in sharper contrast to the perceived political weakness of the Congress Indira Party or a coalition of smaller parties.

Beyond the immediate world of political parties, two developments that were taking place within the country as a whole make the future prospects of the BJP bright. On the political horizon, the growing sense of national identity will encourage belief in the idea that, because India's traditions and culture grow out of Hinduism, India should be recognized and governed as a Hindu country and its people should follow the Hindu way of life. As this ideology of Hindu fundamentalism spreads, the BJP, which gives it a political voice, will gain support. Moreover, as India's economy continues to grow at a respectable pace for the next several years at least, the middle class will also grow. It was already evident from the results of the 1996 General Election that many of the new bourgeoisie were giving their political allegiance to the BJP, and, as the members of the middle class become more numerous, more Indians will be voting for that party's candidates.

It is important to note, however, that, although the BJP's rise during the 1980's and early 1990's to prominence had been spectacular, there are good reasons to expect that, while this rise will continue, its pace will slow down. The major factor that had brought the parties of the 1996 General Election's National Front/Left Front together and had given the Front common cause with the Congress Indira Party was their common realization that the Central Government might be taken over by the BJP and that they would fare badly under a Hindu fundamentalist regime. When the election was over and the BJP had won the most Parliamentary seats, the Front's MP's and the Congress Indira Party's MP's made it known that they would support any government but one led by the BJP. Atal Bihari Vajpayee, the BJP's Parliamentary leader, was appointed Prime Minister and asked to form a government, but his slate of ministers was never sworn in because he could not muster a majority of Parliamentary votes to support them. All of the other parties except the BJP's allies were aware of the threat to the continuation of their activities and influence which would be posed by a Central Government controlled by a Hindu fundamentalist party and, accordingly, were ready to do their utmost to prevent a BJP take-over. One may question the extent to which they were driven by the motive that they publicly professed—that they were fighting to preserve India as a pluralistic secular state—but there could be no doubt that they realized that their political futures depended upon keeping the BJP out of power in Delhi.

It is likely that this broad-based party opposition to the ascendancy of a Hindu fundamentalist party will make it difficult for the BJP to form a Central Government in the near future. The 190 seats which, along with its allies, the BJP holds in the present Parliament are a long way from the 273 that it would have to win to form a BJP government. But the BJP could take a step in that direction by winning enough seats in a general election to be asked by the President to form a government and then finding enough MP's from other parties who would support a coalition government that it would lead. As the Congress Indira Party weakens and as support for Hindu fundamentalism grows, the chances increase that the BJP would come to power in Delhi through a two-step process—first as the leading party in a coalition government and then as the party holding the reins of power on its own.

While such a scenario did not seem to be a likely denouement in May 1996 when A.B. Vajpayee could not muster enough votes to institute a Central Government under his leadership, political events that took place during early 1997 made it appear to be a real possibility, even a probability. First and foremost, the Deve Gowda government fell in April as a result of a clash between the leaders of the United Front and the Congress Indira Party. With the "top guns" of the two major self-designated "secular" political powers at each other's throats, the relative strength of the BJP as the communal alternative received a major boost. In addition, the fact that the United Front coalition government lasted only 10 months when India's two earlier coalition governments had managed to cling to power for two years showed Indian voters, not only that coalition governments at the Center of India's governmental system were fragile political creatures but that they were becoming increasingly fragile. The obvious political lesson from this display was that India needed a strong unified political party to take charge in Delhi. Given the weakness of the Congress Indira Party, the BJP was the only party that could fit this bill.

The prospects of the BJP's winning substantially more Parliamentary seats in the next general election were improved by some concurrent developments that strengthened its political position. The BJP president L.K. Advani, who had been charged in the Jain brothers scandal case, was acquitted. With its president's reputation as an honest politician restored, the BJP could resuscitate the claim which it had made during the 1996 General Election that it did not suffer from the corruption that plagued the Congress Indira Party. In addition to the boost that would come from an image of honesty that would appeal to all segments of India's voters, the BJP electoral fortunes benefited from political successes that it had achieved in two States by showing minority voters that, in spite of the fact that it was the party of the Hindu majority, it was ready to reach out to their constituencies. In Uttar Pradesh, it had worked out a "power-sharing agreement" with the BSP which was backed by that State's lower social orders and had accepted an untouchable woman as the Chief Minister. In the Punjab, it had helped the Akali Dal, the party striving for Sikh autonomy, to wrest control of the State government from the Congress Indira Party.

Internal squabbles that took place during the summer of 1997 within the parties that constituted its principal opponents at the national level also provided the BJP with an opportunity to strengthen itself for the next general election. The Congress Indira Party preoccupied itself during the weeks preceding the celebration of the 50th anniversary of Independence with a contest among its leaders over who should become its regular president. The Janata Dal, which was the keystone of the United Front's coalition government and political home of Prime Minister Gujral, did likewise. The only difference was that the struggle between Laloo Prasad Yadav, its president and Bihar's Chief Minister, and Sharad Yadav, its Parliamentary leader who had shouted down the Prime Minister when the latter tried to move the women's legislative reservation bill, was carried on with a great deal more bitterness. That bitterness became so intense that Laloo Prasad Yadav, blaming Deve Gowda for undermining his presidential position, organized a Rastriya Janata Dal splinter party which, although its emergence did not threaten the stability of the Gujral government, represented a further fragmentation in the opposition to the BJP. While the leaders of the BJP's chief rivals focused their attention on these organizational conflicts, BJP president L.K. Advani put his time and energy into leading a nationwide *rath yatra* (pilgrimage) that was designed to recognize the coming of free India's 50th anniversary celebration by a symbolic action that would recall the pilgrimages which Mahatma Gandhi had undertaken to make Independence possible.

Advani traveled with an entourage of BJP members to cities and towns in all parts of the country. The crowds that he drew varied in size, depending upon the State in which the meeting took place. They were sparse in Tamil Nadu where the BJP had little in the way of a following, but other States gave him a warmer reception. Wherever he spoke, Advani attempted to convince his listeners that the BJP alone had the energy and unity required to govern the nation, citing as his evidence the ongoing internal battles that he said sapped the strength of both the Congress Indira and the Janata Dal parties. When Muslims and untouchables were in the crowd, he tried to assure them that they had nothing to fear from BJP rule because, according to the party's president, a BJP government would pursue the well-being of all Indians regardless of their religion or caste. The degree to which Advani's summer 1997 pilgrimage succeeded in recruiting members for the BJP ranks outside the Hindi-speaking belt and among voters who were not caste Hindus would be seen only when the next general election took place. But, at the very least, it portrayed him as a national political leader who was interested in going to the people to win support for his party rather than one who cared mainly about holding or winning a power position within his party organization. Since his pilgrimage was managed and supported by BJP leaders and followers in all parts of the country, it also displayed a party that was unified rather than riven by factional differences. In both these respects, the pilgrimage took on the aura of a prelude and a preparation for the next general election campaign, both of which would foster the solidarity that the BJP would need to win the next national contest with the Congress Indira Party and the Janata Dal Party.

The first voter test of the future of the BJP that followed the 1996 General Election came at the State level during the early days of October 1996 when elections were held, following a stint of President's Rule, in Uttar Pradesh, India's largest and most populous state. Of the 425 seats in the State Legislature, the BJP and its allied party won 176, far short of a majority but considerably more than any of its principal rivals. The United Front won 135 and the Congress Indira Party, along with a party ally, came in third with 100. Immediately after the election results were announced, United Front and Congress Indira Party leaders agreed to combine their 231 seats to create a "secular" government that would forestall BJP rule. If this intention had been realized, the governmental situation in Uttar Pradesh would have been almost a carbon copy of the Central Government—a United Front-Congress Indira Party coalition put together to prevent a Hindu fundamentalist take-over. What had happened in the Uttar Pradesh State elections in October reflected the same political "handwriting on the wall" that had emerged from the general election. The BJP emerged from both as the strongest party, and, although a combination of "secular" parties had prevented it for the time being from taking over, the forces of Hindu fundamentalism which the BJP represented appeared to be only a step away from seizing political power.

As things turned out in Uttar Pradesh, the effort to put together a "secular" State government came to naught because the United Front and the Congress Indira Party could not agree on who should be its Chief Minister. The Congress Indira Party argued that the post should be given to Mayawati, a leader of the BSP, which had been its ally in the State election. Mayawati was both a woman and an untouchable. United Front leaders refused to support her, with the result that, even though the two parties had a combined strength sufficient to constitute a majority in the Uttar Pradesh Legislative Assembly, they could not get together to form the "secular" government which they had declared to be their objective. At this juncture, the Governor could have given the BJP, the party that had won the most seats, an opportunity to seek the support of enough MLA's from other parties to form a BJP-led coalition government. Instead, he sent a recommendation to the Central Government that President's Rule, which was scheduled to expire in a fortnight, be extended for another six months. As in the case of Gujarat, the Deve Gowda government saw an opportunity to wrest control of a State government from the BJP. It supported the Governor's recommendation, and India's largest and most populous State continued for the time being to be ruled from Delhi.

The political price that the Deve Gowda government had to pay for continuing President's Rule in Uttar Pradesh was much higher than it had cost to use it as a political tool in Gujarat. In the first place, its Constitutionality was much more questionable since there was no threat to law and order. Questionable Constitutionality was nothing new.

During Mrs. Gandhi's regime, President's Rule had frequently been proclaimed in a way very different from the intention of the Constitution's framers, who considered it to be an emergency measure rather than a commonplace event in the functioning of India's political system. In their mind, it was to be used only when a political crisis occurred within a State that threatened a breakdown of law and order. During the first 16 years following the adoption of the Constitution, it was used only eight times by Prime Ministers Nehru and Lal Bahadur Shastri. They had instituted it only in situations where the malfunctioning of State government posed a real threat to law and order. During the 11 years between 1966 and 1977, Mrs. Gandhi imposed President's Rule 39 times. The marked increase in the frequency with which it occurred was explained by the fact that Mrs. Gandhi used President's Rule to dismiss State governments which had come under the control of parties that opposed her Congress Indira Party and which refused to follow the dictates of her Central Governments. In the case of Gujarat, the Deve Gowda government could at least argue that, when the police had to intervene and bodily remove Members of the Legislative Assembly from the building in which they met, there was sufficient evidence of a threat to the maintenance of law and order to warrant the use of the Constitution's President's Rule provision. But no such evidence existed in the case of Uttar Pradesh. Here the BJP could justifiably accuse the Deve Gowda government of following what they called Mrs. Gandhi's "unconstitutional" tradition of imposing President's Rule in order to prevent an opposition party from exercising authority in a State where it had emerged from an election as the voters' favorite.

The BJP's wrath at having the Uttar Pradesh "stolen" from it by the Deve Gowda government was accompanied by the wrath of the Congress Indira Party whose support Deve Gowda needed to remain in power. The Congress Indira Party President attacked the United Front for blocking the formation of a "secular" government in Uttar Pradesh because of its opposition to putting a female untouchable in the post of Chief Minister. The party's leaders in Uttar Pradesh called upon the leaders in Delhi to reconsider its support of the government, but Narasimha Rao, although he was prepared to express verbal criticism, was not willing to take such a step. No doubt, the Congress Indira Party could have won back some of the untouchable votes which it had lost during Mrs. Gandhi's days if it had been willing to take the risk of fighting a general election for which it was not ready in order to stand firmly behind the recommendation of its Uttar Pradesh contingent that an untouchable woman should become that State's Chief Minister. Obviously, that risk was judged to be too great.

In the end, Deve Gowda succeeded in engineering the extension of President's Rule in Uttar Pradesh for a further six months and thus kept the BJP from taking power, but at the price of incurring the wrath of both its political friend, the Congress Indira Party, and its political enemy, the BJP. That this price was more than the political gain was worth became clear before the six months' extension had expired. In March 1997, the BJP and the BSP announced a "power-sharing agreement," under which Mayawati, a BSP leader, would assume the Chief Minister's office during the first six months of the year and Kalyan Singh, a BJP leader, would succeed her for the remaining six months. The working of the "power-sharing agreement" would be monitored by a panel of party leaders made up of L.K. Advani and A.B. Vajpayee, representing the BJP, and Kanshi Ram, representing the BSP. The creation of this panel was to be the first step in a process aimed at creating a consensus between the two parties on national political issues. Since BJP candidates had won 176 seats and the BSP candidates had won 67 seats in the State election that had preceded President's Rule, this "power-sharing agreement" gave the two-party alliance a majority of the 425-member State Assembly. Accordingly, a joint BJP-BSP government was sworn in, with Mayawati as its Chief Minister.

Although the Deve Gowda United Front government could still take comfort from the fact that Uttar Pradesh was not under BJP control, it had to face the fact that it no longer ruled India's largest and most populous State from Delhi. Although the Congress Indira Party could take comfort from the fact that the anti-secular political force represented by the BJP had not taken sole charge of Uttar Pradesh, it had to face the fact that, when the BSP agreed to a "power-sharing agreement" with the BJP, it had lost the political ally with which it had fought the State election. Adding to this political loss was the fact that the increased support of untouchable voters which it had sought to win at the national level by backing Mayawati for the Uttar Pradesh's Chief Minister's post had been stolen by, of all parties, the BJP.

The BJP's success in forging a partnership role in the government of Uttar Pradesh had been preceded a month earlier by a similar success in Punjab State. As a junior partner in the Akali Dal-led coalition government, it not only had a voice in the formulation of that State's policy but a link with a party that had the sympathy of Sikh activists throughout the country. Thus its political fortunes among the Sikh minority had been improved not only at the level of their home State but at the national level. There was a striking political irony in this development similar to the one displayed in Uttar Pradesh. The BJP, as a communal party voicing the cause of Hindu fundamentalism, would appear to be the political bête noire of minorities like the Sikhs and the untouchables. Yet, in the unexpected turns that Indian politics take, during 1977 at least, it had become the ally of the Sikhs in the Punjab and the untouchables in Uttar Pradesh.

Looking beyond Uttar Pradesh and beyond 1997, if a Hindu fundamentalist government headed by the BJP does come to power in Delhi, however much it might soften its Hindutva (Hindu India) agenda during the course of an election as a way of winning "secular" votes, it would be obliged to be authoritarian in order to achieve its ultimate goal of turning India into a Hindu state. Imposition of Hindu law and the Hindu way of life on a large minority like the Muslims and a small but militant minority like the Sikhs would inevitably lead to conflict and violence. Restricting or scrapping the "affirmative action" program, which had assisted a number of India's untouchables in moving up the political and economic ladder, would lead to unrest and agitation among that 15% of the population. Added to these political firestorms would be the defiance that a number of State governments, backed by their linguistically minded constituents, would display when, after a period of relative free wheeling, an authoritarian BJP Central Government tried to bring them under firm control.

Mrs. Gandhi's 1975–79 Emergency regime could well provide a model for such an authoritarian and repressive Hindu fundamentalist government: an all-powerful executive with Parliament and the courts under its control—opposition parties outlawed and their leaders in jail—press censorship and radio and television used for propaganda purposes. Adopting this model would commend itself because of the way in which, during the Emergency, the Indian public at large had quietly accepted a drastic reversal of the democratic political tradition that had been followed during the preceding quarter century. Such a Hindu fundamentalist government might even take a page out of Sanjay Gandhi's book and resurrect the family planning and slum clearance components of his crash program for reforming Indian society. After all, it was the Muslims and untouchables who had borne the brunt of these campaigns, and they were two of the groups which would be targeted by a Hindu fundamentalist regime.

V.S. Naipaul describes what he calls the "million little mutinies" which he saw going on around him in the India of the early 1990's:

"People everywhere have ideas now of who they are and what they owe themselves. The process quickened with the economic development that came after Independence. What was hidden in 1962, or not easy to see, what perhaps was only a state of becoming has become clearer. The liberation that has come to India could not come as release alone. In India, with its layer below layer of distress and cruelty, it has to come as disturbance. It had come as rage and revolt. India was now a country of a million little mutinies. A million mutinies, supported by twenty kinds of group excess, sectarian excess, religious excess, regional excess: the beginnings of self-awareness, it would seem, the beginnings of an intellectual life, already negated by old anarchy and disorder."

If, as Naipaul writes, there were a "million little mutinies" going on during the days of the relatively easy going Congress Indira Party regime led by Narasimha Rao, with an authoritarian and repressive Hindu fundamentalist government in control at the Center, the years ahead could see the number of "little mutinies" increase to several million and some of the "little mutinies" become "big mutinies". To keep the lid on this cauldron of unrest, a Hindu fundamentalist government would have to rely on the armed forces to suppress unrest and insurrections to an even greater extent than had previous Central Governments. Fortunately for India's future as a unified nation state, India's military establishment is strong enough to do this job. It is almost certain that the military would remain as loyal to a BJP-led government as it has been to the secular governments that had previously ruled India. Not only have the army, navy, and air force maintained the tradition inherited from the British of taking their orders from the civilian authorities and refraining from attempts to interfere in the political process, but the BJP has been the champion of the armed forces during the 1990's, calling for increased military spending and the development of nuclear weapons. The armed forces would not be inclined to forget their civilian political friends when these friends make up a Central Government that needs military muscle to enforce its decrees against recalcitrant minority groups.

India's armed forces could be expected to support a government headed by the BJP despite the fact that the largest ethnic contingent among both officers and enlisted men would be Sikhs and Sikhs would be one of the minority groups that would feel the weight of a Hindu fundamentalist regime. Although the largest group within the military, Sikh officers and men would still be less than 20% of the total force, and they would need the support of most of the Hindu officers and men who constitute the 80% majority in order to successfully carry out a military coup. In addition, Sikhs account for only 2% of the Indian population who would have to give its support to a Sikh-led military government if it were to take over from the BJP. It must be remembered that almost all of the Sikhs in India's armed forces remained loyal to Rajiv Gandhi's Hindu dominated government in 1984 even after Hindu mobs had slaughtered thousands of their co-religionists and the Rajiv Gandhi government had done nothing to arrest and punish those who had instigated the bloody mob violence. Having followed the British tradition of supporting the civilian government even in the face of such extreme provocation, it hardly seems likely that Sikhs in the military would try to oust a BJP government which was oppressing but not killing fellow Sikhs.

Playing the role of the military muscle that backed Hindu fundamentalist rule would mean that India's military would have become for the first time since Independence a permanent player in politics. Under the secular governments that have ruled India thus far, the military, since it has been used to put down insurgencies and riots which were sporadic in nature, had entered the domestic political arena only as and when needed. Under a Hindu fundamentalist government, the armed forces would not only carry out these ad hoc assignments but would have to stand by continuously in the wings as the back-up for an authoritarian and repressive civilian regime which would require their support if it were going to hold on to the reins of political power in the face of continuing communal unrest.

The other force besides the military, this one intangible, that would support a Hindu fundamentalist government confronted with "millions of mutinies" spawned by its authoritarian rule would be the sense of nationalism that has been on the increase during free India's first half-century. The growing number of "mutinies" scattered through the country, far from undermining, would add strength to this intangible force. Untouchables agitating and Muslims and Sikhs fighting to protect their rights would convince the caste Hindu majority that India's security was threatened from within as well as from without. They might even become convinced that there was a connection between the internal and the external threat. They might see the possibility of Pakistan taking advantage of communal unrest within India to launch an incursion into Kashmir or one of India's other border areas on the pretext of coming to the aid of their co-religionists who were being suppressed by the Hindu fundamentalist government. With or without such a connection, growing numbers of ardent Indian nationalists would rally round a Hindu fundamentalist government because they would see it as the protector of India's unity and territorial integrity.

The only part of the country where the Indian people would be unlikely to support authoritarian and repressive Hindu fundamentalism rule from Delhi would be the South, for two reasons. In the first place, the dismal showing of the BJP in the 1996 General Election made it clear that commitment to Hindu fundamentalist ideology was most widespread in India's Hindi-speaking North and Northwest. This coupling of Hindu fundamentalism with the Hindi language area would bring back to southern minds memories of the bloody anti-Hindi agitation of the 1950's. For this reason, southern caste Hindus would be much less enthusiastic than their northern counterparts about countrywide Hindu fundamentalist rule because they would see it also as Hindi rule. For those with a longer historical perspective, imposition of Hindu fundamentalist rule with a political base in the North and Northwest would bring back the specter of the age-old attempt of the North to dominate the South that goes back millennia to the time of the Aryan invasion of Dravidian lands. These short-term and long-term historical memories were, no doubt, one of the major reasons why the BJP won only six of South India's 132 Parliamentary seats in the 1996 General Election.

Secondly, the southern States, consisting as they do of the Dravidian language-speaking communities, make up the region where language-based political parties like the Dravida Munnetra Kazagham in Tamil Nadu and the Telegu Desam Party in Andhra Pradesh have their greatest strength. This high degree of linguistic consciousness feeds the desire of the State governments which are its political embodiment to exercise the maximum degree of autonomy vis-à-vis the Central Government. During the era of coalition government in Delhi, which, in all likelihood, would precede a Hindu fundamentalist government's coming to power, these and other State governments would have had a golden opportunity to operate with minimum interference from the Center. Were an authoritarian Hindu fundamentalist Central Government to come to power and crack the whip over them, the golden era of state autonomy would be a thing of the past. State governments like those in Tamil Nadu and Andhra Pradesh which are backed by linguistically minded constituents would probably display the greatest antagonism toward a Central Government that sought to take away the freedom that they had enjoyed in handling their own affairs.

It is impossible to say how strong these two political factors would be in fomenting South Indian opposition to a Hindu fundamentalist government in Delhi. At the very least, they would combine to make it more difficult for the Central Government to rule India's southern precincts. If the Central Government cracked down severely on the southern States to try to bring them into line, the widespread riots that could ensue would require paramilitary police and the Indian Army intervention to bring under control. Recollecting the mob violence and the police and army firings which took place during the 1950's anti-Hindi agitation and which resulted in hundreds of deaths should convince even skeptics that such a bloody South-versus-North scenario could be played out again during the years to come.

If it does come to pass, it is quite likely that South India's Tamils would play leading roles. They have a strong tradition of sectional and linguistic consciousness that goes back to E.V. Ramasamy Nayaker's Self-Respect Movement of the 1920's. This consciousness fueled Tamil resistance to the Central Government's 1950's attempt to make Hindi India's only national language and culminated in the rise of C.N. Annadurai's Dravida Munnetra Kazagham (DMK) Party of the 1960's, which began its political campaign by calling for an independent Tamil state. The DMK today controls the Tamil Nadu State Government.

Both the party and the State Government have a record of supporting the Tamil Tigers fighting for an independent Tamil State in Sri Lanka. Having lost much popular support because of their assassination of Rajiv Gandhi and having been banned in India as a terrorist organization, the Tamil Tigers are no longer openly backed by Tamil Nadu's DMK government, but they still have allies among ultra-nationalist Tamil groups. So, although it is not as bright as it was 10 years ago, the flame of the Tamil cause still burns in Tamil Nadu. If a Hindu nationalist/Hindi-speaking coalition were to attempt to suppress the Tamil people, the latter could take the lead in violent opposition to any serious attack on the autonomy of their homeland. These "freedom fighters" would have behind them a population of 60 million Tamils, many of whom would be prepared to shed blood to fight off domination by a Hindu fundamentalist government backed by Hindi-speaking North Indians. Such a convulsive political scenario may not become a reality, but, if it does, it will be much more difficult for the Central Government, even with the backing of the Indian Army, to contain than the unrest which today besets Kashmir, the Punjab, and Assam.

❖

Future Economic, Social, and Environmental Directions

Looking ahead to the economy of free India's second half-century, it is almost certain that, for the next few years, at least, Central Governments will continue to pursue the free market policies initiated by the Rajiv Gandhi government, expanded by the Narasimha Rao government, and perpetuated by the Deve Gowda and Gujral governments. Even though these policies were the brain child of the Congress Indira Party, they have been followed by coalition governments of which the Communist parties are members and for the simple reason that they have helped to stimulate the Indian economy and to produce remarkable growth in the country's GNP. A BJP-led government would be looking to the past for its political and social models, but, so far as economic policy is concerned, it is not likely that it would return to the socialist inspired and public sector dominated economy that had been the order of the day prior to the 1980's. To take such a step into India's economic past would be tantamount to taking a step toward political disaster because it would undo one of the few recent reforms carried out by the Central Government that had led to unquestionably positive results. In addition, continuing these free market policies would further the growth of the consumption-oriented middle class which had proved to be a rich recruiting ground for the BJP. All indications, political as well as economic, are that India will continue to follow its present course on the economic policy front for some years to come, whatever the complexion of the political parties in power in Delhi.

Despite the Central Government's following the old adage, "if it ain't broke, don't fix it," so far as economic policy is concerned, a future slow-down in the annual rate of economic growth from the

5–7% level achieved between 1995 and 1997 is likely to occur—for several reasons. In the first place, insofar as economic growth has been stimulated by the Central Government's implementation of large scale development projects, coalition governments in charge in Delhi would be too shaky to embark on major new initiatives that require solid political backing to get under way. A Hindu fundamentalist government, on the other hand, would be so preoccupied with keeping the lid on political and social unrest that it would not have the time and energy to focus attention on implementing extensive infrastructure or industrial developments like those carried out during the glory days of Congress Party rule.

Within the industrial component of the private sector, one serious constraint will be a shortage of the power needed to keep the increasing number of factories going at full capacity on a full-time basis. Already during 1996, the rate of increase in power supplies had fallen by 50% compared with the previous year, while the demand for power had shot up higher than ever before. By the end of the year, the shortage in peak power demand was estimated at 20%. On the critically important agricultural front, the rate of increase in crop production had also fallen. In fact, the Central Government's statistical office came up with a negative figure when it compared 1996's agricultural output with that of 1995. Here the problem was a shortage of water for irrigation. The Deve Gowda government had begun its tenure by announcing that one of its priority policies would be to improve India's irrigation facilities, but its first budget allocated only a minuscule share of total expenditures for this purpose. Continuation of such a ridiculously low level of effort on the part of the Central Government is not going to bring about the increase in irrigated acreage that India needs to produce the additional food required for its burgeoning population.

Acting as a millstone slowing down production gains in both the industrial and agricultural sectors will be the growing deterioration of free India's transportation infrastructure, described as follows by the American University's Country Study:

"The transportation system sector has many shortages...despite its importance in moving goods and passengers over large areas... By the early 1980's, many parts of the transportation system were barely meeting current requirements, let alone preparing for further economic growth. Many roads...were breaking up because of over-use and lack of sufficient maintenance, and the railroads required track renewal and replacement of overage rolling stock. Ports needed equipment and facilities, such as that for bulk and container cargo, while the national civil airlines needed supporting equipment, such as that for instrument landings at many airports. Planners were aware of the problems, but the transportation system's requirements far exceeded funds available... Transportation bottlenecks could emerge within a period of sustained economic growth."

Official estimates of the funds needed to make good these infrastructure deficiencies run to very high figures. According to these estimates, $130 billion would have to be spent over the next five years and a total of $200 billion during the next decade. One of the major transportation bottlenecks is the inefficient operation of India's 11 major ports and 23 minor ports. This is a particularly serious transportation deficiency because it impedes shipments of the exports from which the country earns badly-needed foreign exchange. To make it possible for these ports to handle cargo in an efficient manner before the next decade comes to a close will cost $8 billion. Since it is obvious that India cannot raise such large capital funds within its borders, government officials are actively wooing foreign companies that are involved in trade with India to convince them that it is in their interest to put up the money needed to make that trade move more expeditiously. The degree to which its transportation infrastructure meets the future needs of India's expanding economy will depend to a crucial degree upon the success that is achieved in persuading foreign investors to underwrite the cost of putting it in working order.

Although statistical data for portions of one year are not sufficient to establish a long-term trend, they do provide a straw in the wind that could foreshadow some longer term negative economic developments. Industrial growth during the first half of the 1995–96 fiscal year was 9.8% compared with 12.1% during the first half of the 1994–95 fiscal year, and the increase in exports fell from 24% to 6.4%.

If one looks at the third quarter of 1996 alone, the declines were more dramatic. Both industrial production and exports fell by 50% compared with the third quarter of 1995. What is more, these declines had an impact on the prices which Indians had to pay for goods and services. Despite the rapid increase in economic activity that had characterized the early and mid-1990's, the rate of inflation had remained moderate at about 5%. During 1996, however, it steadily increased, and, by the end of December, had approached 8%. No doubt this higher rate is still in the moderate range, but, if this upward trend continues on the 1996 scale or, even worse, if the pace increases, a serious inflation problem would tarnish the bright prospects that otherwise characterize India's future economic development.

On the general social front, coming decades are unlikely to see any major change in the 1990's status quo. The middle class will continue to grow along with economic development, and India will proceed further in the direction of becoming a consumer society. But, since the "trickle down" theory does not work in India any more than it does in any other country, the poor will remain as poor, and there will be many more of them. To make any dent in India's widespread and chronic poverty would require, not only economic development, but major public sector programs to provide the educational opportunities, the health services, and the decent housing that the poor need if they are going to be able to take advantage of improved economic conditions. Neither a coalition government nor a Hindu fundamentalist government ruling at the Center is likely to have the power, the will, and the resources needed to undertake socio-economic reform on the massive scale that would be required to make good these deficiencies. In this regard, the Deve Gowda government's 1996–97 budget was a straw in the wind. Even though the government had said that it was committed to improving the lot of the poor, its first budget included appropriations for education, health services, and housing for slum dwellers that, taken together, constituted less than 1% of total budget outlays.

The one exception to the general rule that the coming years will see a continuation of the social status quo, could come in the area of "affirmative action." Since the BJP has been on record since its early days as opposing any increase in the number of legislative seats, governments posts, and scholarships reserved for members of "backward and scheduled castes and tribes," an increase in that party's political influence will probably lead to cutbacks in this long-standing program for uplifting the untouchable and tribal segments of India's population. The BJP's coming to power in Delhi could spell its death. In that case, Indian society would have changed, but in a negative direction because the status of the downtrodden and the dispossessed would have worsened rather than improved. Ending that program would not only prevent individual untouchables and tribals who could take advantage of "affirmative action" from improving their economic and political lot but would also send a message to all untouchables and tribals that caste Hindus were set on keeping them in their place as the pariahs of Indian society.

Supporters of India's "affirmative action" program might have thought that its immediate future was in good hands when the Deve Gowda government declared that it intended, not only to keep it alive, but to extend its coverage to all of the poor segments of the population. The political reality is that it would be a mistake to treat such commitments as anything more than a statement of good intentions. It would be almost impossible for a shaky coalition government to overcome the fierce political opposition that would be mounted by the elite and middle class who would see themselves as the victims of an even greater measure of "reverse discrimination" because they were the only segment of the population who could not enjoy the benefits of "affirmative action." Given this hard fact of political life, it is almost certain that a pronouncement by any present or future coalition Central Government that it intended to enlarge the scope of "affirmative action" will fall into the category of fine words that are not followed by the actions needed to make them a reality.

Just as the Central Governments that lead India into the 21st century are likely, with the exception of the "affirmative action" program, to pursue policies that maintain the present social order, so too are they likely to follow the status quo course with respect to the environment. In this crucially important sphere of public policy, maintaining the status quo would mean doing little or nothing to control pollution or make good the environmental damage that has already occurred. The result in the country as a whole, and especially in the cities, will be that water and air quality will deteriorate further and more solid waste will accumulate. What is more, the rate of increase in the environmental damage occurring in all three of these problem categories will go up as the population continues to explode and industrial and agricultural development proceeds without environmental controls and environmental repair.

❖

Eschatology and Survival

If India continues to move in these directions on the demographic, political, social, and environmental fronts, what destiny is likely to lie ahead for its people as they live out the second half-century of freedom from colonial rule? The danger of the 1950's, when free India was new and fragile—when regional linguistic divisions shook the land—was that the country would explode, that the process of dividing British India that had begun with Partition would continue and that a collection of autonomous language-based states rather than a unified nation state would emerge. During all of his years in office, Jawaharlal Nehru had constantly warned fledgling India about the danger to national unity posed by what he labeled "fissiparous tendencies." He battled them until his dying day, and that was one of the reasons why the contentious linguistic regions of India stayed together.

That danger is now past. India is firmly established as a unified nation state. The danger that lies ahead is the opposite one, not that India will explode but that India will implode—that under the weight of a burgeoning population, a weak or repressive government that does not come to grips with worsening economic and social problems, and an environment that is moving toward the uninhabitable, the country will fall in on itself and become saturated, stagnated, gridlocked. Since the threat of this danger is presently most apparent in India's major cities, one might describe an imploded India as "Calcutta writ large." What that would look like has been graphically described by V.S. Naipaul:

"In richer countries, where people could create reasonably pleasant home surroundings for themselves, perhaps, after all, public squalor was bearable. In India, where most people lived in such poor conditions, the combination of private squalor and an encompassing squalor outside was quite stupefying. It would have given people a low view of their needs—air, water, space for stretching out—but it must also have given them a low idea of their possibilities, as makers or doers. Some such low idea of human needs and possibilities would surely have been responsible for the general shoddiness of India's industrial goods, the ugliness and unsuitability of so much post-independence architecture, the smoking buses and cars, the chemically treated streets, the smoking of factories. 'Everybody's suffering here,' a famous actor said at a dinner one evening. And that simple word…was like an illumination.

"For years and years, and even during the time of my first visit in 1963, it had been said that Calcutta was dying, that its port was silting up, its antiquated industry dying. But Calcutta hadn't died. It hadn't done much, but it had gone on; and it occurred to me that the prophecy had been excessive. Now it occurred to me that this is what happened when cities died. They didn't die with a bang; they didn't die when they were abandoned. Perhaps they died like this; when everybody was suffering, when transport was so hard that people gave up jobs they needed because they feared the suffering of the travel; when no one had clean water or air and no one could go walking. Perhaps cities died when they lost the amenities that cities provided, the visual excitement, the heightened sense of human possibilities, and became places where there were too many people and people suffered."

If V.S. Naipaul sounds too dismal, too pessimistic, the skeptic can turn to the views of another perceptive observer of the contemporary Indian scene, Ved Mehta, and he will find the writer saying much the same thing. Mehta is writing about Delhi during the 1980's but, in describing its state, he refers to Calcutta: "The city as a whole seemed run down, discouraged, sickly and the situation in other Indian cities was worse. It is as if Calcutta were a sign of the country's future."

This is how Mehta had reacted to Calcutta during an earlier visit:

"I know I cannot accept Calcutta… The perception that Calcutta forces on me is not the fact of death, which perhaps I can accept, but of the process of dying, possibly the dying of an entire population, for Calcutta's spreading population, like the slow strangulation of the

Hooghly River, foreshadows something more frightening than personal death; it forebodes racial extinction... I ask myself how the species could have reached such a point of degradation and yet have adapted itself to that degradation; for the adaptation seems to show only how the will to survive bends us downward."

What is striking about these descriptions of contemporary Calcutta is that both writers use the word "dying." If it sounds extreme—too gloomy, too bleak—to conjure up the image of "death" in writing about the future of India's major cities, one need only remind oneself that history provides numerous examples of cities and countries that had "died" because they were no longer places where their inhabitants could lead a decent life—because they had been overwhelmed by their demographic, political, economic, social, and environmental problems. In some cases, they had ceased to be, but, in other cases, they had remained in existence because their inhabitants had continued to live on in them but had suffered in the process.

It is the danger of moving toward the latter kind of "death" that India faces as it embarks on its second half-century. If it does enter that state, it is the cities that would have led the way. The degradation of life that characterizes today's major cities, described by Naipaul and Mehta, would have spread to the smaller cities and towns. The countryside would have followed as the cities and towns found it more and more difficult to absorb the exploding rural population. Life would go on, but India would have become a country where, in the words of the famous actor whom Naipaul quotes, "Everybody's suffering here."

When one contemplates a dismal future for a country, questions inevitably come to mind: How could its people tolerate such an outcome? Would they not reform their country and deal with its problems before things got that bad? If reform did not occur in time, would they not revolt against the emergence of living conditions that they would consider to be intolerable? In the case of India, based on the long history of the Indian people, the answer to these questions appears to be that it would put up with living as an imploded country, that its people would neither reform it nor revolt against its deleterious quality of life. The "millions of little mutinies" about which Naipaul writes would continue and even increase, but they would take the form of numerous but scattered parochial groups carrying on separate and distinct struggles for a bigger piece of the shrinking political, economic, social, and environmental pie, not a widespread revolt by the people as a whole aimed at increasing the size of the pie so that all groups could have a larger piece. India is not a country where such mass revolts take place because, as Trevor Fishlock points out:

[its people] "have frenzies from time to time and dreadful and bloody ones at that, but no decent long lasting rage, an anger that could be channeled into reform... India's soil is too thin for revolution. It is not a place for mass movements and a determined common purpose... And in its history its people have not often linked arms. India is a land of communities and clans and, therefore, of wariness and mistrust in personal dealings... In keeping their distance and upholding their myriad demarcations, in concentrating on their immediate circles and on themselves, Indians have learned to disregard others... India can be a place of sudden and terrifying violence. Caste and communal stress create an explosive vapor. But India is like the ocean. The waves clash on the surface when storms blow, but the great body of dark water moves relentlessly."

Rather than reform or revolt in an attempt to head off the development of a national state of entropy, "Indians", to quote Ved Mehta, " have a way of living with their problems." They have this ability because, on the religious side of their lives, they have the Hindu religion and, on the cultural side, they have the caste system. Mehta and Fishlock cite these as constituting the intangible and tangible resources which the Indian people use to carry on under the most adverse living conditions. Mehta stresses the role of the caste system: "It may be that the extremely rigid hierarchy of three thousand or more castes and sub-castes in Hinduism—a hierarchy that, although it has always been a pernicious force throughout the society, has always been a source of stability for more than twenty-five hundred years—can play a part in keeping the country together."

Fishlock emphasizes the passivity and fatalism that Indians derive from their Hindu religion:

"For millions of Indians, village life may be brutal, anxious, and violent, with its strong emphasis on caste, its poverty, frustrated hopes, and the ill-treatment of the weak by the strong. There are, therefore, the conditions for revolution, but the poor have never shown any interest in revolt. The passivity of the country people is part of India's easy going massiveness: religious beliefs, the conditions of life, the prod of the police *lathi*, dampen volatility. Fatalism yokes men uncomplainingly to their plows, their lot in life being what they earned in their last existence, their hope in this life being for enough to eat."

Fishlock writes specifically of the 70% of the population who are "country people," but what he has to say applies as well to the millions of poor people who inhabit India's cities. Geographically speaking, they are urbanites, but, socially and religiously speaking, they are predominantly "country people" living in urban surroundings. Even though the physical conditions in which they live are, generally speaking, worse than those that make up the environment of ruralites, thus giving them a greater incentive than their country cousins to revolt against their lot, the urban poor are just as inclined to "live with their problems." Almost all of them are migrants or the children or grandchildren of migrants from the countryside who have brought with them into the city and perpetuated there the Hindu world-view and the caste-based social system that were the foundations of the rural world from which they came. As a result, they share the passivity and fatalism of the country people whom Fishlock describes.

Most of the urban poor, poor as they are, are better off economically than the relatives whom they left behind in their native villages. No doubt, they work at the lowest paying jobs that the city has to offer and, consequently, live at a subsistence level but, unlike American slum-dwellers, they do not suffer from high rates of unemployment. As a matter of fact, some cities show a higher rate of unemployment among the lower ranks of the middle class than among slum-dwellers. The major economic problem of the poor is, not unemployment, but the fact that they are underemployed— underemployed in the sense that they work at low-productivity, and, therefore, low-paying jobs. As a result, they suffer from poverty, not from the resentment and anger that come from sitting around all day with nothing to do but contemplate their misery. Without this anger and resentment to drive them, they are no more inclined to revolt than are the rural poor.

If the prognosis that India faces the danger of entering a state of national entropy during its second half-century were being spelled out from a traditional Indian point of view, it might be said that its future was in the hands of the heavenly bodies and that, if they ordain such a bleak destiny, the Indian people can do nothing to avoid it. But since this prognosis has emerged from looking at the Indian scene from a Western point of view, it has to be followed by saying that India's future is not preordained and that a state of national entropy can be avoided if its people undertake the radical demographic political, economic, social, and environmental reforms that would be necessary to reverse the downward slide of its first half-century. Having said this, one would have to go on and say that, while these reforms could conceivably take place, it would be an historical miracle of the first order, given the state of the nation in 1997, if they became a reality. The actions that would be required would be sweeping in scope and revolutionary in nature because they would involve, not only turning around much of what had transpired during free India's first half-century, but also going against what is in the religious mind and social bones of its people. While such an historical miracle could happen, it is the nature of miracles that they do not occur much more often than they do.

During the 1950's, as free India was beginning its first half-century, it looked as though its end, if it came, would be explosive—that India would break up into a collection of linguistic states. In 1997, as free India marks the end of that half-century, it looks as though its end, if it comes, will be implosive—that the country would have become engulfed by demographic saturation, political and economic stagnation, social gridlock, and environmental decay. Since this study of the history of free India began with a line of poetry—"But where are the snows of yesteryear?"—it might be appropriate to approach its close with some poetic images that express what has just been said but with fewer words and in a more evocative way. When I first came to India in 1952, it was thought that, if free India came to an end, it would be with a "bang." When I revisited India in 1996 and saw what had happened during its first half-century, it seemed to me that free India would end, if it ended, with a "whimper," a state of national life where, in the words of the actor whom V.S. Naipaul met in Calcutta, "Everybody's suffering here." The metaphor at the heart of that personal reflection was obviously produced by my remembering the well-known words with which T.S. Eliot closed his poem, *The Hollow Men*:

"This is the way the world ends,

This the way the world ends

Not with a bang but a whimper."

In my mind, Eliot's words could be easily paraphrased to describe free India's end if what had transpired there during its first half-century continued to be the story of its second half-century:

This is the way India ends,

This is the way India ends

Not with a bang but a whimper."

India's "whimper" would take the form of a national chorus of people from all walks of life who were, in varying ways and to varying degrees depending on their socio-economic status, suffering. That final state could be characterized for the people as a whole in another way by using some words that are less poetic but still well-known. These words were written not, like Eliot's, about the world in general but specifically about India. John Kenneth Galbraith, then the American ambassador, described the India of the early 1960's as a "functioning anarchy." Galbraith's India was much like the India of the previous decade to which I had been introduced when I first arrived in the country, but, by the 1960's, I would not have used the word "anarchy" to describe it. Galbraith was looking at the surface of Indian life and saw it to be disorganized and chaotic but, in a way that was very different from the Western world, orderly. Having, by Galbraith's time, lived and worked in India for 10 years, I could see far enough below the surface to know that, at the deeper level of social and cultural life, it was not disorganized and chaotic. So I would not have agreed with him in characterizing it as an "anarchy." On the other hand, I would have agreed with him that what he saw was "functioning"—that, although it had a long way to go, the India of the 1950's and the early 1960's was moving, albeit slowly and haltingly, toward the day when all its people would have a better life.

Looking to the future from the perspective of 1997, it seemed clear that neither of the terms that Galbraith used to describe the India of his days in Delhi would apply to free India during its second half-century if the trends of its first half-century continue. Indian society and culture would still not be an "anarchy" any more than they were during the early 1960's, but India would no longer be "functioning." It would no longer be "functioning" because it would be moving, not toward a good life for all its people, but toward a life in which all segments of its population, rich and middle class and poor alike, each in its own way and to its own degree, would be suffering.

From the perspective of 1997, a trouble-ridden prognosis for free India's future seemed inescapable—that, barring the implementation of a program of reform that is sweeping in scope, revolutionary in depth, and sustained in duration, India's people will be moving toward a state of national entropy. They will, in a word that is used by both Trevor Fishlock and Ved Mehta, "bend" and live on in this state as they have tolerated their difficult lot for centuries. The process of Indianization that developed during free India's first half-century will continue and grow stronger as the years go by because that process is rooted in the Hindu religion that has always been and continues to be the wellspring of Indian culture. According to the Hindu world view, the Indian people should expect a life of suffering in an unreal world. The only way they can convert this suffering into happiness is to escape into the reality of *nirvana*. The only way they can achieve *moksha* (escape) is to accept the sufferings inflicted by living in a state of *maya* and follow the *dharma* (duty) which their *karma* (destiny) has imposed upon them, difficult as that may be.

In the "tryst with destiny" speech which he delivered when the British flag was lowered over the Red Fort in Delhi and replaced by the flag of free India, Jawaharlal Nehru proclaimed that a new India had been born and that it had replaced the old India. This new India, according to Nehru, would not accept the pessimistic and enervating view of India's worldly lot that had characterized the world view of the old India. It would believe that its destiny did not depend on the alignment of the stars and planets but on the will and actions of its people. It would believe that its people could combine their efforts and build a better life for all. It would believe that the answer to India's predicament was not escape but reform.

The history of free India's first half-century has shown that Nehru was mistaken in thinking that, when India became independent, the old India had passed away and that a new India had been born. He made that mistake because he believed that the soul of India, when it had been freed from foreign suppression, would become enshrined in the new India. In reality, India's soul had all along been enshrined in the old India. So it was not surprising that, during the years that followed Nehru's August 15, 1947, speech, the old India gradually blotted out the new. The worldly goal of the new India, according to Nehru, was to build a humane and prosperous society that would provide a good life for all its people. The worldly goal of the old India was not to remake the world of India but to make the best that it could of its sufferings. Looking back over the 50 years that have elapsed since Nehru spoke to the world from above the gate of the Red Fort in Delhi, one would have to say that, during these five decades, the worldly goal of the new India had been eclipsed by the worldly goal of the old India. Looking forward toward the next 50 years, one would have to say that India will do a better job of achieving the worldly goal of the old India during its second half-century than it did of achieving the worldly goal of the new India during its first half-century.

Index

Gujral, Inder Kumar 191–198, 224